No part of this guide may be reproduced in any form without permission in writing from the publisher except in the case of brief quotations embodied in critical articles or reviews.

Legal & Disclaimer

The information and contents herein are not designed to replace or take the place of any form of medical or professional advice and are not meant to replace the need for independent medical, financial, legal or other professional advice or services, as may be required. The content and information in this book have been provided for educational and entertainment purposes only.

The content and information in this book have been compiled from reliable sources and are accurate to the author's best knowledge, information, and belief. The author cannot guarantee this book's accuracy and validity and cannot be held liable for any errors and/or omissions. Further, changes will be periodically made to this book when needed. It is recommended that you consult with a health professional who is familiar with your personal medical history before using any of the suggested remedies, techniques, or information in this book.

Upon using the contents in this book, you agree to hold harmless the author from and against any damages, costs, and expenses, including any legal fees potentially resulting from the application of the information provided You agree to accept all risks associated with using the information presented inside this book.

Table of Content

Chapter 1 The Basics of Keto Diet

What is a ketogenic diet?

Ketogenic (keto for short) diet is a way to rein in rampant carbohydrates (sugars) in blood and food. There is a lot of science behind even the simplest meals but the problem is how to make it digestible and usable in everyday life. To make matters worse, not all bodies react the same way to same foods. Rather than being a comprehensive fix-all diet, keto is perhaps best used to test how the body tolerates carbohydrates or lack thereof.

Glucose or blood sugar is a fairly simple carbohydrate and is used as an energy source at the core of many bodily processes. Almost all carbohydrates that enter human digestion get broken down to glucose, which then seeps through the intestinal lining into the bloodstream. The more complex the carbohydrate, the longer it takes to create glucose and vice versa, and here is the first problem as modern, processed food is loaded with simple, refined sugars that surge into the bloodstream to wreak havoc on endocrine systems. Body normally has tightly regulated hormonal cycles, but constant glucose barrage flattens the endocrine response and leads to all sorts of health problems.

Is a ketogenic diet healthy?

Each body will respond differently to ketogenic diet but it can never do direct harm. Instead of eating carbohydrates to quickly create an avalanche of glucose, eating proteins and fats, which is what keto diet consists of, will nudge the body towards using other organs in the body, distributing the digestive load. In other words, the body can and does adapt to turning proteins and fats to energy but activates an alternative pathway that uses compounds known as ketones as an intermediary step. Abundance of ketones in the bloodstream is called "ketosis" and can be tested by soaking special keto sticks with urine. People with kidney problems might have additional issues on keto diet as excess ketones are mostly eliminated through urine.

The upside of ketosis is that the body starts preparing itself for using other fats, such as those found in fat cells. Because glucose is the type of fuel used immediately but fats take time to burn, the body starts preemptively burning fats and storing glucose in the liver. Some small amount of glucose is created too, though the process burns more energy than it creates. Having the body naturally use its own systems is the only legitimate way to burn fat, no matter what the latest glitzy food supplement says.

Why should you try this diet?

Keto diet is the perfect starting point for a dietary makeover. Everyone can try it – children have been placed on keto diet and it actually helped them subdue epileptic seizures that do not respond to medication. The mechanism behind this is unknown but may be due to brain cells becoming impervious to glucose; ketones use an alternative pathway to enter cells but are still usable by mitochondria, the powerhouse of the cell. However, microscopic invaders that thrive on glucose, such as fungi and bacteria, suddenly find themselves starved and bayed by the immune system.

Glucose is normally oxidized within the mitochondria to produce energy in a process that's akin to burning and may cause disruption of nearby cells and nerve signals if excessive. By restricting glucose intake this chain disruption slows down and lets the cells and organs self-regulate. In people with type 2 diabetes, keto diet helps control glucose levels and keeps insulin cycles from spiking. The only problem with keto diet is the lack of scientific studies showing just how powerful it is; that's up to the dieter to try and see for themselves.

What to avoid on Keto Diet?

Ketosis is generally achieved when the body has been on 20-50g of carbohydrates a day for 2-3 days. This might sound easy but a single 125g apple has 17g of carbohydrates and a mere 32g slice of rye bread has 15g. Reaching for just one more piece of candy or half a cup of ice cream is enough to stop ketosis and resume the normal glucose digestion cycle. In short, keto diet asks us to drop anything sweet and plenty of foods that don't even taste so but contain carbohydrates nonetheless.

Bread and pasta are by far the worst offenders, as they are eaten habitually with all meals in limitless quantities. Fruit at least has some redeeming qualities, since it consists of 80-90% water that satiates and slows down glucose absorption but also contains dietary fiber that acts as a cleanser when inside the intestines. Note that keto diet rarely produces dramatic results and it might take months or even years before there's a noticeable improvement. This is because health problems often progress for years before any action is taken, so improvement can never come overnight.

Who can benefit from Keto diet plan?

Anyone who's willing to try new diets should also try keto and will receive at least some indirect benefits. The most vulnerable patients, such as elderly and children, can go on keto as well, provided they have strong family support that will cook for them and urge them to stay away from carbohydrates. Those with mystery ailments and skin conditions, especially ones that resist medical treatment, should try keto as well. Note that the most extreme form of keto revolves around eating 0g of carbohydrates, which is emotionally extremely demanding and shouldn't be done without dire need.

Not only does the food nourish the body, but it also sustains the mind; people under severe stress usually take some form of junk food to relieve the pressure and feel at least some joy in the day. Junk food producers are well aware of this emotional need and thus supply the general public with nauseating quantities of carbohydrates in their products. Going on keto diet reveals internal weaknesses and habits that keep the person locked in the cycle of gorging on carbohydrates and experiencing the hormonal crash once the glucose wave passes; this can be a challenge in its own right.

How to transition to a Keto diet, the right way

Correct dietary choices are made every minute of every hour of every day, and the same applies to switching over to keto diet. The main obstacle in adopting keto diet is that the person had already made plenty of wrong choices during childhood and adolescence. Because habits are extremely resilient to change, the switch must be thoroughly prepared. The first step is to examine the environment and identify carbohydrate sources. Candy, potato chips and other sneaky snacks are usually the worst offenders as they don't satiate but still bring in the calories and carbohydrates. Any food that is eaten without conscious thinking should be mercilessly weighed and judged. The second step is to ditch all the carbohydrates in our vicinity, to literally throw them in the trash. Once keto diet starts showing results, it's common for the dieter to feel elated and decide to celebrate with junk food, thus ruining the progress.

Keto diet tips for best results

Prepare keto meals ahead of time and freeze them if possible to help with cravings. Constantly scan the environment for carbohydrate sources and eliminate junk food with extreme prejudice to avoid snacking. Any carbohydrates, such as apples, should be eaten after a hearty meal, preferably one made in accordance with keto principles. Simply eating less bread or pasta takes massive effort to accomplish and is a monumental achievement. Find a community of people on keto diet for recipes, tips and emotional support.

Chapter 2 Breakfast Recipes

Baked Eggs with Bacon and Double Cheese
Serves: 4, Preparation: 5, Cooking: 25

Ingredients
- 8 eggs from free-range chickens
- 1 Tbsp fresh parsley, finely chopped
- 1 tsp of basil, chopped
- Salt to taste
- 1/4 cup of Gruyere cheese, grated
- 4 slices of bacon
- 2 Tbsp olive oil
- 1 scallion, cut into thin slices
- 3/4 cup of goat cheese, crumbled
- 2 cherry tomatoes, quartered

Instructions
1. Preheat the oven to 400 F/200 C.
2. In a bowl, beat eggs, parsley, basil and salt.
3. Heat the oil in a skillet on high fire, pour the olive oil. Sauté the scallion and chopped bacon until get a nice color.
4. Add grated Gruyere cheese and cook, stirring, for further 2 - 3 minutes.
5. Pour the egg mixture and stir.
6. Transfer the egg/bacon mixture in a baking dish. Sprinkle crumbled goat cheese and cover with cherry tomatoes.
7. Bake for about 15 minutes or until cheese melted. Serve hot.

Nutrition information:
Calories: 177.6 Carbohydrates: 4g Proteins: 25g Fat: 45g Fiber: 1g

Zucchini Spaghetti with Melted Cheese
Serves: 4, Preparation: 15 minutes, Cooking: 4 hours and 30

Ingredients
- 1 1/2 lbs. of zucchini sliced
- 1 lb Spaghetti
- 1/2 cup of olive oil
- 2 cloves of garlic
- 1 Tbsp fresh oregano
- 1 Tbsp fresh thyme
- 1/2 cup water
- 1 cup grated parmesan cheese
- Salt and pepper to taste

Instructions
1. Clean and grate zucchini to make a zucchini spaghetti with the help of mandolin.
2. Pour the Olive oil on the bottom of your Crock Pot. Add the garlic, zucchini, oregano, thyme and water. Season with the salt and pepper and stir.
3. Cover and cook on LOW for 4 hours.
4. Open lid and add grated parmesan cheese.
5. Cover again and cook on HIGH for 30 minutes. Serve hot.

Nutrition information:
Calories: 380 Carbohydrates: 6g Proteins: 15g Fat: 35g Fiber: 2g

Coconut and Avocado Almond Milkshake

Serves: 3, Preparation: 5 minutes

Ingredients

- 2 1/2 cups coconut milk (canned)
- 1/2 avocado, pitted and cut in half
- 1/4 cup coconut flakes (unsweetened)
- 2 Tbsp ground nuts
- 2 Tbsp stevia granulated sweetener (optional)
- Ice cubes

Instructions

1. Place all ingredients in your high-speed blender; blend until smooth completely.
2. Serve in chilled glasses.

Nutrition information:

Calories: 476 Carbohydrates: 8g Proteins: 6g
Fat: 50g Fiber: 3.2g

Egg Whites Omelet with Turkey and Mascarpone

Serves: 4, Preparation: 5 minutes, Cooking: 5 minutes

Ingredients

- 8 egg whites
- 4 slices of smoked turkey, finely chopped
- 1 grated tomato
- 1/2 cup of Greek yogurt
- 2 slices of Mascarpone cheese
- 2 Tbsp of olive oil

Instructions

1. In a bowl, beat the egg whites with yogurt, smoked turkey, tomato and cheese.
2. Heat the oil in a non-stick frying pan and pour the egg white mixture.
3. Cook omelet for 2 minutes, flip and cook for 1 minute.
4. Serve immediately.

Nutrition information:

Calories: 182 Carbohydrates: 5.2 Proteins: 10.5g
Fat: 13.5g Fiber: 0.5g

Eggs Stuffed with Spinach and Bacon

Serves: 6, Preparation: 15 minutes, Cooking: 10 minutes

Ingredients

- 6 large eggs, boiled (hard)
- 1/2 cup of olive oil
- 2 slices bacon, chopped
- 1 lb fresh spinach chopped
- 1/2 cup of mayonnaise
- 2 Tbsp of yellow mustard
- 2 Tbsp of grated parmesan cheese
- Salt and pepper to taste

Instructions

1. Place the eggs in a saucepan, cover completely with cold water.
2. Once the water begins to boil, turn off the heat and let cook for 10 minutes.
3. Transfer eggs into a bowl with cold water.
4. Peel eggs, halve and remove the yolks; reserve yolks.
5. Heat the olive oil in a frying skillet over medium-high heat and sauce the bacon and spinach.
6. In a meantime, in a large bowl stir the egg yolks, mayonnaise, mustard, parmesan and salt and pepper.
7. Add spinach with bacon mixture and stir again to combine thoroughly.
8. Fill the egg whites with the mixture and place on a platter.
9. Refrigerate for one hour and serve.

Nutrition information:

Calories: 407 Carbohydrates: 7g Proteins: 12g
Fat: 37.2g Fiber: 2g

Eggs with Smoked Paprika and Pecorino

Serves: 4, Preparation: 5 minutes, Cooking: 15 minutes

Ingredients

- 1/4 cup of fresh butter
- 1 clove of garlic, sliced
- 1 fresh onion finely chopped
- 1 tomato grated
- Salt and freshly ground pepper to taste
- 8 eggs from free-range chickens
- 2 Tbsp smoked paprika
- 1 cup of Pecorino Romano grated
- 2 Tbsp of fresh basil, chopped

Instructions

1. Heat butter in a frying skillet over medium heat; sauté the garlic, the onion, and the tomato.
2. Season with the salt and pepper to taste, and cook, stirring constantly, for about 5 minutes.
3. Add eggs, one at a time and stir; sprinkle with the smoked paprika and stir again.
4. Cook for further 2 - 3 minutes.
5. Sprinkle with grated Pecorino and fresh basil and serve.

Nutrition information:

Calories: 427 Carbohydrates: 6.4g Proteins: 27g Fat: 33g Fiber: 2.6g

Homemade Keto Almond Spread

Serves: 10, Preparation: 15, Cooking: 12 minutes

Ingredients

- 3 cups almonds, roasted
- 1 pinch of salt
- 1 tsp cinnamon
- 1 tsp almond or vanilla extract
- 2 Tbsp of natural granulated sweetener (Stevia, Truvia, Erythritol...etc.)

Instructions

1. Preheat the oven to 350 F/175 C.
2. Line one rimmed sheet with parchment paper and spread almonds.
3. Roast for 10 - 12 minutes. Remove almonds from the oven and let them cool for 5 - 10 minutes.
4. Place almonds in a food processor along with all remaining ingredients.
5. Process for 10 minutes or until completely smooth.
6. Store in a glass jar and keep refrigerated.

Nutrition information:

Calories: 248 Carbohydrates: 8g Proteins: 9g Fat: 22g Fiber: 4.5g

Keto Breakfast Waffles with Crispy Bacon

Serves: 4, Preparation: 10 minutes, Cooking: 10 minutes

Ingredients

- 1/3 cup fresh butter melted
- 4 slices bacon
- 2 eggs from free-range chickens
- 3 cup of almond flour
- 1 1/2 tsp baking soda
- 2 tsp natural sweetener (Stevia, Truvia, Erythritol...etc.)

Ingredients

1. Microwave the butter about 30 seconds; set aside.
2. Heat the frying skillet and brown bacon until crisp.
3. In a small bowl, combine flour, baking soda and sweetener.
4. Add eggs and stir thoroughly. Add melted butter and stir.
5. Preheat the waffle iron according to manufacture instruction.
6. Spoon the batter on the edges and place 2 slices of bacon over.
7. Cook waffles until golden brown; flip once.
8. Serve hot.

Nutrition information:

Calories: 346 Carbohydrates: 1g Proteins: 8g Fat: 35g Fiber: 0g

Keto Coconut Waffles

Serves: 6, Preparation: 10 minutes, Cooking: 10 minutes

Ingredients

- 4 eggs from free-range chickens
- 2 cup almond flour
- 1 Tbsp of coconut flour
- 1/2 tsp baking soda
- 1/2 tsp of sea salt
- 1/2 tsp ground cinnamon
- 1/4 cup coconut milk (canned)
- 1 cup almond milk (unsweetened)
- 1/4 cup shredded coconut, unsweetened
- 2 Tbsp of natural sweetener (Stevia, Erythritol...etc.)
- 1 1/2 tsp vanilla extract

Instructions

1. Preheat your waffle iron according to manufacturer instructions.
2. In a bowl, whisk the eggs yolks.
3. Add the almond flour, coconut flour, baking soda, pinch of salt, cinnamon, almond milk, coconut milk, shredded coconut, and sweetener; stir well.
4. In a separate bowl, beat the egg whites until become froth.
5. Add the egg whites to the egg yolk batter mixture and pour the vanilla extract; stir well.
6. Pour the batter in a waffle iron and cook according to your preference.
7. Serve hot.

Nutrition information:

Calories: 55 Carbohydrates: 1.1g Proteins: 3.5g Fat: 4g Fiber: 0.3g

Keto Dilly - Zucchini and Feta Muffins

Serves: 12, Preparation: 10 minutes, Cooking: 25 minutes

Ingredients

- 1 1/2 cups almond flour
- 2 Tbs natural sweetener (Stevia, Truvia, Erythritol...etc.)
- 2 tsp baking powder
- 1/2 tsp salt
- 3/4 tsp fresh dill
- 1/4 cup almond milk
- 1 butter stick softened
- 2 Eggs from free-range chickens
- 2/3 cup Feta cheese crumbled
- 3/4 cup shredded zucchini

Instructions

1. Preheat oven to 400 F/200 C. Grease one muffin tin; set aside.
2. In a large bowl, combine the almond flour, sweetener, baking powder, salt and dill.
3. In a separate bowl, combine the almond milk, softened butter and eggs.
4. Stir the cheese and shredded zucchini and combined well.
5. Stir the almond milk mixture to the dry ingredients and gently stir.
6. Fill the prepared muffin cups about two-thirds full.
7. Bake for 20 to 25 minutes.
8. Serve warm or cold.

Nutrition information:

Calories: 157 Carbohydrates: 1g Proteins: 2.5g Fat: 16.5g Fiber: 0.1g

Lemonito Zucchini Muffins

Serves: 12, Preparation: 10 minutes, Cooking: 25 minutes

Ingredients

- 2 cups of almond flour
- 1/2 cup of natural granulated sweetener (Stevia, Truvia, Erythritol...etc.)
- 1 Tbsp baking powder
- 1 tsp salt
- Grated peel of 1/2 lemon
- 3/4 cup roasted almonds, finely chopped
- 2 eggs, beaten
- 1/2 cup almond milk
- 1/3 cup olive oil
- 1 cup zucchini, shredded and drained

Instructions

1. Preheat the oven to 400 F/200 C.
2. Grease with the oil one 12-cup muffin tin.
3. In a bowl, combine together the flour, sweetener, baking powder, salt and lemon peel; stir. Add finely chopped almonds and stir again.
4. In a separate bowl, whisk the eggs, almond milk and olive oil.
5. Combine dry ingredients with egg mixture; stir until just combines and add shredded zucchini.
6. Spoon the batter into prepared muffin tin. Bake for 20 to 25 minutes.
7. Serve warm or cold.

Nutrition information:

Calories: 118.5 g Carbohydrates: 2.2g Proteins: 3gFat: 12g Fiber: 1g

Spinach with Eggs Dish Recipe

Serves: 4, Preparation: 5 minutes, Cooking: 20 minutes

Ingredients

- 1 1/2 lb frozen spinach, thawed and drained
- 2 spring onions finely chopped
- 1 bunch of dill chopped
- 6 large eggs
- 2 Tbsp olive oil
- Salt and pepper to taste

Instructions

1. Heat a non-stick frying pan over high heat.
2. Add the spinach, chopped spring onion, and dill. Stir and cook for about 5 - 6 minutes.
3. Add chopped onion and dill and stir well.
4. When the water is completely evaporated pour the olive oil, stir and crack the eggs.
5. Season the salt and pepper to taste.
6. Lower the heat, cover and let it cook for 10 - 12 minutes or until the eggs are done. Serve hot.

Nutrition information:

Calories: 203 Carbohydrates: 5.6g Proteins: 14g Fat: 15.5g Fiber: 3.5g

Marinated Corned Beef with Eggs

Serves: 4, Preparation: 15 minutes, Cooking: 15 minutes

Ingredients

- 2 Tbsp of butter softened on room temperature
- 2 green onions, finely diced
- 1/2 cup red bell pepper finely diced
- 1 lb corned beef, finely diced
- 1 Tbsp mustard (Dijon, English, ground stone)
- 1 Tbsp Worcestershire Sauce
- 1/4 tsp ground nutmeg
- 8 eggs
- Salt and freshly ground black pepper to taste

Instructions

1. Heat butter in a pan over medium heat.
2. Sauté the green onions with a pinch of salt until softened.
3. Add bell pepper and cook for 2 - 3 minutes.
4. Transfer the mixture to a mixing bowl and add the corned beef, Worcestershire sauce, mustard, pepper and nutmeg. Place the mixture in a container, cover and refrigerate overnight.
5. Remove corned beef from the fridge for 15 minutes before cooking,
6. Heat some oil in a large frying pan and add the corned beef; cook for 5 minutes.
7. Crack the eggs, one by one, over corned beef and cook for 3 minutes.
8. Serve hot.

Nutrition information:

Calories: 492 Carbohydrates: 3.2g Proteins: 44g Fat: 33g Fiber: 1g

Maxelan Blueberry and Coconut Smoothie

Serves: 4, Preparation: 5 minutes

Ingredients

- 1/2 avocado pitted
- 1 1/4 cup of fresh raspberries
- 3/4 cup coconut milk
- 1/2 cup water
- 1 cup of fresh baby spinach leaves
- 1 tsp pure vanilla extract
- Ice cubes (optional)

Instructions

1. Place all ingredients from the list in a high-speed blender; blend until smooth well.
2. Serve.

Nutrition information:

Calories: 221 Carbohydrates: 8.8g Proteins: 3.5g Fat: 17g Fiber: 10g

melet with Prosciutto, Halloumi and Basil

Serves: 4, Preparation: 10 minutes, Cooking: 15 minutes

Ingredients

- 8 eggs from free-range chicken
- 7 oz of prosciutto finely chopped
- 8 oz grated Halloumi (pr Paneer cheese)
- 1/2 cup of yogurt
- 1 bunch of fresh basil, chopped
- Salt and pepper
- Olive oil for frying

Instructions

1. Heat the oil in a frying skillet and brown smoked pork until crispy.
2. Transfer to a plate with kitchen paper towel to drain.
3. In a bowl, beat the eggs with yogurt, Halloumi, basil, and the salt and pepper.
4. Heat the oil in a non-stick frying pan and pour the egg mixture.
5. Cook for 2 - 3 minutes, and then flip and cook for 1 - 2 minutes.
6. Serve immediately.

Nutrition information:

Calories: 499 Carbohydrates: 3.7g Proteins: 45g Fat: 41g Fiber: 0g

Oven Baked Mushrooms & Beet Greens Omelet

Serves: 6, Preparation: 10 minutes, Cooking: 30 minutes

Ingredients

- 2 Tbsp of olive oil, divided
- 2 scallions finely chopped
- 1 clove garlic, minced
- 2 cups beet leaves chopped
- 2 cup of mushrooms sliced
- 8 eggs from free-range chickens
- 1/2 tsp ground thyme
- 1/2 tsp salt and ground black pepper
- 1 cup grated parmesan cheese

Instructions

1. Preheat oven to 400 F/200 C.
2. Heat the oil in a large frying pan, and sauté chopped scallions and garlic until softened.
3. Add beet greens and mushrooms; cook, stirring occasionally, until beet greens is softened or for about 10 minutes.
4. In a large bowl, whisk together eggs, thyme, salt, and pepper.
5. Add egg mixture to the beet greens mixture.
6. Add the parmesan cheese and stir until well combined.
7. Pour the batter in one oiled baking dish.
8. Bake 10 - 12 minutes or until cooked through.
9. Slice and serve warm.

Nutrition information:

Calories: 244.5 Carbohydrates: 7g Proteins: 17g Fat: 17g Fiber: 2.5g

Roly-poly Scrambled Eggs

Serves: 4, Preparation: 10 minutes, Cooking: 5 minutes

Ingredients

- 12 eggs from free-range chickens
- Sea salt to taste
- 1/4 cup of almond milk
- 1/3 cup of fresh butter
- Sweet red paprika for serving

Instructions

1. Beat the eggs and almond milk with a pinch of salt.
2. Heat butter in a small non-sticking skillet at medium heat.
3. Pour the egg mixture into the pan and cook in a low heat, stirring continuously for 2 - 3 minutes.
4. Remove the eggs from heat and place on plates.
5. Sprinkle with red paprika and serve.

Nutrition information:

Calories: 335 Carbohydrates: 1.4g Proteins: 17g Fat: 28.5g Fiber: 0.05g

Baked Broccoli with Eggs and Feta

Serves: 6, Preparation: 15 minutes, Cooking: 25 minutes

Ingredients

- 1 large head of broccoli
- 6 eggs from free range chickens
- 8 oz Feta cheese crumbled
- 1/2 cup olive oil
- 1/2 Tbsp of sweet paprika
- 1 tsp finely chopped parsley
- 1/2 tsp dry thyme
- 2 pinches salt, freshly ground pepper

Instructions

1. Preheat oven to 360 F/182 C.
2. Boil the broccoli in pot with salted water until softened, for about 6 - 7 minutes.
3. Heat the large baking pan.
4. Transfer cooked broccoli in a baking pan.
5. Crack the eggs over the broccoli one by one.
6. Season the salt, pepper and, paprika and thyme.
7. Add crumbled Feta cheese evenly.
8. Drizzle with the oil, place in oven, and bake for about 10 - 15 minutes or until the eggs are done.
9. Serve hot.

Nutrition information:

Calories: 357 Carbohydrates: 6.2g Proteins: 14g Fat: 31g Fiber: 0.4g

Piquant Eggs Mash

Serves: 4, Preparation: 10 minutes, Cooking: 3 hours

Ingredients

- 1 Tbsp of tallow
- 2 green onions finely sliced
- 2 cloves garlic finely chopped
- 2 pinch grated hot pepper (or to taste)
- 1 tsp cumin
- 8 free-range eggs
- 1/2 tsp ground hot pepper or hot paprika
- Salt to taste
- 1 Tbsp fresh chopped dill and parsley for serving

Instructions

1. Heat the tallow in skillet, and sauté the green onions and garlic until soft, for about 3 - 4 minutes. Season it with the salt, hot pepper and cumin.
2. Transfer the onion to the inner stainless pot in the Crock Pot.
3. In a bowl, whisk the eggs with a pinch of salt and red hot pepper.
4. Pour the egg mixture over the green onions in your Crock Pot.
5. Cover and cook on HIGH for 2 - 3 hours.
6. Sprinkle with chopped parsley or dill and serve hot.

Nutrition information:

Calories: 202 Carbohydrates: 6g Proteins: 14g Fat: 13g Fiber: 1.5g

Chapter 3 Vegetable recipes

Keto Aubergines Bourgeoises
Serves: 6, Preparation: 10 minutes, Cooking: 40 minutes

Instructions

- 2 scallions finely chopped
- 2 Tbsp of olive oil
- 1 cup of small white mushrooms
- 2 eggplants cut into slices
- 3 cloves garlic
- 2 Tbsp of almond flour
- 2 Tbsp tomato puree
- 1 1/2 cups of red wine
- 1 cup of water
- 1 cup of bone broth
- 1/4 cup of fresh thyme finely chopped
- Salt and ground pepper to taste

Instructions

1. Heat the olive oil in a skillet. Sauté scallions and mushrooms for 2 - 3 minutes.
2. Add the eggplant and sauté for 2-3 minutes until golden.
3. Add sliced garlic and stir for 2 - 3 minutes.
4. Sprinkle with the almond flour and stir with a wooden spoon.
5. Add the tomato paste and stir again. Pour wine, water and bone broth and stir well.
6. Cover and cook for 30-35 minutes at medium - low temperature
7. Add chopped thyme, stir and cook for 5 minutes.
8. Adjust salt and pepper and serve hot.

Nutrition information:
Calories: 110 Carbohydrates: 8.2g Proteins: 3.5g Fat: 5.4g Fiber: 7g

Cauliflower Mash in Red Sauce
Serves: 6, Preparation: 10 minutes, Cooking: 15 minutes

Ingredients

- 2 Tbsp of olive oil
- 1 medium head of cauliflower cut in florets
- 1 medium onion, finely chopped
- 2 garlic cloves, finely sliced
- 1/2 cup of chopped chives
- Chopped parsley to taste
- 1 Tbsp of coconut aminos
- 2 cups of water
- 1 pinch of turmeric
- 1 pinch of black pepper powder
- Salt to taste

Instructions

1. Heat the oil in a large pot at medium-high heat.
2. Sauté the onion and the garlic until soft.
3. Add the coconut aminos and sauté for 2 minutes at low heat.
4. Pour water and add all remaining ingredients.
5. Cook for 10 - 12 minutes; stir.
6. Transfer the cauliflower mixture in a blender and blend for 30 - 45 seconds.
7. Return it in a pot, drizzle with olive oil, adjust seasonings and serve.

Nutrition information:
Calories: 96 Carbohydrates: 5.3g Proteins: 2.5g Fat: 8g Fiber: 2.5g

Roasted Brussels sprouts with Bacon
Serves: 4, Preparation: 10 minutes, Cooking: 30 minutes

Ingredients
- 1 ½ lbs of Brussels sprouts
- 2 Tbsp of olive oil
- Salt and pepper to taste
- 6 slices bacon cut into pieces

Instructions
1. Preheat oven to 400 F/200 C.
2. Clean and cut the Brussels sprouts.
3. Place Brussels sprouts in a large baking dish and drizzle with olive oil.
4. Season with the salt and pepper.
5. Sprinkle chopped bacon evenly over Brussels sprouts.
6. Bake for 20-30 minutes. Serve hot.

Nutrition information:
Calories: 395 Carbohydrates: 11g Proteins: 12.5g Fat: 33g Fiber: 4.1g

Boosting Kale, Cucumber and Avocado Smoothie
Serves: 6, Preparation: 10 minutes

Ingredients
- 1 cup fresh kale leaves, finely chopped
- 1 cup cucumber, chopped
- 1/3 cup avocado cut in cubes
- 1/2 cup celery, chopped
- 2 Tbsp of fresh mint leaves
- 1 cup water
- 1 cup ice cubes, or as needed

Instructions
1. Place all ingredients in your fast-speed blender.
2. Blend until smooth.
3. Serve in chilled glasses and drink.

Nutrition information:
Calories: 31 Carbohydrates: 2g Proteins: 1g Fat: 2g Fiber: 1.5g

Crispy Cheddar Kale Chips

Serves: 4, Preparation: 15 minutes, Cooking: 10 minutes

Ingredients

- 1/4 cup garlic-infused olive oil
- Sea salt and ground black pepper to taste
- 1/2 cup Cheddar cheese grated
- 1 lb Kale roughly chopped soft stems

Instructions

1. Preheat oven to 400 F/200C.
2. Rinse and place the kale on a few sheets of kitchen paper towel to dry.
3. Clean and break kale into small pieces.
4. Pour the olive oil and season salt and pepper to taste. Toss to coat.
5. Line a baking dish with parchment paper.
6. Spread kale pieces in a single layer in a baking dish and sprinkle with grated Cheddar cheese.
7. Bake for about 10 minutes, or until the kale pieces become crispy.
8. Serve.

Nutrition information:

Calories: 114 Carbohydrates: 9g Proteins: 7g Fat: 6g Fiber: 2g

Green Beans Soup with Red Pepper Flakes

Serves: 8, Preparation: 5 minutes, Cooking: 45 minutes

Ingredients

- 2 Tbsp of olive oil
- 1 green onion, diced
- 2 clove garlic, minced
- 1 lb fresh green beans
- 1/2 cup fresh cilantro, chopped
- 1 carrot finely sliced
- 2 cup water
- 1 cup bone broth (or water)
- 1 tsp crushed red pepper flakes
- 1/4 tsp chili powder
- 1 tsp cumin
- Salt and ground pepper to taste

Instructions

1. Heat the oil in a large pot and sauté the onion and garlic with a pinch of salt until soft.
2. Add the green beans and cilantro and stir for further 2 minutes.
3. Add all remaining ingredients and give a good stir.
4. Cover and cook for 30 - 35 minutes or until green beans are soft.
5. Adjust salt and pepper and serve hot.

Nutrition information:

Calories: 127 Carbohydrates: 8.5g Proteins: 11g Fat: 9g Fiber: 2g

Green Keto Puree

Serves: 6, Preparation: 10 minutes, Cooking: 20 minutes

Ingredients

- 1 scallion, chopped
- 2 Tbsp extra virgin olive oil
- 1 lb fresh spinach leaves
- 1/2 lb Swiss chard, tough stems removed
- 3 cups water
- 1/4 cup coconut milk
- Sea salt and black ground pepper to taste

Instructions

1. Heat the olive oil in a skillet and sauté the scallion for about 2-3 minutes.
2. Add the Swish chard and spinach leaves, water and salt and pepper to taste; stir.
3. Bring to the boil and let it simmer for 15 minutes.
4. Transfer spinach mixture in a food processor along with the coconut milk and blend until creamy.
5. Adjust salt and pepper and serve.

Nutrition information:

Calories: 85 Carbohydrates: 4.5g Proteins: 3g Fat: 7g Fiber: 2.5g

Hearty Asparagus Salad with Creamy Dressing

Serves: 4, Preparation: 10 minutes

Ingredients

- 10 ounces frozen cut asparagus, thawed
- 1/2 avocado, chopped
- 2 small spring onions finely chopped
- Sea salt to taste
- 1/2 cup Greek yogurt
- 3 Tbsp of grated Parmesan cheese
- 1 Tbsp mustard (Dijon, English, ground stone)
- 2 Tbsp extra virgin olive oil

Instructions

1. In a salad bowl, combine the asparagus, avocado, and onions; sprinkle with a pinch of the salt, and set aside.
2. In a separate bowl, whisk together Greek yogurt, Parmesan cheese and mustard.
3. Add to the asparagus mixture and toss until well coated.
4. Drizzle with little olive oil and serve immediately or refrigerate until serving.

Nutrition information:

Calories: 143 Carbohydrates: 6g Proteins: 5g Fat: 12g Fiber: 2.4g

Heavy - Creamy Spinach Puree

Serves: 4, Preparation: 10 minutes, Cooking: 15 minutes

Ingredients

- 1 Tbsp tallow
- 1 lb of frozen spinach drained
- 2 clove garlic, minced
- Salt and fresh-ground black pepper to taste
- 1/2 cup water
- 1 cup heavy cream
- 3/4 cup grated parmesan cheese

Instructions

1. Thaw (about two hours) and drain the spinach in a colander.
2. Heat the tallow in a large pot and sauté garlic, spinach with a pinch of salt and pepper.
3. Pour water, cover and boil for three minutes or until spinach begins to wilt.
4. Transfer spinach in a blender along with cream and parmesan cheese; blend for 25 - 35 seconds or until combined well.
5. Taste and adjust salt and ground pepper.
6. Serve.

Nutrition information:
Calories: 327 Carbohydrates: 8g Proteins: 13g Fat: 28g Fiber: 4g

Mayo- Mustard Asparagus and Mushrooms Salad

Serves: 4, Preparation: 15 minutes, Cooking: 15 minutes

Ingredients

- 20 large spears of asparagus
- 2 cups mushrooms
- 1/2 cup of mayonnaise
- 2 Tbsp yellow mustard
- 1 lemon juice
- Salt and ground pepper to taste

Instructions

1. Cut the woody part of the asparagus, rinse, and place in pot with salted water.
2. Boil asparagus for 10 minutes over medium-high heat. Remove asparagus in colander, allow it to cool, and cut into pieces.
3. Place the asparagus pieces in a large salad bowl.
4. Rinse the mushrooms and cut them into thin slices. Put them in a bowl with asparagus
5. Season with the salt and pepper to taste, add the mayonnaise and mustard and stir; pour lemon juice to taste, stir and serve.

Nutrition information:
Calories: 101 Carbohydrates: 4g Proteins: 4g Fat: 6g Fiber: 3g

Oriental Spiced Cucumber and Fennel Salad

Serves: 4, Preparation: 10 minutes, Cooking: 20 minutes

Ingredients

- 1 lb cucumber cut into pieces
- 2 fennel bulb thinly sliced
- 3 hot peppers
- 3 cloves garlic (peeled and left whole)
- 1 Tbsp of coriander seeds
- 1 cinnamon sticks (broken into several pieces)
- 2 cups white vinegar
- 1/2 tsp red pepper flakes
- 1 cup water
- 3 Tbsp of stevia sweetener granulated
- 2 Tbsp of kosher salt
- 1 bay leaf
- 1 tsp black peppercorns
- Olive oil for serving

Instructions

1. Place all ingredients in a large and deep pot. Cook covered for about 15 - 20 minutes over medium heat.
2. Transfer mixture in colander to drain.
3. Remove all ingredients from colander in a salad bowl, drizzle with olive oil and serve.

Nutrition information:

Calories: 148 Carbohydrates: 8g Proteins: 7g Fat: 14g Fiber: 4.5g

Steamed "Italiano" Broccoli

Serves: 5, Preparation: 10 minutes, Cooking: 10 minutes

Ingredients

- 1 1/2 lb of fresh broccoli florets (or thawed frozen)
- 1/2 cup Italian salad dressing

Instructions

1. Place broccoli florets in steamer basket above 2 inches boiling water.
2. Cover and steam for about 4 minutes or until broccoli is soft.
3. Remove from the steam, drain and place broccoli in serving plate.
4. Drizzle with Italian dressing and toss to coat. Serve.

Nutrition information:

Calories: 60 Carbohydrates: 6g Proteins: 14g Fat: 11g Fiber: 2g

Warm Avocado - Zucchini Salad

Serves: 5, Preparation: 5 minutes, Cooking: 20 minutes

Ingredients
- 2 Tbsp olive oil
- 1 spring onion finely chopped
- 2 cloves of garlic
- 3 zucchini
- 1 large avocado
- 1 Tbsp of fresh thyme finely chopped
- Salt and black ground pepper to taste
- 1 lemon (zest and juice)

Instructions
1. Heat the olive oil in a frying skillet over medium-high heat.
2. Sauté the onion and garlic with a pinch of salt until soft, for about 4 - 5 minutes.
3. Add the zucchini and cook for about 2 - 3 minutes.
4. Add the lemon zest, thyme, and season with the salt and pepper; stir well.
5. Add avocado and lemon juice and cook for further 3 - 4 minutes.
6. Remove from the heat; let cool for 10 minutes and serve.

Nutrition information:
Calories: 171 Carbohydrates: 7g Proteins: 7g Fat: 19g Fiber: 5g

Wild Greens, Asparagus with Cheese Sauce

Serves: 6, Preparation: 10 minutes, Cooking: 25 minutes

Ingredients
- 1 1/4 lb mustard greens or amaranth cut coarsely
- 1 bunch of asparagus green (about 10 - 12 pieces), cleaned, and cut 4 pieces
- Salt and ground black pepper to taste
- For the cheese sauce
- 1/2 cup of olive oil
- 1 clove of garlic, cleaned finely minced
- 1 Tbsp rosemary leaves, finely chopped
- 1 tsp hot dried paprika
- 1 cup cream cheese (full-fat)

Instructions
1. Boil salted water in a saucepan with plenty of salted boiling water.
2. Boil the greens and asparagus for about 7 to 10 minutes.
3. Drain well and put in a salad bowl.

Cheese sauce:
1. In a frying pan heat the olive oil and heat the garlic over medium heat.
2. Add the cheese, rosemary leaves, and hot dried paprika, salt and freshly ground pepper; stir well.
3. Stir for 15 - 20 seconds and remove from the heat.
4. Pour hot cheese salad over the greens and asparagus. Serve.

Nutrition information:
Calories: 261 Carbohydrates: 7g Proteins: 10g Fat: 22g Fiber: 5.5g

Creamy Broccoli and Bacon Casserole

Serves: 4, Preparation: 15 minutes, Cooking: 35 minutes

Ingredients

- 1 Tbsp of olive oil
- 2 cups of broccoli florets, cooked
- 8 eggs
- 1/4 cup water
- 1 cup of Cottage cheese
- 1 tsp of fresh thyme
- Salt and ground black pepper to taste
- 3 ounces of bacon, crumbled
- 2 Tbsp of Feta cheese, crumbled

Instructions

1. Preheat the oven to 380 F/190 C.
2. Coat the casserole dish with olive oil.
3. Place the broccoli florets (cooked) on a bottom of casserole dish; sprinkle with the pinch of salt and pepper.
4. Add the Cottage cheese and fresh thyme over the broccoli.
5. n a bowl, whisk the eggs with 1/4 cup of water; season with the salt and pepper.
6. Pour the egg mixture over the broccoli, and sprinkle with crumbled bacon and crumbled feta cheese.
7. Place the casserole in the oven, and bake for 35 minutes.
8. Let rest for 10 minutes before slicing and serving.

Nutrition information:

Calories: 325 Carbohydrates: 5g Proteins: 22g
Fat: 24g Fiber: 0.2g

Delicious Spinach - Bacon Casserole

Serves: 5, Preparation: 15 minutes, Cooking: 15 minutes

Ingredients

- 1 tsp of tallow
- 8 slices bacon (pancetta)
- 3/4 lb fresh spinach chopped
- 8 eggs from free-range chickens
- 1 cup Parmesan cheese grated
- 2 pinch salt and pepper

Instructions

1. Preheat the oven to 400 F/200 C.
2. Grease one casserole dish with the tallow.
3. Lay the bacon slices on the bottom of casserole dish.
4. Sprinkle chopped spinach leaves over the bacon, and sprinkle with little salt.
5. In a bowl, whisk the eggs along with Parmesan cheese and the pinch of salt and pepper.
6. Pour the egg mixture over the spinach evenly.
7. Place in oven and cook for 20 minutes.
8. Turn off the oven but leave the casserole for 10 - 15 minutes inside.
9. Serve hot.

Nutrition information:

Calories: 502 Carbohydrates: 4.5g Proteins: 27g
Fat: 42g Fiber: 1.5g

Steak Strips and Zucchini Omelet Casserole

Serves: 5, Preparation: 10 minutes, Cooking: 30 minutes

Ingredients

- 1 Tbsp lard
- 1 lb bacon, cut into strips
- 1 spring onion, finely diced
- 3 large sized zucchinis, grated
- 1 tsp of sea salt and ground black pepper
- 6 free range eggs
- 1/2 can of feta cheese, crumbled

Instructions

1. Preheat oven to 350 F/175 C.
2. Grease one large casserole dish with the lard.
3. Place the bacon strips in a casserole dish, and cover with sliced green onion and zucchini rings.
4. Season with the salt and pepper.
5. Beat the eggs in a bowl with a pinch of salt and crumbled feta cheese.
6. Pour the egg mixture in a casserole dish.
7. Bake for 30 minutes or until the eggs are cooked.
8. Serve hot.

Nutrition information:

Calories: 496 Carbohydrates: 5g Proteins: 19g Fat: 48g Fiber: 1.5g

Zucchini Noodles with Parmesan

Serves: 4, Preparation: 15 minutes, Cooking: 5 minutes

Ingredients

- 2 cups zucchini noodles (zoodles)
- Salt and fresh cracked pepper to taste
- 2 Tbsp olive oil
- 2 cloves garlic, minced
- 1 Tbsp green pepper chopped
- 3 Tbsp fresh basil (chopped)
- 1 tsp red pepper flakes
- 1 cup water
- 1/4 cup Parmesan cheese

Instructions

1. Pour oil to the inner stainless steel pot in the Instant Pot.
2. Cut zucchini into thin, noodle-like strips with a mandolin. Season zucchini noodles with the salt and pepper.
3. Place zucchini in Instant Pot, and add minced garlic, green pepper, fresh basil, red pepper flakes and water over zucchini.
4. Lock lid into place and set on the MANUAL setting for 5 minutes.
5. When the timer beeps, press "Cancel" and carefully flip the Quick Release valve to let the pressure out.
6. Remove zucchini noodles on a serving plate, sprinkle with Parmesan and serve.

Nutrition information:

Calories: 113 Carbohydrates: 4g Proteins: 7g Fat: 10g Fiber: 3g

Brown Cremini Mushrooms Gravy

Serves: 8, Preparation: 5 minutes, Cooking: 4 hours

Ingredients

- 1 lb of Cremini mushrooms (or white mushrooms, shiitake mushrooms)
- 1 medium onion finely chopped
- 1 cup of cream
- 1 cup of almond milk (unsweetened)
- 1/4 cup white dry wine
- 1 Tbsp butter
- Salt and red ground pepper to taste

Instructions

1. Place mushrooms along with all ingredients in Slow Cooker; stir gently to combine.
2. Cover and cook on HIGH for 1 - 2 hours or on LOW for 3 - 4 hours.
3. Open lid, stir well, adjust salt and pepper and allow to cool.
4. Store in glass jar and keep refrigerated.

Nutrition information:

Calories: 150 Carbohydrates: 4g Proteins: 3g Fat: 14g Fiber: 0.2g

Creamed Portobello Mushrooms

Serves: 4, Preparation: 10 minutes, Cooking: 3 hour and 30 minutes

Ingredients

- 1 1/2 lbs of Portobello mushrooms, halved
- Salt and ground white pepper
- 1 Tbsp of butter
- 1/2 cup of bone broth
- 2 Tbsp of brandy
- 1 Tbsp of almond flour
- 3/4 cup of fresh cream
- 2 Tbsp of chopped fresh parsley

Instructions

1. Place mushrooms in your Slow Cooker along with salt and pepper, butter, bone broth, brandy and almond flour.
2. Cover and cook on HIGH for 3 hours.
3. Open lid and stir cream; cover and cook on HIGH for further 25 - 30 minutes.
4. Serve hot with chopped parsley.

Nutrition information:

Calories: 236 Carbohydrates: 5g Proteins: 7g Fat: 21g Fiber: 2g

Dense Green Squash Puree

Serves: 6, Preparation: 5 minutes, Cooking: 9 hours

Ingredients

- 2 Tbsp garlic-infused olive oil
- 1 lb green squash, sliced
- 2 cups green olives, pitted and chopped
- 1 grated tomato
- 2 tsp capers
- 1 Tbsp fresh basil finely chopped
- Salt and pepper, to taste
- 2 Tbsp sesame seeds toasted (for serving)

Instructions

1. Add all ingredients from the list in your Slow Cooker and stir well.
2. Cover and cook on LOW 7 - 9 hours.
3. Transfer the mixture into blender or food processor and blend it until smooth.
4. Taste and adjust salt and pepper to taste.
5. Sprinkle with toasted sesame and serve.

Nutrition information:

Calories: 152 Carbohydrates: 6g Proteins: 2.5g Fat: 14g Fiber: 4g

Easy Cauliflower Mousse with Sesame

Serves: 4, Preparation: 10 minutes, Cooking: 4 hours

Ingredients

- 1 lb cauliflower florets
- 1 Tbsp fresh butter
- 1 small onion, chopped small
- 1 cup cooking cream
- Salt and pepper to taste
- 1/2 cup toasted sesame
- Fresh parsley leaves, for garnish (or cilantro)

Instructions

1. Add the cauliflower florets together with all ingredients in your Slow Cooker.
2. Cover and cook on LOW for 6 hours or on HIGH for 4 hours.
3. Taste and adjust salt; stir well.
4. Serve with chopped parsley.

Nutrition information:

Calories: 180 Carbohydrates: 8g Proteins: 6g Fat: 14g Fiber: 4g

Savory Zucchini Cream with Nuts

Serves: 6, Preparation: 10 minutes, Cooking: 3 hours

Ingredients

- 6 medium zucchini
- 4 Tbsp of ground almonds
- 1 cup almond milk
- Seasoned salt and ground white pepper
- 1/3 cup of garlic-infused olive oil

Instructions

1. Rinse, clean and cut zucchini in slices.
2. Place all ingredients in your Slow Cooker.
3. Cover and cook on HIGH for 3 hours.
4. Transfer zucchini mixture in a blender; blend for 25 - 30 seconds or until smooth.
5. Adjust salt and pepper and blend again.
6. Serve immediately or keep refrigerated.

Nutrition information:

Calories: 72 Carbohydrates: 5g Proteins: 4g Fat: 7g Fiber: 3g

Bok Choy Stir-Fry

Serves: 2, Preparation: 10 minutes, Cooking: 15 minutes

Ingredients

- 20 oz Bok choy, fresh
- 2 Tbsp garlic-infused olive oil
- 2 green onions finely chopped
- 2 cloves garlic minced
- 1 Tbsp of oyster sauce (made with stevia sweetener)
- Salt to taste
- 1 tsp almond flour
- 4 Tbsp water

Instructions

1. Rinse your Bok Choy and drain well.
2. Heat the oil in a skillet and sauté the onion and garlic for 3 - 4 minutes.
3. Add Bok Choy and stir for approximately 2 - 3 minutes.
4. In a bowl, whisk the oyster sauce, salt, almond flour and water.
5. Pour the mixture over Bok Choy, turn off the heat, stir, and let sit for 5 minutes.
6. Serve hot.

Nutrition information:

Calories: 134 Carbohydrates: 2.5g Proteins: 1g Fat: 14g Fiber: 0.5g

Chapter 4 Side Dish & Salad Recipes

Almond - Lemon Spinach Salad
Serves: 6 , Preparation: 10 minutes

Ingredients
- 1 1/2 lbs torn spinach leaves
- 1/4 cup finely chopped green onions
- 1/2 green bell pepper, sliced or diced
- 2 tsp grated fresh ginger
- 2 Tbsp fresh lemon juice or to taste
- 1/3 cup olive oil
- 1/4 tsp salt
- 1/8 tsp red pepper flakes
- 2/3 cup chopped almonds, toasted

Instructions

1. Rinse and clean spinach from any dirt and add in a large salad bowl.
2. In a bowl, whisk lemon juice, olive oil, ginger, salt and red pepper flakes.
3. Toss spinach with dressing mixture and sprinkle toasted sliced almonds on top.
4. Serve.

Nutrition information:
Calories: 229.5 Carbohydrates: 7.5g Proteins: 7.g
Fat: 20.6g Fiber: 4.5g

Savory and Sour Chicken Salad
Serves: 4, Preparation: 20 minutes, Cooking: 35 minutes

Ingredients
- 4 small chicken breasts
- 1 bay leaf
- 6 black peppercorns
- 1 onion, quartered
- 2 garlic cloves, halved
- 1 ¼ cup of white wine
- 2 ½ cups of water
- ½ cup of apple cider vinegar
- ½ cup of white vinegar
- 2 cups of extra virgin olive oil
- Pinch of salt
- 2 rosemary sprigs
- 2 thyme sprigs

For the salad:
- ½ cup of extra virgin olive oil
- 2 Tbsp of wine vinegar
- Salt and black pepper
- 2 cups of mixed salad leaves
- 2 avocados, chopped
- 2 boiled eggs, chopped

Instructions
1. Place the chicken breasts in a pan with the bay leaf, peppercorns, onion, garlic, wine, water and vinegar.
2. Pour the olive oil over the chicken, season with the salt, and add the herbs.
3. Cover and let the chicken simmer gently for 30-35 minutes.
4. When cooked, let it cool and keep it in the fridge overnight.

Salad
1. Combine the olive oil, vinegar, salt and pepper in a bowl and blend it using a hand mixer.
2. Place the mixed salad leaves in a large bowl.
3. Drain the chicken and cut it into strips.
4. Put the chicken strips on top of the salad leaves.
5. Add sliced avocado and garnish with the boiled egg.
6. Finally, pour the vinaigrette over the salad and serve immediately.

Nutrition information:
Calories: 405 Carbohydrates: 12 g Proteins: 32g
Fat: 19g Fiber: 7g

Green Beans Salad with Creamy Cracked Pepper

Serves: 6, Preparation: 15 minutes, Cooking: 3 minutes

Ingredients

- 1 lb green beans, fresh
- 2 green onion (white and green parts), chopped
- 1/2 tsp salt and ground black pepper to taste
- 1 cup water
- 1/2 cup cream cheese (full-fat)
- 1/2 cup sour cream
- Ground black pepper to taste
- 1/4 cup Parmesan cheese - grated

Instructions

1. Clean and rinse green beans in cool water.
2. Use a sharp knife cut off the ends.
3. Place the green beans in your Instant Pot and finely chopped green onions and water. Season salt and pepper to taste.
4. Lock lid into place and set on the MANUAL setting for 3 minutes.
5. Use Quick Release - turn the valve from sealing to venting to release the pressure.
6. Transfer green bans mixture to serving bowl.
7. In a bowl, stir cream cheese, sour cream and cracked black pepper; pour over green beans.
8. Sprinkle creamy green beans with grated parmesan cheese and serve.

Nutrition information:

Calories: 108 Carbohydrates: 4g Proteins: 7g Fat: 10g Fiber: 2g

Warm Spinach - Basil and Parmesan Salad

Serves: 6, Preparation: 10 minutes, Cooking: 6 hours

Ingredients

- 2 Tbsp olive oil
- 1 1/2 lbs. spinach chopped
- 1 green onion, diced
- 2 cloves garlic, sliced
- 1/2 cup basil, fresh
- Pinch of ground nutmeg
- 1/4 cup water
- Salt and pepper to taste
- 3/4 cup Parmesan cheese - grated
- 1 lemon wedges for serving

Instructions

1. Grease the bottom and sides of Crock Pot with olive oil.
2. Add all ingredients in Crock Pot and give a good stir.
3. Cover and cook on LOW for 4 - 6 hours.
4. Transfer creamy vegetables on a serving plate.
5. Serve hot with lemon wedges.

Nutrition information:

Calories: 125 Carbohydrates: 4g Proteins: 9g Fat: 10g Fiber: 3g

Herbed Brussels Sprouts Salad

Serves: 6, Preparation: 10 minutes, Cooking: 3 minutes

Ingredients

- 2 lbs Brussels sprouts
- 1 Tbsp fresh parsley finely chopped
- 1 tsp of fresh dill finely chopped
- 1 tsp fresh chives chopped
- Salt and pepper to taste
- 1 cup water
- Salt and ground black pepper to taste
- 2 Tbsp of olive oil for serving
- Lemon juice for serving (freshly squeezed)

Instructions

1. Place Brussels sprouts into your Instant Pot.
2. Add fresh herbs, salt and pepper to taste and pour water.
3. Lock lid into place and set on the MANUAL setting for 3 minutes.
4. When the timer beeps, press "Cancel" and carefully flip the Quick Release valve to let the pressure out.
5. Open the lid and transfer Brussels sprouts in a salad bowl.
6. Drizzle with olive oil and lemon juice, and serve.

Nutrition information:

Calories: 107 Carbohydrates: 9g Proteins: 5g Fat: 7g Fiber: 6g

Warm Bok Choi Salad with Mustard Dressing

Serves: 6, Preparation: 5 minutes, Cooking: 15 minutes

Ingredients

- 1 1/2 lbs of Bok choy, trimmed
- 1 cup or more water
- Seasoned salt to taste
- 1 cup olive oil
- 1 1/2 Tbsp of lime juice
- 2 Tbsp yellow mustard

Instructions

1. Rinse and clean Bok Choy from any dirt.
2. Pour Bok Choy in your Instant Pot, sprinkle with a pinch of seasoned salt and pour water.
3. Lock lid into place and set on the MANUAL setting for 15 minutes.
4. Use Quick Release - turn the valve from sealing to venting to release the pressure.
5. Open lid, and with tongue transfer Bok Choy in a large salad bowl.
6. In a bowl, whisk olive oil, mustard, seasoned salt and lime juice.
7. Pour dressing over Bok choy salad, toss and serve.

Nutrition information:

Calories: 327 Carbohydrates: 1.5g Proteins: 1g Fat: 37g Fiber: 0.6g

Broccoli Salad with Melted Cheese

Serves: 4, Preparation: 15 minutes, Cooking: 3 hours

Ingredients

- 1 1/2 lbs. broccoli florets cut into small pieces
- 1 cup of water
- 1/4 cup olive oil
- 1/2 lemon zest
- 1 1/2 tsp lemon juice, freshly squeezed
- Salt and pepper to taste
- 1 can ground parmesan Cheese

Instructions

1. Wash the broccoli thoroughly and clean from any dirt.
2. Cut the broccoli in florets, and then cut them in small pieces
3. Place broccoli in your oiled Crock Pot.
4. Pour water, oil, lemon zest and lemon juice into Crock Pot.
5. Season salt and black pepper, stir and cover.
6. Cook on LOW for 2-3 hours.
7. Open lid, and sprinkle grated parmesan cheese in your Crock Pot.
8. Cover again, and cook on HIGH for 15 minutes. Serve hot.

Nutrition information:

Calories: 280 Carbohydrates: 7g Proteins: 15g Fat: 33g Fiber: 0.1g

Warm Spinach - Basil and Parmesan Salad

Serves: 6, Preparation: 10 minutes, Cooking: 6 hours

Ingredients

- 2 Tbsp olive oil
- 1 1/2 lbs. spinach chopped
- 1 green onion, diced
- 2 cloves garlic, sliced
- 1/2 cup basil, fresh
- Pinch of ground nutmeg
- 1/4 cup water
- Salt and pepper to taste
- 3/4 cup Parmesan cheese - grated
- 1 lemon wedges for serving

Instructions

1. Grease the bottom and sides of Crock Pot with olive oil.
2. Add all ingredients in Crock Pot and give a good stir.
3. Cover and cook on LOW for 4 - 6 hours.
4. Transfer creamy vegetables on a serving plate.
5. Serve hot with lemon wedges.

Nutrition information:

Calories: 125 Carbohydrates: 4g Proteins: 9g Fat: 10g Fiber: 3g

Bitter Turnip Greens and Almond Salad

Serves: 4, Preparation: 10 minutes, Cooking: 30 minutes

Ingredients
- 1 Tbsp tallow
- 3 cups turnip greens
- 1/2 cup slivered almonds, lightly toasted
- 1/4 tsp of salt and black pepper freshly ground
- 1 Tbsp apple vinegar (optional)

Instructions
1. Rinse and clean the turnip greens from any dirt.
2. Heat tallow in a skillet over medium heat.
3. Add turnip greens; season with the pinch of the salt and pepper and sauté for 20 minutes.
4. Add finely chopped almonds, stir and cook for further 10 minutes; stir.
5. Stir in apple cider vinegar.
6. Taste and adjust salt and pepper.
7. Transfer to the salad bowl, and allow it to cool before serving.

Nutrition information:
Calories: 113 Carbohydrates: 7.4g Proteins: 6.7g Fat: 9.4g Fiber: 5g

Hearty Artichokes, Green Beans and Eggs Salad

Serves: 6, Preparation: 15 minutes, Cooking: 35 minutes

Ingredients
- 4 artichokes (cooked)
- 2 cups green beans (cooked)
- 4 boiled eggs (hard)
- 2 scallions finely chopped
- 2 Tbsp of fresh mint finely chopped
- 2 Tbsp of fresh dill finely chopped
- 3 Tbsp of capers
- 10 olives, pitted, finely chopped (optional)

Dressing
- 1/2 cup olive oil
- 2 Tbsp of lemon juice
- Sea salt and freshly ground black pepper

Instructions
1. Bring to boil pot with the salted water.
2. Add artichokes and boil for 2 - 3 minutes.
3. Reduce heat; simmer, covered, for about 20 to 30 minutes.
4. Cut artichokes in quarters and place in a salad bowl.
5. Add green beans, eggs quartered, spring onions, dill, mint, caper and olives.

For the dressing:
1. In a bowl, combine olive oil, salt, pepper, lemon juice and stir well.
2. Pour dressing over the artichokes salad and toss to combine well.
3. Serve immediately.

Nutrition information:
Calories: 493 Carbohydrates: 12g Proteins: 21g Fat: 24g Fiber: 2.4g

Lobster, Eggs and Mayonnaise Salad
Serves: , Preparation: 10 minutes

Ingredients
- 2 can (11 oz) lobster meat
- 1 cup mayonnaise
- 2 boiled eggs, finely chopped
- 3 Tbsp scallions, green parts only, chopped
- 1 Tbsp mustard (Dijon, English, or whole grain)
- Salt and ground pepper
- 1 Tbsp capers
- 1 lettuce heart

Instructions

1. Place the lobster meat, mayonnaise, eggs, green onions, mustard in a salad bowl.
2. Stir to combine well.
3. Season the salt and pepper to taste.
4. Sprinkle with a capers and garnish with lettuce hearts.
5. Serve and enjoy!

Nutrition information:
Calories: 374 Carbohydrates: 9g Proteins: 21g Fat: 25.5g Fiber: 13g

Tuna - Avocado Salad with Mayo-Mustard Dressing
Serves: 4, Preparation: 15 minutes

Ingredients
- 1 avocado, sliced
- 6 oz of tuna fish in water
- 1 tomato, coarsely chopped
- 3 Tbs fresh basil, finely chopped
- 1 tsp chives, chopped, for garnish
- For the sauce
- 1 Tbsp stone-ground mustard
- 2 Tbs mayonnaise
- 1 tsp apple cider vinegar
- Sea salt and ground black pepper ti taste

Instructions
1. Place the tuna fish, tomato, onion, avocado, basil in a shallow ball and stir well.

For the sauce:
1. In a small bowl stir the mayonnaise, mustard and apple cider vinegar and salt and pepper.
2. Pour the sauce over the salad.
3. Taste and adjust salt and pepper to taste.
4. Sprinkle with chopped chives and serve.

Nutrition information:
Calories: 292 Carbohydrates: 9g Proteins: 33g Fat: 14g Fiber: 5.4g

Chicken Salad with Dandelion Greens & Chicory

Serves: 6, Preparation: 10 minutes

Ingredients

- 10 oz dandelion greens, trimmed and thinly sliced
- 10 oz chicory greens
- 1 chicken breast, cooked and sliced
- 1/4 cup extra-virgin olive oil
- 3 Tbsp of fresh lemon juice (about 2 lemons)
- Sea salt and freshly ground black pepper, to taste

Instructions

1. Clean and rinse from any dirt dandelion greens and chicory, and add in a large salad bowl.
2. Add sliced chicken breast in a salad bowl; toss. Season the chicken with the salt.
3. Whisk the olive oil and lemon juice and pour over the salad; toss to combine well.
4. Serve immediately.

Nutrition information:

Calories: 182 Carbohydrates: 5.6g Proteins: 18g Fat: 10g Fiber: 3g

Delicious Avocado Puree

Serves: 8, Preparation: 15 minutes

Ingredients

- 4 ripe avocados
- Juice of 1 lemon
- 1 onion finely chopped
- 1 ripe tomato finely chopped
- Salt to taste
- 1 cup of fresh parsley finely chopped

Instructions

1. Peel and cut avocado in the middle.
2. Remove the pit with a teaspoon, remove the flesh and place into a bowl.
3. Add the onion and tomato and drizzle with lemon juice.
4. Place the mixture in a blender and blend until softened.
5. Season with the salt and blend for 20 further seconds.
6. Transfer the avocado pour into glass bowl and sprinkle with chopped parsley.
7. Refrigerate until serving.

Nutrition information:

Calories: 159 Carbohydrates: 8.8g Proteins: 2.4g Fat: 14g Fiber: 7g

Festive Red Cabbage Salad

Serves: 6, Preparation: 15 minutes

Ingredients

- 1 lb red cabbage, finely chopped or shredded
- 2 garlic cloves, finely sliced
- 4 slices crispy bacon, crumbled
- 1/2 cup olive oil
- 2 Tbsp of fresh lemon juice
- 1/2 tsp of mustard seeds
- 1/2 tsp of tarragon

Instructions

1. Rinse cabbage and clean from any dirt or yellow outer leaves.
2. Place the cabbage in a food processor and finely chopped or shred.
3. Place shredded cabbage in a large salad bowl.
4. Sprinkle with the salt and pepper; add crumbled bacon and sliced garlic. Toss to combine well.
5. In a small bowl, whisk the olive oil, lemon juice, mustard seeds and tarragon.
6. Pour dressing over cabbage salad, and toss to combine well.
7. Serve.

Nutrition information:

Calories: 200 Carbohydrates: 8.5g Proteins: 6.3g Fat: 15.5g Fiber: 4.3g

Garlic Sauce for Poultry

Serves: 6, Preparation: 5 minutes

Ingredients

- 1 cup olive oil
- 1/2 cup fresh lemon juice
- 6 large garlic cloves, finely chopped
- Salt and freshly ground black pepper to taste
- 1 peel from one lemon
- 1/4 tsp dried sage
- 1/4 tsp dried marjoram
- 1/4 tsp of nutmeg

Instructions

1. Add all ingredients in a high-speed blender; blend for 15 - 20 seconds or until all ingredients combined well.
2. Pour in a glass container, cover and refrigerate before serving.
3. Serve with any kind of poultry.

Nutrition information:

Calories: 328 Carbohydrates: Proteins: 2.6g Fat: 36g Fiber: 0.3g

Green Salad a la Italian

Serves: 8, Preparation: 10 minutes

Ingredients

- 10 oz green salads such as lettuce, cos, romain
- 1 can (11 oz) artichoke hearts, drained and quartered
- 1 can (11 oz) tuna in water or oil, drained, flaked
- 1/2 lb green beans, cooked, drained
- 1 pinch salt to taste
- 1 cup Italian dressing

Instructions

1. Place all ingredients from the list above in a large salad bowls.
2. Pour Italian dressing, and gently stir to combine evenly.
3. Taste and adjust salt if needed.
4. Serve immediately.

Nutrition information:

Calories: 167 Carbohydrates: 7.6g Proteins: 12 g Fat: 9.8g Fiber: 2.8g

Hearty Autumn Salad

Serves: 4, Preparation: 10 minutes

Ingredients

For the salad:
- 3/4 lb of lettuce salad
- 1 avocado
- 1 carrot
- 1/2 cup of almonds, finely chopped

For the vinaigrette:
- 4 Tbsp olive oil
- 2 Tbsp lemon juice (freshly squeezed)
- 1 - 2 Tbsp of mayonnaise
- Salt and black pepper to taste

Instructions

1. Rinse and chop lettuce, peel avocado and carrot, and place all together in a large salad bowl.
2. In a bowl, whisk all ingredients for dressing.
3. Sprinkle almonds over salad.
4. Pour dressing and toss to combine well.
5. Serve immediately.

Nutrition information:

Calories: 223 Carbohydrates: 8.7g Proteins: 3.8g Fat: 19.5g Fiber: 6g

Homemade Spicy Harissa Paste

Serves: 6, Preparation: 15 minutes, Cooking: 10 minutes

Ingredients

- 5 red chili peppers
- 2 Tbsp of extra-virgin olive oil
- 4 cloves of garlic, sliced
- 2 tsp cumin seeds
- 2 tsp coriander seeds
- 2 Tbsp of white wine
- 3 Tbsp of chopped fresh parsley
- Salt to taste

Instructions

1. Heat the oil in a non-stick skillet, and fry the chili peppers for 2-3 minutes.
2. Put peppers in a bowl, cover with aluminum foil and allow it to cool.
3. In a skillet roast the cumin and coriander seeds for two minutes.
4. When the peppers cooled down completely, remove the peel with gloves and cut them in the middle to remove the seeds.
5. Place cleaned peppers in mortar along with garlic, cumin and coriander seeds; beat until you get a smooth mixture.
6. Stir in the wine, add a little bit of oil and beat until you get a smooth paste.
7. Add chopped parsley and season the salt.
8. Serve or keep refrigerated.

Nutrition information:
Calories: 27 Carbohydrates: 4g Proteins: 1.1g Fat: 1g Fiber: 1g

Keto Canary Island Red Sauce

Serves: 6, Preparation: 10 minutes, Cooking:

Ingredients

- 2 large red bell peppers cut into chunks
- 1 bunch fresh cilantro
- 3 cloves garlic
- 1 Tbsp ground sweet paprika
- 1/4 cup olive oil
- 1 chili pepper
- 2 Tbsp ground almonds

Instructions

1. Combine all ingredients in a blender; blend until finely smooth.
2. Place in a glass jar and refrigerate for one hour.
3. Serve.

Nutrition information:
Calories: 101 Carbohydrates: 4.2g Proteins: 0.8g Fat: 9.2g Fiber: 1.4g

Keto Hollandaise Sauce

Serves: 4, Preparation: 5 minutes, Cooking: 10 minutes

Ingredients
- 3 egg yolks from free-range chickens
- 1/4 cup water
- 2 Tbsp of lemon juice , freshly squeezed
- 1/2 cup cold butter, cut into 8 pieces
- 1/8 tsp cayenne pepper
- 1/8 tsp paprika
- Salt to taste

Instructions
1. Separate the eggs. Heat the egg yolks, water and lemon juice in a small saucepan over low heat.
2. Cook, stirring constantly, until the mixture begins to bubble.
3. Add the butter, and stir until melted and sauce is thickened.
4. Add the paprika and cayenne pepper, and season with the salt to taste.
5. Remove from heat and allow it to cool.
6. Serve. Keep refrigerated.

Nutrition information:
Calories: 246 Carbohydrates: 1g Proteins: 2.3g Fat: 26.4g Fiber: 0.1g

Nutty Sauce for Roast

Serves: 6, Preparation: 5 minutes, Cooking: 2 hours

Ingredients
- 1 cup bone broth (preferable homemade)
- 1 cup water
- 1 cup red wine
- 1 Tbsp fresh parsley finely chopped
- 1 Tbsp fresh basil finely chopped
- 1/3 cup ground almonds
- 1 Tbsp fresh butter
- Lemon juice, to taste
- Salt and freshly ground white pepper to taste

Instructions
1. Add all ingredients to the inner pot in the Crock Pot.
2. Cover and cook on LOW setting for 1 - 2 hours.
3. Serve warm or cold.
4. Keep refrigerated.

Nutrition information:
Calories: 39 Carbohydrates: 1.5g Proteins: 1.5g Fat: 8g Fiber: 1g

Keto Mock Hollandaise Sauce

Serves: 6, Preparation: 5 minutes, Cooking: 10 minutes

Ingredients

- 2 egg whites from free-range chickens
- 1 cup mayonnaise
- 2 Tbsp lemon juice (freshly squeezed)
- 1/2 tsp dry mustard
- Salt to taste

Instructions

1. Separate the eggs.
2. In a saucepan, beat slightly the egg whites.
3. Add mayonnaise, lemon juice, dry mustard, and salt; beat until combined well.
4. Place the saucepan over medium-low heat and stirring constantly, cook the sauce until thick, but do not boil.
5. Remove the saucepan from the heat and let it cool.
6. Serve or keep refrigerated.

Nutrition information:

Calories: 34 Carbohydrates: 3.2g Proteins: 1.3g Fat: 1g Fiber: 0.1g

Marinated Olives

Serves: 4, Preparation: 5 minutes, Cooking:

Ingredients

- 24 large olives, black and green
- 2 Tbsp of extra-virgin olive oil
- 2 Tbsp red wine
- 2 cloves garlic, thinly sliced
- 2 tsp coriander seeds, crushed
- 1/2 tsp crushed red pepper
- 1 tsp dried thyme
- 1 tsp dried rosemary, crushed

Instructions

1. Place olives and all remaining ingredients in a large container or bag, and shake to combine well.
2. Cover (if in container), and refrigerate to marinate overnight.
3. Serve.

Nutrition information:

Calories: 102 Carbohydrates: 2.7g Proteins: 0.5g Fat: 10g Fiber: 1.5g

Mornay Sauce for Seafood

Serves: 4, Preparation: 5 minutes, Cooking: 10 minutes

Ingredients

- 3 egg yolks from free-range chickens
- 1 cup Béchamel classic sauce
- 1/4 cup whipped cream
- 1 tsp of lemon juice, freshly squeezed
- 1/4 cup Parmesan cheese

Instructions

1. In a saucepan, whisk eggs yolks with the cream.
2. Add the Béchamel sauce mix and simmer over low heat; stir to avoid sauce burning.
3. Remove from heat and stir ground cheese. Serve.

Nutrition information:

Calories: 134 Carbohydrates: 2.2g Proteins: 5.g Fat: 12g Fiber: 0.02g

Mushrooms and Wine Steak Sauce

Serves: 8, Preparation: 5 minutes, Cooking: 15 minutes

Ingredients

- 3 Tbsp of fresh butter grass-fed
- 4 oz fresh button mushrooms, rinsed
- 1/4 cup onion, finely chopped
- 1 clove garlic, minced
- 1 cup bone broth (preferable homemade)
- 1 1/2 Tbsp of grated tomato
- 1/8 tsp ground black pepper, freshly ground
- 2 tsp almond flour
- 1 Tbsp of water
- 2 Tbsp dry red wine

Instructions

1. Heat butter in a saucepan over medium heat. Add mushrooms, onion and garlic; sauté for about 3 - 4 minutes.
2. Stir in bone broth, tomato paste and black pepper. Bring to the boil; reduce heat to low and simmer, covered, for 5 minutes.
3. Blend the almond flour with water. Add some of the hot mushroom sauce into almond mixture and return to saucepan.
4. Pour wine and stir sauce until thickened.
5. Serve hot or cold.
6. Keep refrigerated.

Nutrition information:

Calories: 55 Carbohydrates: 1.4g Proteins: 5.g Fat: 5.5g Fiber: 0.4g

Provençal Black Olive Paste

Serves: 4, Preparation: 5 minutes

Ingredients

- 1/2 lb black olives pitted
- 4 Tbsp capers
- 2 cloves garlic finely chopped
- 2 Tbsp of mustard
- 1/2 cup of olive oil
- Freshly ground black pepper
- Fresh thyme (optional)

Instructions

1. Place all ingredients in a high-speed blender and blend until smooth.
2. Place in a glass jar or container and refrigerate for 2 hours.
3. Serve.

Nutrition information:

Calories: 125 Carbohydrates: 6.2g Proteins: 1.5g Fat: 11g Fiber: 4g

Roasted Radicchio Salad

Serves: 4, Preparation: 10 minutes, Cooking: 20 minutes

Ingredients

- 1 lb radicchio (cut in wedges)
- 1/4 cup olive oil
- 1 Tbsp fresh thyme, chopped
- 2 Tbsp lemon juice (freshly squeezed)
- Salt and pepper to taste

Instructions

1. Preheat oven to 450°F.
2. Cut radicchio into wedges and rinse in cold water; gently shake off excess water.
3. Place radicchio in large bowl; drizzle with olive oil, sprinkle with thyme, salt, and pepper and toss to coat.
4. Arrange radicchio wedges on rimmed baking sheet.
5. Roast for about 10 - 13 minutes.
6. Stir and bake for further 6 - 7 minutes.
7. Arrange radicchio on platter, sprinkle with a pinch of salt and pepper, drizzle generously with lemon juice and serve.

Nutrition information:

Calories: 153 Carbohydrates: 5.4g Proteins: 2g Fat: 15g Fiber: 1.2g

Romaine Lettuce with Roquefort Dressing

Serves: 8, Preparation: 15 minutes

Ingredients

- 1 lbs Romaine lettuce
- 3 cherry tomatoes, chopped
- 1 green onion, sliced thin rings
- 1/2 cup white mushrooms, well cleaned, and thinly sliced
- 1/4 cup of extra-virgin olive oil
- 1/2 cup cream cheese (full-fat)
- 1/3 cup Roquefort cheese
- Freshly-ground black pepper, to taste

Instructions

1. Rinse and clean the lettuce and place in a salad bowl.
2. Add cherry tomatoes, green onion and mushrooms; toss to combine.
3. In a bowl, whisk the olive oil, cream cheese, ground pepper and Roquefort cheese. Pour the dressing over salad and toss to combine well.
4. Serve.

Nutrition information:

Calories: 101 Carbohydrates: 5.11g Proteins: 7g Fat: 6.5g Fiber: 2.5g

Savory and Sweet Rhubarb Puree

Serves: 4, Preparation: 15 minutes Cooking: 15 minutes

Ingredients

- 1 lb of rhubarb, cut into slices
- 2 Tbsp of olive oil
- 2 Tbsp of water
- 1 piece of fresh ginger, peeled, finely shredded
- 1/4 cup stevia sweetener, granulated
- 1 cinnamon stick
- 2 Tbsp of mustard (Dijon, English, ground stone)

Instructions

1. Clean and cut rhubarb into slices.
2. Place the rhubarb into a saucepan with water, ginger, stevia sweetener and the cinnamon stick.
3. Simmer over low heat about 10 - 12 minutes or until the rhubarb is tender.
4. Remove the cinnamon stick and ginger, and transfer the rhubarb mixture in a blender or food processor.
5. Blend on high to create a smooth puree.
6. Add mustard and stir for 20 - 30 seconds.
7. Serve.

Nutrition information:

Calories: 39 Carbohydrates: 6.2g Proteins: 1.5g Fat: 5g Fiber: 4.5g

Tangy Lemon and Dill Vinaigrette

Serves: 4, Preparation: 10 minutes, Cooking:

Ingredients

- 4 Tbsp of white wine vinegar
- 4 Tbsp of Dijon mustard
- 4 Tbsp of fresh dill, chopped
- 2 tsp finely chopped garlic
- 2 fresh lemon juice, or to taste
- 1/3 cup extra-virgin olive oil
- Salt and freshly ground black pepper to taste

Instructions

1. Stir vinegar and mustard together in a small bowl until smooth.
2. Stir the dill, chopped garlic, and lemon juice into vinegar mixture.
3. Slowly, pour the olive oil into the mixture while whisking continuously until the dressing is creamy and smooth.
4. Season with the salt and ground black pepper.
5. Ready!

Nutrition information:

Calories: 181 Carbohydrates: 3.7g Proteins: 1g Fat: 19g Fiber: 0.5g

"Mimosa" Stuffed Eggs

Serves: 4, Preparation: 10 mins, Cooking: 20 mins

Ingredients
- 8 eggs, hard boiled
- 2 tbs vinegar
- 4 tbs mayonnaise
- 2 tbs of mustard
- Salt and ground pepper to taste
- For serving
- 2 tsp spring onions, sliced
- 1 tsp sweet red paprika

Instructions
1. Boil eggs and allow them to cool; peel.
2. Cut the eggs lengthwise.
3. Remove the yolks, and place in a bowl.
4. Add vinegar, mayonnaise, mustard, and the salt and pepper; stir well.
5. Fill the eggs with the mayonnaise mixture.
6. Serve with fresh chopped onions and paprika.

Nutrition information:
Calories: 208.96 Carbohydrates: 5,54g Proteins: 13.14G Fat: 14.83 Fiber: 0,43G

Aromatic Almond Kale and Zucchini Mash

Serves: 6, Preparation: 5 minutes, Cooking: 20 minutes

Ingredients
- 1/2 cup of ground almonds
- 1 1/2 cups of water
- 1 tsp of ground cumin
- 1 tsp of turmeric powder
- Salt and ground black pepper
- 1 Tbsp of fresh grated ginger
- 4 oz kale
- 2 Tbsp of olive oil
- 2 large zucchini
- Juice from 1 lemon
- 1 scallion chopped
- For serving
- Chopped fresh spearmint
- Chili powder

Instructions
1. In a pot add water, ground almonds, cumin, turmeric, ginger and the salt and pepper; bring to boil and cook for 10 minutes at low temperature.
2. Add kale in a pot, and stir with a wooden spoon.
3. Heat the olive oil in a pan at medium temperature.
4. Cut the zucchini into slices and sauté for 2-3 minutes until golden.
5. Place zucchini in a pot and sprinkle with lemon juice; stir to combine well.
6. Finally, add chopped scallion in a pot and stir.
7. Serve into warm plates with a slotted spoon.
8. Sprinkle with chopped spearmint and chili powder to taste.

Nutrition information: Calories: 135.42
Carbohydrates: 5.84g Proteins: 4g Fat: 10.9g
Fiber: 2.55

Baked Savory Shrimp Cupcakes

Serves: 12, Preparation: 25 minutes, Cooking: 20 minutes

Ingredients
- 1/2 cup of olive oil
- 1 cup of almond flour
- 1 Tbsp stevia granulated sweetener
- 2 tsp baking powder
- 1 tsp baking soda
- 1 tsp of onion powder
- 1 tsp of sweet ground paprika
- 1 tsp of cumin
- 1 pinch of cayenne pepper
- 1 tsp garlic powder
- 3 medium eggs
- 3/4 cup of water
- 2 tsp of tomato puree
- For the glaze
- 1/2 cup of stevia granulated sweetener
- 2 Tbsp of cognac

For shrimps
- 1 Tbsp of olive oil
- 12 medium shrimp
- Salt and black ground pepper
- 1 Tbsp chives

Instructions
1. Preheat the oven to 360 F/180 C.
2. Grease 12 cup cakes and set aside.
3. Heat the olive oil in a frying skillet. Add almond flour and salt.
4. Add the flour and stir with a wire just for one minute to get a golden-brown color.
5. Remove the mixture from the saucepan and transfer to the food processor.
6. Add the sweetener, baking powder, soda, onion, paprika, cumin, cayenne pepper, garlic, and blend at medium speed for 1-2 minutes until all ingredients to combine well.
7. Add the eggs, one by one, water and tomato paste. Beat to combine well.
8. Pour dough in each muffin cup, about 3/4.
9. Bake for 20 minutes or until the cupcakes are golden.
10. Remove from the oven and allow it to cool.

For the glaze
1. Combine the sweetener with cognac until get a smooth glaze.
2. Spread little bit of glaze over each cup cake.

For shrimps
1. Heat the olive oil in a frying pan on high temperature.
2. Season shrimp with the salt and pepper.
3. Sauté shrimp for two minutes in total.
4. Place one shrimp in each cup cake.
5. Sprinkle with chives and serve.

Nutrition information: Calories: 124.43 Carbohydrates: 1.2g Proteins: 2.46g Fat: 11.4g Fiber: 0.1g

Braised Mushrooms with Thyme and Lemon

Serves: 4 , Preparation: 5 minutes, Cooking: 15 minutes

Ingredients

- 2 Tbs of olive oil
- 1 tsp of butter
- 1 lb of fresh mushrooms, halved or quartered
- 1 clove of garlic grated,
- 1 lemon, juice
- 1 tsp of lemon zest,
- 1 Tbs of fresh thyme leaves
- Salt and ground pepper to taste

Instructions

1. Heat the olive oil and the butter in a large frying pan.
2. Add the mushrooms and cook, without stirring, for 3 minutes.
3. Stir mushrooms and continue to cook for further 5 - 6 minutes.
4. Add garlic and lemon zest and cook for 1 minute.
5. Season mushrooms with thyme and with the salt and pepper.
6. Drizzle mushrooms with the lemon juice, stir and serve.

Nutrition information: Calories: 100.56 Carbohydrates: 5.6g Proteins: 3.7g Fat: 8.22g Fiber: 1.65g

Fried Artichokes with Kefalotyri

Serves: 6, Preparation: 15, Cooking: 10

Ingredients

- 6 artichokes, cleaned
- 1/2 cup of almond flour
- Salt and ground black pepper
- 4 Tbsp grated kefalotyri (Romano or Parmesan)
- 2 Eggs from free-range chickens
- Olive oil for frying

Instructions

1. Rinse and thoroughly clean; cut them in 8 pieces and place in a water with lemon.
2. In a bowl, combine the almond flour, salt, pepper and ground Kefalotyri.
3. Beat the egg and pour it into the flour mixture; stir well.
4. If the butter is too thick, add some water.
5. Heat the oil on a large frying skillet.
6. Roll the artichokes in the batter and fry them for 3-4 minutes turning once.
7. Serve warm.

Garlic Marinated Mushrooms

Serves: 8, Preparation: 5 minutes, Cooking: 60 minutes

Ingredients

- 2 1/2 lbs fresh white mushrooms
- 2 cups vinegar (distilled)
- 6 cloves garlic
- 1/2 tsp salt

Instructions

1. Blanch mushrooms in distilled vinegar, chopped garlic and salt for about one hour.
2. Remove mushrooms from the pot and place in colander to drain.
3. Keep refrigerated.

Nutrition information: Calories: 40 Carbohydrates: 5.3g Proteins: 4.52g Fat:1g Fiber: 1.5g

Green Beans and Tuna Salad

Serves: 8, Preparation: 10 minutes, Cooking Time: 20 minutes

Ingredients

- 3/4 lb of green beans, boiled
- 1 cucumber
- 1 small green hot pepper
- 1 avocado
- 1 large zucchini
- Juice and zest of 2 limes
- 3 Tbsp of olive oil
- Salt and ground black pepper
- 2 can (11 oz) tuna fish
- 3 Tbsp of sesame seeds
- 2 Tbsp of fresh mint, finely chopped

Instructions

1. Place green beans in a large salad bowl.
2. Cut the cucumber in half, and then in slices.
3. Clean and slice the pepper, avocado, zucchini and put in a salad bowl; gentle stir to combine.
4. Season the salad with the salt and pepper, and pour the lime juice, lime zest and olive oil; toss to combine.
5. Finally, add tuna fish over salad.
6. Sprinkle with sesame and fresh mint and refrigerate for 20 minutes.
7. Serve.

Nutrition information:
Calories: 158.5 Carbohydrates: 7.8g Proteins: 8g Fat: 11g Fiber: 4.4g

Ground Turkey Cocktail Bites

Serves: 6, Preparation: 10 minutes, Cooking: 5 minutes

Ingredients

- 1 lb ground turkey breast
- 3 Tbsp mayonnaise
- 2 Tbsp grated onion
- 1/2 tsp celery salt
- 2 Tbsp fresh parsley finely chopped
- 1 tsp of garlic powder
- 1/2 tsp of Tabasco sauce
- 3 Tbsp ground almonds
- Lemon wedges for serving

Instructions

1. In a large bowl, combine all ingredients in compact mixture.
2. Refrigerate for 2 hours.
3. Shape the turkey mixture into small bite-size pieces.
4. Heat one non-stick frying pan and cook turkey balls for 5 minutes or until crisp.
5. Serve hot with lemon wedges.

Nutrition information: Calories: 140.5 Carbohydrates: 7.5g Proteins: 14.5 Fat: 6g Fiber: 2g

Halloumi Cheese Wrapped with Prosciutto

Serves: 6, Preparation: 5 minutes, Cooking: 5 minutes

Ingredients

- 1/2 lb of halloumi cheese (or Paneer)
- 6 thin slices of prosciutto
- 1 Tbsp of fresh chopped oregano
- 3 Tbsp of extra-virgin olive oil
- Lemon wedges for serving

Instructions

1. Cut halloumi cheese in 6 sticks.
2. Sprinkle chopped oregano over halloumi sticks.
3. Wrap each stick of halloumi with a strip of prosciutto, and then drizzle with olive oil.
4. Heat one non-stick frying skillet and fry halloumi sticks with prosciutto for about one minute on each side.
5. Serve hot with lemon wedges.

Nutrition information:
Calories: 265 Carbohydrates: 4g Proteins: 19g Fat: 20g Fiber: 1.2g

Herbed Cheese Spread

Serves: 10, Preparation: 5 minues, Cooking: 0

Ingredients

- 8 oz cream cheese, full-fat
- 6 oz goat cheese
- 1/4 cup Greek yogurt
- 1 clove garlic, finely sliced
- 1/2 tsp dried thyme
- 1 Tbsp of chopped chives
- 1 pinch of cayenne pepper (optional)
- Salt and ground black pepper to taste

Instructions

1. In a bowl, stir all ingredients and stir until thoroughly combined.
2. Place the mixture into a glass bowl and refrigerate for at least 2 hours.
3. Serve cold.

Nutrition information:

Calories: 75 Carbohydrates: 2.4g Proteins: 7g Fat: 11g Fiber: 0.05g

Oregano - Parmesan Shrimp Oven Baked

Serves: 6 , Preparation: 15 minutes , Cooking: 12 minutes

Ingredients

- 2 lbs of shrimp, peeled
- Salt and ground pepper
- Zest and juice from 1 lemon
- 1/3 cup of olive oil
- 2 Tbsp of fresh oregano
- 1/4 cup of ground almonds
- 2 cloves of garlic
- 1/2 cup of grated parmesan
- Pinch of chili flakes
- 1 bunch of fresh parsley, chopped
- 1 Tbsp of fresh basil
- Lemon wedges for serving

Instructions

1. Preheat the oven to 400 F/200 C.
2. In a bowl, combine shrimp, lemon zest and juice, olive oil, and the salt and pepper; stir with the spoon.
3. Add fresh chopped oregano, stir and set aside.
4. Place the garlic, ground almonds, parmesan, chili flakes, fresh oregano, lemon zest in high-fast blender.
5. Blend until the mixture combined well.
6. Add the mixture to the bowl with the shrimps; gentle stir.
7. Lay shrimp in an oven proof baking dish and bake for 10 - 12 minutes.
8. Serve with lemon wedges.

Nutrition information:

Calories: 295 Carbohydrates: 5.7g Proteins: 26g Fat: 19g Fiber: 2.5g

Roasted Cocktail Mussels

Serves: 6, Preparation: 20 minutes, Cooking: 20 minutes

Instructions

- 2 lbs of mussels
- 3/4 cup of water
- Coarse salt for baking dish
- 3/4 cup of ground almond
- 1/3 cup of olive oil
- 4 Tbsp of grated parmesan
- 2 cloves of garlic, chopped
- 1 bunch of parsley, finely chopped
- 1 tsp fresh oregano
- 2 pinches of salt

Instructions

1. Preheat the oven to 450 F/230 C.
2. Rinse and clean mussels under cold water.
3. Heat the water in a large pot, add mussels, cover and boil for 5 -6 minutes.
4. Transfer mussels with pierced ladle to a bowl; reserve cooking liquid.
5. Remove the half shell and hold the other half with the mussel.
6. Sprinkle thick salt in a baking pan, lay the mussels and pour with some liquid.
7. In a bowl, stir ground almonds, olive oil, parmesan, garlic, parsley, oregano and the salt. Divide the mixture evenly over mussels.
8. Bake for 15 minutes and serve hot.

Nutrition information:
Calories: 355 Carbohydrates: 8g Proteins: 23g
Fat: 25g Fiber: 2g

Smoked Pink Trout Dip

Serves: 6, Preparation: 15 minutes

Ingredients

- 1 1/2 cups of cream cheese, softened
- 2 Tbsp of sour cream
- 1 Tbsp of lemon juice
- 1 tsp of grated lemon zest
- 1 spring onion finely chopped
- 2 tsp of finely chopped dill
- 5 ounces of smoked pink trout, chopped
- Salt and ground black pepper to taste

Instructions

1. In a bowl, add cream cheese and sour cream, and beat with an electric mixer until fluffy.
2. Add lemon juice and lemon zest; beat until all ingredients combined well.
3. Season the salt the pepper, and add chopped fresh onion and dill; stir.
4. Finally, add chopped smoked trout and gently stir with the spoon.
5. Taste and adjust salt to taste.
6. Transfer cream cheese/fish dip in a glass container and cover with plastic membrane.
7. Keep refrigerated until serving.

Nutrition information:
Calories: 247 Carbohydrates: 2g Proteins: 10g
Fat: 22g Fiber: 0.2g

Spicy Cheese Salad

Serves: 6, Preparation: 10 minutes

Ingredients
- 1 clove garlic, finely sliced
- 3 Tbsp of extra-virgin olive oil
- 1 chili pepper, finely sliced
- 1 tsp ground hot pepper
- 3/4 lb of feta cheese
- 1 cup of Greek yogurt

Instructions

1. Add all ingredients in a blender.
2. Blend only for 20 - 30 seconds.
3. Store the cheese salad in a glass bowl.
4. Keep refrigerated until serving.

Nutrition information:
Calories: 152 Carbohydrates: 3g Proteins: 9g Fat: 12g Fiber: 2.5g

Savory and Sour Chicken Salad

Serves: 4, Preparation: 20 minutes, Cooking: 35 minutes

Ingredients
- 4 small chicken breasts
- 1 bay leaf
- 6 black peppercorns
- 1 onion, quartered
- 2 garlic cloves, halved
- 1 ¼ cup of white wine
- 2 ½ cups of water
- ½ cup of apple cider vinegar
- ½ cup of white vinegar
- 2 cups of extra virgin olive oil
- Pinch of salt
- 2 rosemary sprigs
- 2 thyme sprigs

For the salad:
- ½ cup of extra virgin olive oil
- 2 Tbsp of wine vinegar
- Salt and black pepper
- 2 cups of mixed salad leaves
- 2 avocados, chopped
- 2 boiled eggs, chopped

Instructions

1. Place the chicken breasts in a pan with the bay leaf, peppercorns, onion, garlic, wine, water and vinegar.
2. Pour the olive oil over the chicken, season with the salt, and add the herbs.
3. Cover and let the chicken simmer gently for 30-35 minutes.
4. When cooked, let it cool and keep it in the fridge overnight.

Salad

1. Combine the olive oil, vinegar, salt and pepper in a bowl and blend it using a hand mixer.
2. Place the mixed salad leaves in a large bowl.
3. Drain the chicken and cut it into strips.
4. Put the chicken strips on top of the salad leaves.
5. Add sliced avocado and garnish with the boiled egg.
6. Finally, pour the vinaigrette over the salad and serve immediately.

Nutrition information:
Calories: 405 Carbohydrates: 12 g Proteins: 32g
Fat: 19g Fiber: 7g

Green Beans Salad with Creamy Cracked Pepper

Serves: 6, Preparation: 15 minutes, Cooking: 3 minutes

Ingredients

- 1 lb green beans, fresh
- 2 green onion (white and green parts), chopped
- 1/2 tsp salt and ground black pepper to taste
- 1 cup water
- 1/2 cup cream cheese (full-fat)
- 1/2 cup sour cream
- Ground black pepper to taste
- 1/4 cup Parmesan cheese - grated

Instructions

1. Clean and rinse green beans in cool water.
2. Use a sharp knife cut off the ends.
3. Place the green beans in your Instant Pot and finely chopped green onions and water. Season salt and pepper to taste.
4. Lock lid into place and set on the MANUAL setting for 3 minutes.
5. Use Quick Release - turn the valve from sealing to venting to release the pressure.
6. Transfer green bans mixture to serving bowl.
7. In a bowl, stir cream cheese, sour cream and cracked black pepper; pour over green beans.
8. Sprinkle creamy green beans with grated parmesan cheese and serve.

Nutrition information:

Calories: 108 Carbohydrates: 4g Proteins: 7g
Fat: 10g Fiber: 2g

Herbed Brussels Sprouts Salad

Serves: 6, Preparation: 10 minutes, Cooking: 3 minutes

Ingredients

- 2 lbs Brussels sprouts
- 1 Tbsp fresh parsley finely chopped
- 1 tsp of fresh dill finely chopped
- 1 tsp fresh chives chopped
- Salt and pepper to taste
- 1 cup water
- Salt and ground black pepper to taste
- 2 Tbsp of olive oil for serving
- Lemon juice for serving (freshly squeezed)

Instructions

1. Place Brussels sprouts into your Instant Pot.
2. Add fresh herbs, salt and pepper to taste and pour water.
3. Lock lid into place and set on the MANUAL setting for 3 minutes.
4. When the timer beeps, press "Cancel" and carefully flip the Quick Release valve to let the pressure out.
5. Open the lid and transfer Brussels sprouts in a salad bowl.
6. Drizzle with olive oil and lemon juice, and serve.

Nutrition information:

Calories: 107 Carbohydrates: 9g Proteins: 5g
Fat: 7g Fiber: 6g

Warm Bok Choi Salad with Mustard Dressing

Serves: 6, Preparation: 5 minutes, Cooking: 15 minutes

Ingredients

- 1 1/2 lbs of Bok choy, trimmed
- 1 cup or more water
- Seasoned salt to taste
- 1 cup olive oil
- 1 1/2 Tbsp of lime juice
- 2 Tbsp yellow mustard

Instructions

1. Rinse and clean Bok Choy from any dirt.
2. Pour Bok Choy in your Instant Pot, sprinkle with a pinch of seasoned salt and pour water.
3. Lock lid into place and set on the MANUAL setting for 15 minutes.
4. Use Quick Release - turn the valve from sealing to venting to release the pressure.
5. Open lid, and with tongue transfer Bok Choy in a large salad bowl.
6. In a bowl, whisk olive oil, mustard, seasoned salt and lime juice.
7. Pour dressing over Bok choy salad, toss and serve.

Nutrition information:

Calories: 327 Carbohydrates: 1.5g Proteins: 1g Fat: 37g Fiber: 0.6g

Broccoli Salad with Melted Cheese

Serves: 4, Preparation: 15 minutes, Cooking: 3 hours

Ingredients

- 1 1/2 lbs. broccoli florets cut into small pieces
- 1 cup of water
- 1/4 cup olive oil
- 1/2 lemon zest
- 1 1/2 tsp lemon juice, freshly squeezed
- Salt and pepper to taste
- 1 can ground parmesan Cheese

Instructions

1. Wash the broccoli thoroughly and clean from any dirt.
2. Cut the broccoli in florets, and then cut them in small pieces
3. Place broccoli in your oiled Crock Pot.
4. Pour water, oil, lemon zest and lemon juice into Crock Pot.
5. Season salt and black pepper, stir and cover.
6. Cook on LOW for 2-3 hours.
7. Open lid, and sprinkle grated parmesan cheese in your Crock Pot.
8. Cover again, and cook on HIGH for 15 minutes. Serve hot.

Nutrition information:

Calories: 280 Carbohydrates: 7g Proteins: 15g Fat: 33g Fiber: 0.1g

Warm Mushrooms Parmesan

Serves: 4, Preparation: 5 minutes, Cooking: 10 minutes

Ingredients

- 3 Tbsp butter (grass fed), softened
- 1 1/2 lb fresh mushrooms, whole
- 4 Tbsp Parmesan cheese, grated
- 1/8 tsp black pepper (freshly ground)

Instructions

1. Heat butter in a large frying skillet over medium heat.
2. Add mushrooms and cook over medium-high heat until golden.
3. Sprinkle with grated cheese and pepper and cook for further 1 minute.
4. Serve hot.

Nutrition information:

Calories: 136 Carbohydrates: 5g Proteins: 7.5g Fat: 11g Fiber: 7.3g

Chapter 5 Snack Food Recipes

"Crocked" Button Mushrooms
Serves: 6, Preparation: 5 minutes, Cooking: 10 minutes

Ingredients
- 1 1/2 lbs fresh button mushrooms, rinsed
- 1 cup white wine
- 2 Tbsp of vinegar
- 1/2 cup olive oil
- 1/2 tsp garlic powder
- salt and freshly ground pepper to taste
- 1 dash hot pepper powder
- 1 pinch parsley flakes
- 1 pinch of dry basil

Instructions

1. 1. In a large pot, place all ingredients and cook for 3 - 4 minutes on medium-high heat.
2. Remove from the heat, and allow to cool completely.
3. Place mushrooms in colander to drain.
4. Serve or keep refrigerated.

Nutrition information:
Calories: 218 Carbohydrates: 4.5g Proteins: 4g Fat: 18.5g Fiber: 1.2g

Baked Almond Crusted Zucchini Slices
Serves: 6, Preparation: 15 minutes, Cooking: 15 minutes

Ingredients
- 2 large zucchini, sliced into rings
- 1 cup almond flour
- 1 egg from free range chickens
- Sea salt and ground black pepper to taste
- 1 tsp garlic powder
- 1 tsp onion powder
- 1 tsp fresh thyme (chopped fine)

Instructions
1. Preheat oven to 450 F/230 C.
2. Line a baking sheet with parchment paper and set aside.
3. In a bowl, beat the egg.
4. In a separate bowl, combine almond flour, salt and black pepper, garlic and onion powder, thyme.
5. Dip zucchini slices in the egg and let excess drip off, drop in the almond flour mixture to coat.
6. Place coated zucchini slices onto prepared baking sheet.
7. Bake for 13 - 15 minutes flipping once.
8. Serve warm.

Nutrition information:
Calories: 165 Carbohydrates: 6g Proteins: 8g Fat: 13g Fiber: 3.4g

Mini Bacon-Chicken Skewers

Serves: 6, Preparation: 15 minutes, Cooking: 35 minutes

Ingredients

- 2 chicken breast fillets, cut into cubes
- Salt and ground pepper
- 10 slices of bacon
- 1 cup of cream cheese
- 1 cup of yogurt
- 2 Tbsp of mayonnaise
- 2 Tbsp of mustard

Instructions

1. Cut the chicken into small pieces; season the salt and pepper.
2. In a bowl, combine mayonnaise, yogurt, mustard, and the salt and pepper.
3. Add the chicken pieces and stir.
4. Cover and refrigerate for 2 - 3 hours.
5. Preheat the oven to 360 F/180 C.
6. Cut bacon into bits.
7. Thread chicken and bacon on skewers one after another.
8. Place the chicken-bacon skewers in a baking dish.
9. Bake for 15 minutes, and then, turn and bake for further 10 minutes.
10. Serve hot.

Nutrition information:

Calories: 561 Carbohydrates: 3g Proteins: 29g Fat: 46g Fiber: 0.2g

Grilled Goat Skewers with Yogurt Marinade

Serves: 4, Preparation: 20 minutes, Cooking: 10 minutes

Ingredients

- 1 lb boneless goat loin, cut into 1/2" cubes
- Marinade
- 1 Tbsp lemon juice
- 1 cup yogurt
- 1/4 tsp ground ginger
- 1/2 tsp turmeric
- 1/2 tsp ground cumin
- 1 Tbsp ground coriander
- 1/2 tsp salt

Instructions

1. Cut boneless goat loin, cut into 1/2" cubes.
2. In a bowl, whisk together all ingredients for marinade. Add the goat to the bowl and stir to coat with the marinade evenly. Cover and refrigerate overnight.
3. Remove the bowl with marinated goat 15 - 20 minutes before grilling.
4. Preheat your grill (pellet, gas, charcoal) to HIGH according to manufacturer instructions.
5. Remove the meat from the marinade, and dry on kitchen paper towel. Thread goat meat on skewers.
6. Grill for about 4 - 5 minutes on each side.
7. Serve hot.

Nutrition information:

Calories: 131 Carbohydrates: 1.4g Proteins: 24g Fat: 3g Fiber: 1g

Pancetta Muffins

Serves: 12, Preparation: 15 minutes, Cooking: 3 hours

Ingredients

- 6 slices pancetta cut in small cubes
- 2 cups of almond flour
- 2 tsp baking soda
- 1/4 tsp salt
- 2 Tbsp spring onion chopped (only white parts)
- 1 1/2 cup grated Parmesan cheese
- 1 1/2 tsp allspice (ground)
- 2 Eggs from free-range chickens
- 3/4 cup almond milk (unsweetened)
- 1/2 cup olive oil
- 1 cup water for Instant Pot

Instructions

1. Lightly grease a muffin cups; set aside.
2. In a bowl, stir the almond flour, baking soda, salt, allspice powder, spring onion, parmesan cheese and pancetta.
3. In a second bowl, whisk almond milk, eggs, olive oil, and salt.
4. Combine the almond flour mixture with egg mixture and stir well.
5. Pour the batter in muffins cups (3/4 of each muffins cup)
6. Pour water to the inner stainless steel pot in the Crock Pot, and place the trivet inside (steam rack or a steamer basket).
7. Place the muffins cups on trivet, cover and cook on HIGH for 2 - 3 hours.
8. Serve warm or cold.

Nutrition information:

Calories: 233 Carbohydrates: 1.5g Proteins: 8g Fat: 22g Fiber: 0.1g

Almond Jade Stir-Fry

Serves: 4, Preparation: 5 minutes, Cooking: 20 minutes

Ingredients

- 2 Tbsp olive oil
- 1 cup whole almonds
- 2 cloves garlic, halved
- 1 lb of button mushrooms
- 2-3 tsp minced fresh ginger
- 1/3 cup water
- 3 Tbsp coconut aminos (from coconut sap)
- 2 Tbsp almond flour
- Salt to and d black pepper to taste

Instructions

1. Heat the olive oil in large skillet over medium heat.
2. Add almonds, and cook and stir for about 8 minutes until lightly browned.
3. Remove almonds with slotted spoon on a plate, and set aside.
4. In a same skillet add little oil, and sauté garlic with a pinch of salt for 2 - 3 minutes.
5. Add mushrooms and ginger, and. stir-fry about 5 minutes.
6. In small bowl combine water, coconut aminos and almond flour and mix thoroughly.
7. Add the mixture to skillet; cook and toss about 2 minutes.
8. Taste and adjust the salt and pepper.
9. Serve hot.

Nutrition information:

Calories: 304 Carbohydrates: 8g Proteins: 17g Fat: 27g Fiber: 5g

Chili Almond Coated Turkey Bites

Serves: 6, Preparation: 15 minutes

Ingredients

- 1 lb ground turkey meat
- 3 Tbsp mayonnaise
- 2 Tbsp onion grated
- 2 Tbsp parsley minced
- Salt to taste
- 3 drops of hot pepper sauce as Tabasco (optional)
- 4 Tbsp ground almonds

Instructions

1. In a bowl, stir all (except almonds) ingredients until well combined.
2. Shape the mixture into small bite-size pieces and roll in ground nuts.
3. Cover and refrigerate until serving.

Nutrition information:

Calories: 177 Carbohydrates: 4g Proteins: 16.5g Fat: 12g Fiber: 0.8g

Cold Cheese-Mayo Dip

Serves: 6, Preparation: 15 minutes, Cooking: 5 minutes

Ingredients

- 4 bacon slices, cooked and crumbled
- 2 Tbs chopped green onions
- 1 cup shredded emmental or beaufort cheese
- 3/4 cup cream cheese, softened
- 1/2 cup mayonnaise
- 1/2 tsp yellow mustard
- 1/8 tsp freshly ground black pepper

Instructions

1. In a skillet fry the bacon until crispy; remove from heat and let cool on kitchen paper towel.
2. Chop green onion in thin slices.
3. Combine all ingredients in a large bowl, along with crumbled bacon, and stir with a spoon.
4. Cover ball with plastic membrane and refrigerate for 2 hours.
5. Serve.

Nutrition information:

Calories: 355 Carbohydrates: 3g Proteins: 9.5g Fat: 33g Fiber: 0.1g

Creamy Chicken Topped Cucumbers

Serves: 18, Preparation: 15 minutes

Ingredients

- 8 oz chicken breast finely chopped
- 4 Tbsp of mayonnaise
- 2 Tbsp of yellow mustard
- 2 Tbsp green onions finely chopped
- 1/8 tsp garlic powder
- Ground black pepper to taste
- 3 cucumbers cut into thin slices

Ingredients

1. Line a shallow dish with the parchment paper.
2. Slice cucumbers into thin slices and place on a dish.
3. In a bowl, combine chicken, mayonnaise, mustard, green onion, ground powder and ground black pepper.
4. Top each cucumber slice with 1 or 1 1/2 tablespoon chicken mixture.
5. Refrigerate for 2 hours or more and serve.

Nutrition information:

Calories: 28 Carbohydrates: 2g Proteins: 1.5g Fat: 2g Fiber: 0.5g

Baby Bella Mushrooms Stuffed with Olives

Serves: 10, Preparation: 15 minutes

Ingredients

- 20 Baby Bella (crimini) Mushrooms
- 2 cups cream cheese, at room temperature
- 20 olives green or black
- 1/4 cup fresh parsley finely chopped
- 1/2 tsp Salt and ground black pepper

Instructions

1. In a bowl, stir well cream cheese.
2. Shape balls from cream cheese and put one olive in a center.
3. Place mushrooms on a serving plate, and place the cream cheese balls on each mushroom.
4. Generously sprinkle with chopped parsley.
5. Refrigerate for 4 - 6 hours.
6. Serve cold.

Nutrition information:

Calories: 179 Carbohydrates: 3,5g Proteins: 4g Fat: 17g Fiber: 0,7g

Curry Seasoned Almonds

Serves: 12, Preparation: 15 minutes, Cooking: 5 minutes

Ingredients

- 1 Tbsp curry powder
- 1 Tbsp chili powder
- 1 1/2 Tbsp celery salt
- 1 Tbsp stevia sweetener, granulated
- 2 Tbsp of olive oil
- 1 lb of whole almonds

Instructions

1. In a bowl, combine curry and chili powder, celery salt and stevia : set aside.
2. Heat the olive oil in a large frying skillet and fry almonds for 2 - 3 minutes (stir frequently).
3. Sprinkle almonds curry mixture and stir until well coated.
4. Transfer almonds on a baking pan and let cool for 15 minutes.
5. Serve.

Nutrition information:

Calories: 222 Carbohydrates: 7g Proteins: 7.2g Fat: 20g Fiber: 4g

Dark Avocado Bars

Serves: 8, Preparation: 15 minutes

Ingredients

- 1/2 cup coconut oil, melted
- 3 Tbsp of coconut butter
- 2 medium avocados
- 1/3 cup dark cacao nibs (60 - 69% cacao solid)
- 1/4 cup stevia sweetener, granulated
- 1 tsp pure vanilla extract

Instructions

1. Melt coconut oil and coconut butter in microwave oven for 10 - 13 seconds.
2. Line with parchment paper a large shallow dish and pour the coconut mixture.
3. Freeze for 4 hours or overnight.
4. Remove dish from freezer and cut into pieces. Serve.
5. Store in a container and keep in freezer.

Nutrition information:

Calories: 214 Carbohydrates: 5.5g Proteins: 2g Fat: 22g Fiber: 3.7g

Fried Kale Fritters

Serves: 4, Preparation: 10 minutes, Cooking: 10 minutes

Ingredients

- 1 cup almond flour
- 1/4 cup water
- 1 green chili chopped finely
- 1/4 tsp red chili powder
- 1/4 tsp turmeric powder
- 1 tsp cumin seed powder
- Ground black pepper
- 1 tsp cooking soda
- 1 bunch of kale finely chopped
- 1/2 cups olive oil for frying

Instructions

1. In a large bowl, combine the almond flour, water, chili pepper and the spices and stir well,
2. Add kale to the almond flour mixture and toss to coat well.
3. Heat the oil in a large frying pan on high-medium heat.
4. Scoop a tablespoon of the mixture and place in a pan.
5. Fry kale until golden color and crisp from both sides.
6. Remove kale fritters with slotted spoon and place on plate lined with absorbent paper.
7. Serve hot.

Nutrition information:

Calories: 128 Carbohydrates: 9g Proteins: 4g Fat: 15g Fiber: 2.6g

Frozen Coconut Mocha Smoothie
Serves: 2, Preparation: 10 minutes

Ingredient
- 2 cups unsweetened coconut milk canned
- 2 tsp instant coffee granules
- 1 tsp cocoa powder
- 2 - 3 Tbsp of natural sweetener such Stevia, Truvia, Erythritol...etc.
- 1/2 tsp vanilla extract
- 1 cup Ice cubes crushed (optional)

Instructions

1. Add all ingredients in a blender and blend until combined well.
2. Pour the mixture in a freezer-safe container and freeze for about 4 hours.
3. Remove from the fridge 15 minutes before serving.
4. Give a good stir and serve.

Nutrition information:
Calories: 456 Carbohydrates: 8g Proteins: 5g Fat: 48.5g Fiber: 1g

Goat Cheese Spread
Serves: 6, Preparation: 10 minutes

Ingredients
- 1 cup goat cheese crumbled
- 1 cup of cream cheese
- 1/4 cup plain yogurt
- 1 clove of garlic sliced
- 1 Tbsp chopped chives
- 1/2 tsp dried thyme
- Salt and freshly ground black pepper to taste

Instructions
1. In a bowl, combine all ingredients until thoroughly combined.
2. Refrigerate the mixture for 3 - 4 hours.
3. Serve cold.

Nutrition information:
Calories: 143 Carbohydrates: 3.5g Proteins: 13g Fat: 8.5g Fiber: 3g

Hot Bacon Fat Bombs
Serves: 8, Preparation: 15 minutes

Ingredients
- 3 slices bacon crumbled
- 3 slices pancetta, cut in small cubes
- 1 cup cream cheese
- 1 chili pepper
- Hot smoked paprika
- 1/2 tsp dried basil
- 1/4 tsp onion powder
- 1/4 tsp garlic powder
- Salt and pepper to taste

1. In a bowl, stir all ingredients until combined well.
2. Shape mixture into balls and place on a baking sheet lined with parchment paper.
3. Refrigerate for at least 4 hours.
4. Serve cold.
5. Keep refrigerated.

Nutrition information:
Calories: 216 Carbohydrates: 6.5g Proteins: 6g Fat: 19g Fiber: 1g

Instructions

Keto "Buffalo" Cauliflower

Serves: 6, Preparation: 10 minutes, Cooking: 35 minutes

Ingredients

- 1 Tbsp of fresh butter softened
- 2 Tbsp of olive oil
- 1 cup water
- 1 cup coconut aminos (from coconut sap)
- 1 cup almond flour
- 1 tsp garlic powder
- 1/2 tsp onion powder
- 1 tsp salt and ground black pepper to taste
- 1 large head of cauliflower, cut into florets

Instructions

1. Preheat oven to 400 F/200 C.
2. Add all ingredients (except cauliflower in a blender; blend until smooth.
3. Place the cauliflower florets in oiled large rimmed baking sheet and pour the sauce to over them.
4. Bake in the oven for 30 - 35 minutes.
5. Serve hot or cold.

Nutrition information:

Calories: 58 Carbohydrates: 3g Proteins: 3g Fat: 7g Fiber: 1g

Keto Choco Mousse

Serves: 3, Preparation: 15 minutes

Ingredients

- 4 Tbsp of cocoa powder, unsweetened
- 1 1/2 cup coconut oil melted
- 1/4 cup of heavy cream
- 3 Tbsp stevia granulated sweetener (or to taste)
- 1 Tbsp of pure vanilla extract
- Shredded coconut, unsweetened

Ingredients

1. Melt the coconut oil in a microwave oven.
2. In a mixing bowl, beat the coconut oil and heavy cream with an electric about 3 to 4 minutes or until soft and creamy.
3. Add the remaining ingredients and mix on LOW speed for 2-3 minutes until the mixture is thick.
4. Serve with unsweetened shredded coconut.

Nutrition information:

Calories: 234 Carbohydrates: 6g Proteins: 2g Fat: 23g Fiber: 2g

Peanut Cinnamon Fat Bombs

Serves: 12, Preparation: 10 minutes

Ingredients

- 3/4 cup coconut oil, melted
- 3/4 cup peanut butter
- 3/4 cup butter, salted and melted
- 3/4 cup of natural sweetener (Stevia, Truvia, Erythritol...etc.)
- 1/2 tsp cinnamon
- 4 Tbsp of cocoa powder
- 1/4 cup peanut, ground

Instructions

1. Melt the coconut butter in a microwave oven for 20 -25 seconds.
2. Place all ingredients in your fast-speed blender (except ground peanuts); and blend to combine well.
3. Make small balls and roll each ball in a ground peanut.
4. Place on a baking sheet lined with parchment paper. Freeze for 3 hours.
5. Serve and enjoy!

Nutrition information:

Calories: 263 Carbohydrates: 4.5g Proteins: 5g Fat: 27g Fiber: 2g

Roasted Cheesy Snack

Serves: 6, Preparation: 15 minutes, Cooking: 15 minutes

Ingredients

- 1 Tbsp of almond butter (unsweetened)
- 1/2 cup of almond flour
- 1 1/2 cup of parmesan cheese
- 1/4 tsp fresh oregano, finely chopped
- 1/4 tsp rosemary, finely chopped
- 1/4 tsp fresh basil, finely chopped
- 1 large egg from free-range chickens

Instructions

1. Preheat the oven to 350 Fahrenheit/175C.
2. In a bowl, combine the almond flour, almond butter and grated parmesan cheese.
3. Add fresh herbs and stir well.
4. Add the egg and stir again.
5. Scoop a tablespoon of mixture and place on a baking sheet lined with parchment paper.
6. Bake for 12 - 15 minutes.
7. Remove from the oven and allow to cool.
8. Serve.

Nutrition information:

Calories: 119 Carbohydrates: 1.3g Proteins: 10g Fat: 8g Fiber: 0.3g

Roasted Kale Chips with Lemon Zest

Serves: 4, Preparation: 10 minutes, Cooking: 15 minutes

Ingredients

- 3/4 lb curly kale
- 2 Tbsp of olive oil
- 2 tsp lemon juice (freshly squeezed)
- 2 Tbsp lemon zest (from about 2 large lemons)
- Kosher salt

Instructions

1. Preheat the oven to 350 F175 C.
2. Place the curly kale leaves on a baking sheet, and pour the olive oil and lemon juice Season with the salt, and sprinkle the lemon zest.
3. Bake for 10 - 15 minutes, turning 2 - 3 times (do not burn).
4. Serve warm or cold.

Nutrition information:

Calories: 104 Carbohydrates: 6g Proteins: 9g Fat: 8g Fiber: 2g

Roasted Smoky Spiced Almonds

Serves: 6, Preparation: 10 minutes, Cooking: 1 hour

Ingredients

- 1 cup stevia granulate sweetener (or to taste)
- 2 Tbsp of water
- 1/2 tsp smoked paprika
- 1/4 tsp cayenne pepper
- 3/4 tsp of seasoned salt
- 2 cups whole natural almonds

Instructions

1. Preheat oven to 350 F/175 C.
2. In a bowl, combine stevia sweetener, water, smoked and cayenne pepper and salt and spices in bowl.
3. Add almonds in a spice mixture, toss until combined well.
4. Spread coated almonds in a baking sheet to dry for about 1 hour.
5. Serve.

Nutrition information:

Calories: 275 Carbohydrates: 9g Proteins: 10g Fat: 24g Fiber: 5g

Savory Spinach and Mushrooms Frittata

Serves: 6, Preparation: 15 minutes, Cooking: 25 minutes

Ingredients

- 8 large eggs from free-range chickens
- 1 cup almond milk
- 1 cup parmesan cheese
- Salt and pepper to taste
- 3 cloves garlic, minced
- 2 Tbsp of green onions finely sliced
- 1 cup spinach, frozen and drained
- 4 oz mushrooms, sliced

Instructions

1. Preheat oven to 375 F185 C.
2. In a large mixing bowl, combine all ingredients and whisk with the help of an electric mixer.
3. Pour the mixture into oiled baking pan and bake for 20-25 minutes, Let cool on a wire rack for 15 minutes, and then cut and serve.
4. Keep refrigerated in container.

Nutrition information:

Calories: 103 Carbohydrates: 0.5g Proteins: 11g Fat: 8g Fiber: 0.5g

Spicy Spinach Squares

Serves: 14, Preparation: 15 minutes, Cooking: 35 minutes

Ingredients

- 1 cup almond flour
- 1/2 tsp salt and ground black pepper
- 1 tsp baking soda
- 1 Tbsp cayenne pepper
- 1 cup almond milk
- 2 eggs from free-range chicken
- 3/4 cup fresh butter, melted and cooled
- 1 green onion (only white parts finely chopped)
- 1 lb frozen chopped spinach, defrosted
- 3/4 cup grated parmesan or cheddar cheese

Instructions

1. Preheat the oven to 350 F/175 C.
2. Line a baking dish with parchment paper.
3. In a bowl, combine the almond flour, salt and pepper, baking soda, and cayenne pepper until combine well.
4. Beat the almond milk, eggs, and butter with the help of electric mixer.
5. Combine almond mixture with almond milk mixture and beat again until combined well.
6. Fold in the cheese, onion and spinach and stir well with spatula.
7. Pour the mixture in a prepared baking dish, place in oven and bake for 35 minutes.
8. Let it cool and slice into squares. Keep refrigerated.

Nutrition information:

Calories: 79 Carbohydrates: 3g Proteins: 3g Fat: 7g Fiber: 1.5g

Chapter 6 Sauces, Dressing& Dip

American Jack Daniel's Sauce (Keto version)
Serves: 8, Preparation: 10 minutes, Cooking: 25 minutes

Ingredients
- 1 cup water
- 2 tsp garlic minced
- 1 1/2 cups of natural granulated sweetener such Stevia
- 2 Tbsp of hot sauce
- 2 Tbsp of Coconut Aminos
- 1 cup of lemon juice
- 1/4 cup of Jack Daniels Whiskey
- 2 Tbsp fresh butter
- 1/4 tsp cayenne pepper

Instructions
1. In a small saucepan, pour the water, garlic, stevia sweetener, hot sauce and Cococnut aminos.
2. Cook and stir over moderate heat for about 15 -20 minutes until sweetener dissolve, and the sauce thickens.
3. Remove from heat and add the lemon juice, whiskey, butter and cayenne pepper; stir well until sauce is smooth and shine.
4. Let it cool, and keep refrigerated in a glass container up to 3 months.

Nutrition information:
Calories: 61 Carbohydrates: 5g Proteins: 1g Fat: 4g Fiber: 0.2g

Fresh Mushroom Sauce
Serves: 6, Preparation: 10 minutes, Cooking: 15 minutes

Ingredients
- 1/4 cup of garlic-infused olive oil
- 1 tsp of garlic minced
- 1 lb fresh white mushrooms, sliced
- 1 cup of cherry tomatoes, cut into halves
- 1/2 cup green onions (scallions) finely chopped
- 1/2 tsp salt and ground black pepper to taste

Instructions
1. Heat the olive oil in a frying skillet.
2. Add minced garlic along with mushrooms, and cook, stirring frequently, until mushroom liquid starts to evaporate, about 5 - 6 minutes.
3. Add cherry tomatoes, green onions, and season with the salt and black pepper.
4. Bring to boil, reduce heat, cover and cook for about 5 minutes or until the sauce is done.
5. Remove from heat and serve hot or cold.
6. Keep refrigerated in a covered glass bowl.

Nutrition information:
Calories: 105 Carbohydrates: 4g Proteins: 3g Fat: 10g Fiber: 1.3g

Hot Citrus BBQ Sauce

Serves: 6, Preparation: 10 minutes, Cooking: 15 minutes

Ingredients

- 2 Tbsp of olive oil
- 1 large onion finely chopped
- 1/2 tsp ground red pepper (cayenne)
- 1 chili pepper, seeded and finely chopped
- 1 1/2 cups lime juice (freshly squeezed)
- 2 Tbsp of stevia granulate sweetener (or to taste)
- 1 Tbsp of fresh cilantro finely chopped
- 1/4 tsp salt or to taste

Instructions

1. Heat the olive oil in a saucepan, and cook the onion, ground red pepper, and chili pepper, stirring frequently, until onion is tender, about 5 minutes. At this point, add all remaining ingredients.
2. Bring to boil, and reduce heat to the lowest; cook for further 10 minutes, stirring occasionally.
3. Remove the sauce from heat and allow it to cool.
4. Serve immediately or keep refrigerated.

Nutrition information:

Calories: 61 Carbohydrates: 6g Proteins: 1g Fat: 5g Fiber: 0.7g

Italian Pesto Dip with Ground Almonds

Serves: 4, Preparation: 10 minutes

Ingredients

- 2 cup of fresh basil
- 2 cloves of garlic minced
- 3 Tbsp of ground almonds, salted
- 3/4 cup extra virgin olive oil
- 1 Tbsp of lemon juice
- Salt and ground black pepper
- 4 Tbsp of ground Parmesan cheese

Instructions

1. Place all ingredients (except Parmesan) in a food processor and beat thoroughly until combine well.
2. Add the parmesan cheese and beat for 30 - 45 seconds.
3. Taste and adjust salt and pepper to taste.
4. Keep refrigerated.

Nutrition information:

Calories: 426 Carbohydrates: 3g Proteins: 4g Fat: 45g Fiber: 1g

Keto "Chimichurri" Sauce

Serves: 6, Preparation: 10 minutes

Ingredients

- 1/2 cup of fresh oregano leaves finely chopped
- 1/2 cup of fresh parsley finely chopped
- 1/2 cup fresh cilantro finely chopped
- 3 fresh bay leaves
- 2 jalapenos pepper, chopped
- 3 cloves garlic
- 1 Tbsp salt
- 1 Tbsp of chili powder
- 1/2 cup apple-cider vinegar
- 1/2 cup of olive oil

Instructions

1. Add ingredients from the list above in your food processor or blender.
2. Blend or process until smooth and all ingredients are united well.
3. Serve immediately or keep refrigerated.

Nutrition information:

Calories: 201 Carbohydrates: 8g Proteins: 1.2g Fat: 19g Fiber: 4g

Keto Bearnaise Sauce

Serves: 6, Preparation: 15 minutes, Cooking: 20 minutes

Ingredients

- 1 onion finely chopped
- 1/2 cup fresh tarragon finely chopped
- 2 tsp crushed black pepper grains
- 1/2 cup of dry white wine
- 1/3 cup of vinegar
- 6 egg yolks
- 2 sticks of fresh butter
- 2 tsp of fresh parsley finely chopped
- Salt and ground black pepper to taste

Instructions

1. In a saucepan, combine the onions, half of tarragon, pepper grains, wine and vinegar.
2. Bring to boil, and cook stirring until 1/3 of the liquid evaporate.
3. Transfer the mixture in a metal bowl. Place the bowl over heated bath (Bain-marie).
4. Add the egg yolks one by one stirring continuously until the sauce begins to tie.
5. Add the butter cut in small pieces stirring all the time until our sauce become shine and smooth.
6. Remove the bowl from the Bain-marie and add the remaining tarragon and chopped parsley: stir well.
7. Season the salt and pepper to taste, and allow the sauce to cool. Keep refrigerated.

Nutrition information:

Calories: 364 Carbohydrates: 4g Proteins: 4g Fat: 36g Fiber: 1,2g

Mustard Sauce with Rosemary
Serves: 6, Preparation: 10 minutes, Cooking: 35 minutes

Ingredients
- 2/3 cup of stone ground mustard (or yellow)
- 2/3 cup of garlic-infused olive oil
- 2 Tbsp of fresh rosemary
- 2 tsp fresh thyme
- 1 Tbsp of Coconut Aminos
- Salt and ground black pepper to taste

Instructions

1. Pour all ingredients in a food processor or in a blender, and beat for 30 - 45 seconds or until the sauce is shine and smooth.
2. Keep refrigerated in a glass container.

Nutrition information:
Calories: 357 Carbohydrates: 3g Proteins: 2g Fat: 39g Fiber: 4g

Olives and Almond Dip
Serves: 6, Preparation: 15 minutes

Ingredients
- 2 cups of black olives, pitted
- 1/4 cup olive oil
- 1/2 cup of mayonnaise
- 1/4 cup ground almonds (without salt)
- 1 Tbsp fresh lemon juice
- Pinch of salt

Instructions
1. Rinse the olives and remove pits.

2. Place olives in your fast-speed blender along with all ingredients: blend until shine and smooth.
3. Serve immediately or keep refrigerated in a covered glass bowl.

Nutrition information:
Calories: 162 Carbohydrates: 7g Proteins: 2g Fat: 14g Fiber: 2g

Perfect Basting Sauce (for chicken grilling)
Serves: 6, Preparation: 10 minutes, Cooking: 15 minutes

Ingredients
- 4 cups apple cider vinegar
- 1/2 cup coconut aminos
- 1 tsp garlic powder
- 1 tsp poultry seasoning
- 6 bay leaves
- 1 tsp crushed red pepper
- 1 tsp fresh thyme (chopped fine)
- 1 tsp fresh rosemary (chopped)
- 1 tsp lemon pepper

Instructions

1. Combine all ingredients in a saucepan and bring to boil; stir well. Remove the saucepan from the heat, cover and let it cool completely.
2. Remove bay leaves and keep refrigerated in a glass container up to 2 months.

Nutrition information:
Calories: 34 Carbohydrates: 1,5g Proteins: 0.2g Fat: 5g Fiber: 0,2g

Smoky Peppercorn Baste for Poultry

Serves: 6, Preparation: 10 minutes

Ingredients

- 1/2 cup coconut aminos or teriyaki sauce
- 1/4 cup mustard (Dijon, English, ground stone)
- 1/4 cup chicken fat, melted
- 1/2 tsp coarsely ground black pepper
- 1/2 tsp liquid smoke
- 1/8 tsp salt and crushed red pepper flakes

Instructions

1. Combine all ingredients in a bowl, and whisk with a fork or spoon until all ingredients are united well.
2. Use immediately or keep refrigerated in a glass container or a bowl.

Nutrition information:

Calories: 152 Carbohydrates: 7g Proteins: 2g Fat: 13g Fiber: 0,2g

Sour Sauce with Feta, Yogurt and Green Onions

Serves: 8, Preparation: 5 minutes, Cooking: 15 minutes

Ingredients

- 2 cups of almond milk
- 1 cup of chopped fresh onion
- 3/4 lb grated Feta cheese
- 1 cup of Greek yogurt
- Juice of 2 limes
- Zest from the 2 limes
- 1 Tbsp of fresh mint leaves, finely chopped
- Salt and freshly ground black pepper

Instructions

1. Heat the milk in a saucepan over medium heat.
2. Add grated Feta cheese, fresh onions, and lime juice; stir briefly to dissolve the cheese and the sauce to thicken.
3. Remove from the heat and let cool for a while.
4. Finally, add the yogurt, mint, lemon zest and stir well.
5. Sprinkle with the salt and the freshly ground pepper and let cool completely before serving.
6. Keep refrigerated.

Nutrition information:

Calories: 195 Carbohydrates: 4.5g Proteins: 17g Fat: 13g Fiber: 0.6g

Spicy and Creamy Horseradish Dip

Serves: 6, Preparation: 10 minutes

Ingredients

- 1 cup fresh cream
- 1/2 cup freshly ground pure horseradish
- 1/2 cup mayonnaise
- 2 Tbsp ground stone mustard or yellow
- Generous dash of cayenne pepper

Instructions

1. Whip cream with a hand mixer in a bowl until it forms stiff peaks.
2. Fold all remaining ingredients and continue to beat with mixer for further 30 - 45 seconds.
3. Serve or keep refrigerated.

Nutrition information:

Calories: 221 Carbohydrates: 6g Proteins: 2g Fat: 22g Fiber: 0.01g

Spicy Citronna Sauce

Serves: 6, Preparation: 10 minutes, Cooking: 10 minutes

Ingredients

- 1 onion, finely chopped
- 1 tsp red chili pepper (chopped)
- 1/4 tsp ground red pepper
- 1 Tbsp of olive oil
- 1/2 cup grapefruit juice (freshly squeezed)
- 1/2 cup lemon juice (freshly squeezed)
- 1/2 cup lime juice
- 5 - 6 drops of liquid Stevia sweetener
- 1 Tbsp of fresh cilantro

Instructions

1. Place all ingredients in a saucepan over moderate heat.
2. Stir for 8 - 10 minutes, and remove from the heat.
3. Let the sauce cool, and keep it refrigerated in a glass bowl or container.

Nutrition information:

Calories: 49 Carbohydrates: 6g Proteins: 1g Fat: 3g Fiber: 0.7g

Delicious Ground Meat Sauce

Serves: 4, Preparation: 10 minutes, Cooking: 8 hours

Ingredients

- 1 Tbsp of tallow
- 1 lb ground beef
- Salt and ground black pepper to taste
- 2 scallions finely chopped
- 1 small hot red pepper chopped
- 2 cloves garlic (minced)
- 1 grated tomato
- 1/2 cup canned mushrooms
- 2 Tbsp coconut aminos
- 1 bay leaf
- 1 Tbsp of fresh oregano (minced)

Instructions

1. Grease the inner pot of your Crock Pot with tallow.
2. Add ground beef and generously sprinkle with salt and ground pepper to taste.
3. Add all remaining ingredients and give a good stir.
4. Cover and cook on LOW for 8 hours.
5. Taste and adjust salt and pepper.
6. Serve hot.

Nutrition information:

Calories: 241 Carbohydrates: 4g Proteins: 15g Fat: 19g Fiber: 1.5g

Spicy Mustard - Avocado Dip

Serves: 6, Preparation: 15 minutes

Ingredients

- 2 large avocados
- 1 onion (large, finely chopped)
- 1/2 cup fresh cilantro coarsely chopped
- 3 Tbsp fresh lemon juice
- 1/4 tsp crushed red pepper flakes
- Kosher salt
- 3 Tbsp mustard (Dijon, English, ground stone)
- 2 Tbsp mayonnaise (optional)

Instructions

1. Slice avocado and remove the skin and a pit.
2. Place all ingredients in your high-speed blender and blend until smooth.
3. Keep refrigerated in a covered glass bowl or container.

Nutrition information:

Calories: 142 Carbohydrates: 8g Proteins: 2g Fat: 12g Fiber: 5g

Zesty and Sweet Basting Sauce

Serves: 6, Preparation: 5 minutes, Cooking: 10 minutes

Ingredients

- 1/4 cup onion finely diced
- 1 cup chili sauce (sugar free)
- 10 drops of liquid Stevia sweetener
- 1 Tbsp ground stone mustard
- 1 Tbs Worcestershire sauce
- 1/4 cup dry red wine

Instructions

1. Combine all ingredients from the list above in saucepan; bring to boil and stir periodically.
2. Reduce heat to low, and cook for further 5 minutes.
3. You can use this sauce for basting or as a dipping sauce.

Nutrition information:

Calories: 46 Carbohydrates: 8g Proteins: 1g Fat: 1g Fiber: 0.3g

Chapter 7 Soup & Stew Recipes

Antioxidant Cabbage Soup

Serves: 6, Preparation: 10 minutes, Cooking: 45 minutes

Ingredients

- 2 Tbsp of olive oil
- 1 small onion cut in slices
- 2 cloves of garlic
- 1 red bell pepper
- 3 sticks of celery
- 1 Tbsp of tomato paste
- 1 lb of cabbage, roughly chopped
- 1 Tbsp of coconut aminos
- 1 tsp of fresh oregano
- 1 cup of bone broth
- 3 cups of water
- Salt and ground black pepper
- Juice from 1 lemon

Instructions

1. Heat the olive oil in a deep pot at medium temperature.
2. Sauté the onion, garlic, bell pepper and celery for 3 minutes.
3. Add the tomato paste and sauté for 1 - 3 minutes.
4. Add chopped cabbage and add all remaining ingredients; give a good stir to combine well.
5. Cover and cook at moderate-low temperature for 30 - 40 minutes.
6. Taste and adjust seasonings to taste. Serve warm.

Nutrition information:

Calories: 110 Carbohydrates: 10.2g Proteins: 3g
Fat: 7.3g Fiber: 3.5g

Creamy Antioxidant Cauliflower Soup

Serves: 6, Preparation: 15 minutes, Cooking: 25 minutes

Ingredients

- 1 green onion, sliced
- 3 sticks of celery, chopped
- 2 cloves of garlic
- 1/4 cup of olive oil
- 1 head of cauliflower florets
- 1 Tbsp fresh ginger, finely chopped
- 1 tsp ground turmeric
- 1 tsp of cumin
- 3 cups of water
- 1 cup of bone broth
- Salt and ground pepper to taste
- 1 cup of canned coconut milk
- 1 bunch of parsley, finely chopped

Instructions

1. Heat the olive oil in a pot at medium-high temperature, and sauté the onion, garlic and cauliflower florets for 2-3 minutes.
2. Add ginger, turmeric and cumin; stir and sauté for one minute.
3. Pour water, broth, and the salt and pepper to taste.
4. Cover and cook for 20 minutes or until vegetables softened.
5. Transfer the mixture into your food processor or blender, and blend to make a puree.
6. Pour coconut milk and blend for further 30 - 45 seconds.
7. Taste and adjust seasonings to taste. Serve with chopped parsley.

Nutrition information:

Calories: 200.1 Carbohydrates: 7.8g Proteins: 4g
Fat: 18g Fiber: 2.6g

Beurre Blanc Sauce

Serves: 8, Preparation: 15 minutes, Cooking: 1 hour

Ingredients

- 4 spring onions, only white parts
- 1/2 cup white wine
- 4 Tbsp white wine vinegar
- 3/4 cup fresh butter, softened
- 1/3 cup heavy cream
- 1 tsp of garlic powder
- Salt and ground white pepper

Instructions

1. Clean, rinse and chop spring onions (use only white parts).
2. In a saucepan, boil spring onions along with wine and vinegar.
3. Reduce heat to low and simmer until only one tablespoon of liquid remains.
4. Place onion along with remaining ingredients in your Slow Cooker.
5. Cover and cook on LOW for 1 hour.
6. Open lid and give a good stir Transfer in a glass jar and refrigerate until consuming.

Nutrition information:

Calories: 202 Carbohydrates: 1.5g Proteins: 1g Fat: 21g Fiber: 0.2g

Carne-de-sol Stew - Keto Gourmet Dish

Serves: 6, Preparation: 10 minutes, Cooking: 20 minutes

Ingredients

- 1 lb of Carne-de-sol, cut into strips
- 12 oz of bacon cut into cubes
- 2 Tbsp of lard
- 2 small green onions, sliced
- 1 Tbsp of chopped coriander
- 1 Tbsp chopped parsley
- 1/2 Tbsp chopped fresh chives (optional)
- 1/2 cup of almond flour
- 1/4 cup water

Instructions

1. Soak meat in water overnight.
2. Heat the lard in a frying skillet, and fry bacon and green onions.
3. Add meat and cook for 10 minutes or until soft.
4. Combine the almond flour with water and pour over meat.
5. Sprinkle with seasonings, give a good stir, cover and cook for 7 - 8 minutes at low heat. Serve hot.

Nutrition information:

Calories: 442 Carbohydrates: 1.3g Proteins: 18g Fat: 40.5g Fiber: 0.5g

Chilly Chicory and Avocado Soup

Serves: 4, Preparation: 10 minutes

Ingredients

- 3 chicory leaves
- 1 avocado peeled and cut small cubes
- 1 yellow pepper finely chopped
- 1 spring onion finely chopped
- 4 leaves of fresh mint
- 1 cup coconut milk
- 1 Tbsp of olive oil
- 2 cardamom seed
- Salt (optional)

Instructions

1. Wash and clean your chicory, avocado, yellow pepper and mint.
2. Place all ingredients in a high speed blender. Blend until completely smooth and creamy.
3. Refrigerate for 2 hours and serve cold.

Nutrition information:

Calories: 155 Carbohydrates: 8.6g Proteins: Fat: 5g Fiber: 3g

Instant Chicken and Bacon Stew

Serves: 6, Preparation: 10 minutes, Cooking: 20 minutes

Ingredients

- 2 Tbsp olive oil
- 1 1/2 lbs chicken breast, skinned boneless
- 4 slices bacon
- 1 green onion, chopped (or scallion)
- 2 green bell pepper, chopped
- 2 celery sprigs, diced
- 1/2 tsp dried thyme
- 2 cloves garlic, minced
- 2 cup bone broth (preferable homemade)
- 3 Tbsp of almond flour
- Salt and ground black pepper to taste

Instructions

1. Press SAUTÉ button on your Instant Pot when the word "hot" appears on the display, add the oil and sauté the chicken for about 5 minutes.
2. Add the green onions, bell pepper, celery, garlic and thyme and stir for 2 minutes.
3. Add the flour, and cook, stirring frequently two-three minutes.
4. Stir the bone broth and almond flour and pour into Instant Pot.
5. Season with the salt and ground pepper, stir and turn off the SAUTÉ button.
6. Lock lid into place and set on the SOUP/STEW setting to high heat for 8 minutes.
7. When the timer beeps, press "Cancel" and carefully flip the Quick Release valve to let the pressure out.

Nutrition information:

Calories: 388 Carbohydrates: 5g Proteins: 49.5g Fat: 22g Fiber: 1,5g

Chilly Lobster Soup

Serves: 4, Preparation: 5 minutes, Cooking: 10 minutes

Ingredients

- 2 can (15 oz) lobster meat
- 2 Tbsp extra virgin olive oil
- 1 Tbsp fresh chives, chopped
- 1 large grated tomato
- Salt and ground pepper to taste
- 1/4 cup ground almonds
- 2 tsp cardamom seeds
- 1 cup of red wine
- 1 cup of water

Instructions

1. Add the lobster meat in a large pot; drizzle with extra virgin olive oil and season with the salt and pepper, cardamom and chopped chives.
2. Add grated tomato, red wine and water; cook for 6 - 7 minutes at medium heat.
3. Add the ground almonds and stir well.
4. Taste and adjust seasoning.
5. Serve immediately.

Nutrition information:

Calories: 255.5 Carbohydrates: 2.2g Proteins: 38g Fat: 9g Fiber: 0.7g

Spicy Cabbage Soup

Serves: 6, Preparation: 5 minutes, Cooking: 15 minutes

Ingredients

- 1 Tbsp of tallow
- 1 medium onion, chopped;
- 2 cloves garlic, minced;
- 1/2 medium head sliced cabbage
- 1 grated tomato, chopped
- 1 Tbsp coconut aminos (from coconut sap)
- 1/4 cup ground almonds
- Salt to taste
- 4 cups of water
- Spicy ground paprika to taste

Instructions

1. In a non-stick frying pan heat the tallow.
2. Sauté the onion and garlic until soft and golden brown.
3. Add grated tomato and coconut aminos: stir well.
4. Add cabbage, water, seasonings, and ground almonds; cover and simmer at medium heat for 10 minutes.
5. Add spicy ground paprika to taste and cook for further 2 - 3 minutes.
6. Adjust salt and serve hot.

Nutrition information:

Calories: 94 Carbohydrates: 9g Proteins: 3.5g Fat: 6g Fiber: 3.7g

Thick Chicken Breast Soup with Herbs
Serves: 6, Preparation: 10 minutes, Cooking: 8 hours

Ingredients
- 1 green onion finely sliced
- 1 lb of chicken breast, boneless
- 1 grated tomato
- 1 tsp of dry coriander
- 1 tsp of red ground paprika
- 1 tsp of fresh ginger, grated
- Salt and ground pepper to taste
- 1/2 tsp of turmeric
- 1/4 tsp of ground cinnamon
- 1/2 tsp of garlic powder
- 1 cup water
- 3 Tbsp of almond flour
- 1 1/2 Tbsp of cold water

Instructions
1. Season chicken breast with the salt and pepper and place in your Crock Pot.
2. In a medium-sized bowl, combine tomatoes, coriander, paprika, ginger, turmeric, cinnamon and garlic powder; add water, stir and pour in Crock Pot.
3. Cover and cook on LOW for 8 hours or at HIGH for 4-5 hours.
4. In a small bowl, dilute the almond flour in water and pour the mixture into Crock Pot
5. Cover again and cook on HIGH for further 15-20 minutes or until thickened.
6. Adjust salt, stir and serve hot.

Nutrition information:
Calories: 30 Carbohydrates: 3.5g Proteins: 3g Fat: 1g Fiber: 4g

Green Beans Power Soup
Serves: 6, Preparation: 5 minutes, Cooking: 8 hours

Ingredients
- 2 lbs green beans - trimmed and cut diagonally in half
- 1 small onion, diced
- 1 clove garlic, minced
- 1 carrot, sliced
- 2 Tbsp fresh cilantro, chopped
- 2 cups bone broth (preferable homemade)
- 2 cups water
- 1 tsp chili powder
- 1 tsp cumin
- Salt and ground pepper to taste

Instructions
1. Place all ingredients in the Slow Cooker, and stir well.
2. Cover and cook on LOW for 6-8 hours.
3. Taste and adjust seasonings.
4. Serve hot.

Nutrition information:
Calories: 65 Carbohydrates: 4g Proteins: 6g Fat: 1g Fiber: 0.2g

Keto Kimchi Soup

Serves: 6, Preparation: 10 minutes, Cooking: 3 hours

Ingredients

- 1/2 lb of fresh pork belly
- Sea salt and black pepper or to taste
- 3/4 lb of Napa cabbage, chopped
- 1/2 cup of spring onions finely chopped
- 1/4 cup of fresh button mushrooms
- 1 tsp of stevia sweetener
- 1 tsp ground paprika
- 2 Tbsp of coconut aminos
- 3 Tbsp of sesame oil
- 4 cups of water

Instructions

1. Cut pork belly into pieces and season with the salt and pepper.
2. Place meat in Slow Cooker and add chopped Napa cabbage, spring onions and mushrooms.
3. In a small bowl, stir water, sesame oil, stevia, ground paprika and coconut aminos.
4. Pour mixture in your Slow Cooker over meat and vegetables.
5. Cover and cook on HIGH for 3 hours.
6. Taste and adjust seasonings.
7. Serve.

Nutrition information:

Calories: 110 Carbohydrates: 2g Proteins: 1g Fat: 12g Fiber: 0.4g

Weight-Loss Broccoli Cream Soup

Serves: 4, Preparation: 10 minutes, Cooking: 20 minutes

Ingredients

- 1 lb broccoli
- 2 green onions, finely chopped
- 2 stalks celery white
- 1 cup cauliflower floweret
- 3 Tbsp olive oil
- 2 cup water
- 1/2 tsp garlic powder
- Salt and pepper to taste

Instructions

1. In a deep pan heat the oil, and sauté the green onion and chopped celery.
2. Add in the broccoli and cauliflower.
3. Season the salt and pepper to taste, and add the garlic powder.
4. Pour water into pot, stir and cook for 15 - 20 minutes.
5. When ready, pour the soup into blender and bit to a very fine cream.
6. Serve.

Nutrition information:

Calories: 164 Carbohydrates: 8g Proteins: 5g Fat: 17g Fiber: 1.5g

Wild Mushrooms Soup with Eggs

Serves: 4, Preparation: 5 minutes, Cooking: 20 minutes

Ingredients

- 2 Tbsp of extra-virgin olive oil
- 1 lb wild mushrooms (chanterelles or porcini)
- 1 scallion, finely chopped
- 2 garlic clove, finely chopped
- 2 cups bone broth (preferable homemade)
- 2 cups water
- 2 egg yolks from free-range chicken
- 2 Tbsp of lemon juice
- Salt and freshly ground pepper to taste

Instructions

1. Heat the oil in a pot over medium-high heat.
2. Add mushrooms and stir for 3 minutes; season the salt and pepper.
3. Reduce the heat to medium, add the scallion and garlic, and cook for 3 minutes.
4. Pour the bone broth and water, stir, cover and cook for 10 - 12 minutes.
5. In a bowl, whisk egg yolks with a pinch of salt and lemon juice.
6. Pour the egg mixture in a pot, turn off heat, and stir for further 2 - 3 minutes.
7. Taste and adjust the salt and pepper to taste. Serve hot.

Nutrition information:

Calories: 130 Carbohydrates: 2g Proteins: 18g Fat: 13g Fiber: 0.3g

Winter Cabbage and Celery Soup

Serves: 6, Preparation: 5 minutes, Cooking: 30 minutes

Ingredients

- 2 Tbsp olive oil
- 2 cloves garlic, minced
- 1/2 head cabbage, shredded
- 2 stalks celery, chopped
- 1 grated tomato
- 3 cups bone broth (preferable homemade)
- 3 cups water
- 1/2 tsp ground black pepper

Instructions

1. Heat the oil in a large pot over medium heat.
2. Sauté the garlic, celery and cabbage, stirring, for about 8 minutes.
3. Add grated tomato, and continue to cook for further 2 - 3 minutes.
4. Pour the broth and water. Bring to a boil, lower heat to low, cover and simmer for 20 minutes or until cabbage softened.
5. Sprinkle with ground black pepper, stir and serve.

Nutrition information:

Calories: 85 Carbohydrates: 2g Proteins: 17g Fat: 11g Fiber: 1g

Spinach Soup with Shiitake mushrooms

Serves: 4, Preparation: 10 minutes, Cooking: 15 minutes

Ingredients

- 2 Tbsp of olive oil
- 1 medium onion, chopped
- 2 cloves garlic, minced
- 2 cups of water
- 1/2 bunch of spinach
- 2 cups shiitake mushrooms, chopped
- 2 Tbsp of almond flour
- 1 Tbsp of coconut aminos
- 1 tsp coriander dry
- 1/2 tsp of ground mustard
- Salt and ground black pepper to taste

Instructions

1. Heat the olive oil and sauté the garlic and onion until golden brown.
2. Add the coconut aminos and the mushrooms and stir for a few minutes.
3. Pour water, chopped spinach and all remaining ingredients.
4. Cover and cook for 5 - 6 minutes or until spinach is tender.
5. Taste and adjust salt and the pepper.
6. Stir for further 5 minutes and remove for the heat.
7. Serve hot.

Nutrition information:

Calories: 175 Carbohydrates: 12g Proteins: 21g Fat: 8g Fiber: 43g

Vegan Artichoke Soup

Serves: 6, Preparation: 15 minutes, Cooking: 1 hour 5 minutes

Ingredients

- 1 Tbsp of butter
- 6 artichoke hearts, halved
- 2 cloves garlic, minced
- 1 small onion, chopped
- 1 cup bone broth
- 2 cups of water
- 2 Tbsp of almond flour
- Salt and ground black pepper to taste
- 2 Tbsp of olive oil
- Fresh chopped parsley to taste
- Fresh chopped fresh basil to taste

Instructions

1. Heat the butter in a large pot, and add artichoke hearts, garlic and chopped onion.
2. Stir and cook until artichoke hearts tender.
3. Add bone broth, water and almond flout: season with the salt and pepper.
4. Bring soup to boil, and cook for 2 minutes.
5. Add little olive oil, parsley and basil, stir and cook uncovered for 1 hour.
6. When ready, push the soup through sieve.
7. Taste and adjust salt and pepper.
8. Serve.

Nutrition information:

Calories: 145 Carbohydrates: 6g Proteins: 7g Fat: 12g Fiber: 0.5%

Bouyambessa" Seafood Soup
Serves: 6, Preparation: 10 minutes, Cooking: 25 minutes

Ingredients

- 1/2 cup of olive oil
- 1 spring onion cut in cubes
- 2 Tbsp of fresh celery, chopped
- 2 cloves of garlic minced
- 1 tomato, peeled and grated
- 2 bay leaves
- 1 tsp of anise
- 6 large, raw shrimps
- 1 sea bass and 1 sea bream fillets cut in pieces; about 1 1/2 lbs
- 12 mussels, rinsed in plenty of cold water
- Salt and ground black pepper
- 3 Tbsp of chopped parsley for serving
- 6 cups of water

Instructions

1. Heat the olive oil in a large pot and sauté in the onion, garlic and celery for 4 -5 minutes over medium heat.
2. Add bay leaves, anise and grated tomato; stir and cook for further 5 minutes.
3. Add seafood and fish and pour 6 cups of water; season with little salt and pepper.
4. Cover and cook for 10 - 12 minutes on low heat. Serve hot with chopped parsley.

Nutrition information:
Calories: 272.5 Carbohydrates: 2g Proteins: 19g Fat: 20g Fiber: 0.5g

"Classico" Beef Stew
Serves: 8, Preparation: 5 minutes, Cooking: 1 hour 35 minutes

Ingredients

- 1 1/2 lb beef filed, cut in cubes
- 1 green onion (white and green parts), chopped
- 2 cloves garlic, minced
- 1 small carrot
- 1 grated tomato
- 1 tsp fresh basil (chopped)
- 1 tsp fresh oregano chopped
- 3 cups bone broth (or water)
- 1/2 cup white vinegar
- 1 tsp salt
- 1 Tbsp lard

Instructions

1. Heat the lard in a large skillet and sauté beef meat with a pinch of salt.
2. Add the onion and garlic, and cook until soft.
3. Add grated tomato and the carrot and stir for further 2 minutes.
4. Add all the other ingredients cover and cook on very low heat for about 1 1/2 to 1 3/4 hours, until the beef is tender.
5. Serve hot.

Nutrition information:
Calories: 498 Carbohydrates: 3g Proteins: 46g Fat: 42g Fiber: 1g

Chicken and Greens Soup

Serves: 8, Preparation: 12 minutes, Cooking: 1 hour 50 minutes

Ingredients

- 1/4 cup of olive oil
- 1 1/2 lbs chicken breast, boneless, cut into cube
- 1 spring onion, cut into cubes
- 1 clove of garlic, finely chopped
- 1 1/2 lettuce cos or romain, chopped
- 1 cup of fresh spinach finely chopped
- 1 bunch of dill finely chopped, without the thick stalks
- 1/2 Tbsp of sweet chill powder
- 1 tsp of fresh mint, chopped
- 1 tsp of fresh thyme, chopped
- Salt and freshly ground pepper
- 5 cups of water

Instructions

1. In a deep pot, heat the olive oil to a high heat and sauté the chicken for about 5 - 6 minutes.
2. Add the onion and sauté for about 3 minutes until softened.
3. Add the garlic, the lettuce, spinach, dill, mint, thyme and sauté for about 3-4 minutes, stirring with a wooden spoon.
4. Sprinkle with chili, salt, freshly ground pepper and pour 5 cups of water.
5. Bring to boil, and cook for 1 1/2 hours on low heat.
6. Serve hot.

Nutrition information:

Calories: 181 Carbohydrates: 4.5g Proteins: 20g Fat: 10g Fiber: 3g

Chicken and Shredded Cabbage Stew

Serves: 4, Preparation: 10 minutes, Cooking: 50 minutes

Ingredients

- 2 Tbsp of chicken fat
- 1/2 cup of green onions, chopped
- 2 cloves garlic, sliced
- 2 chicken breast cut in pieces
- 1/2 tsp nutmeg
- 2 Tbsp of yellow mustard
- 1 3/4 cups water
- 1 cup white wine
- 1/4 cup apple cider vinegar
- 6 whole cloves
- 1 carrot, peeled, sliced
- 1/2 tsp salt
- 1/4 tsp pepper
- 1 cup shredded cabbage

Instructions

1. Heat chicken fat in a large Dutch oven over medium high temperature.
2. Add green onions, garlic chicken and cook about 5 - 6 minutes.
3. Spread mustard over chicken pieces; stir nutmeg, salt and pepper, water, wine, vinegar, cloves and carrot; bring to a boil.
4. Cover, reduce heat to low and cook 20 minutes.
5. Add shredded cabbage, stir, cover and cook for about 10 - 12 minutes.
6. Taste and adjust salt and pepper to taste.
7. Serve hot in a bowls.

Nutrition information:

Calories: 191 Carbohydrates: 6g Proteins: 26g Fat: 5g Fiber: 2g

Cold Cauliflower and Cilantro Soup

Serves: 4, Preparation: 5 minutes, Cooking: 25 minutes

Ingredients

- 1 1/2 lbs. cauliflower (previously steamed)
- 1 cup almond milk
- 1/2 tsp fresh ginger grated
- 3 bunches fresh cilantro
- 3 Tbsp garlic-infused olive oil
- 2 pinch of salt

Instructions

1. Heat water in a large pot until boiling. Place the steamer in a pot and put in the cauliflower.
2. Cover and steam cauliflower for 6 - 7 minutes.
3. Remove the cauliflower along with all ingredients from the list above in a high-speed blender.
4. Blend until smooth or until desired texture is achieved.
5. Pour the soup in a glass container, cover and refrigerate for 2 - 3 hours.
6. Serve cold.

Nutrition information:

Calories: 132 Carbohydrates: 7.5g Proteins: 3.5g Fat: 11g Fiber: 3.5g

Creamy Broccoli Soup with Nutmeg

Serves: 6, Preparation: 15 minutes, Cooking: 20 minutes

Ingredients

- 2 Tbsp of olive oil
- 2 green onions finely chopped
- 1 lb broccoli floret, frozen or fresh
- 6 cups of bone broth (cold)
- 1 cup of cream
- Salt and ground pepper to taste
- 1 Tbsp of nutmeg

Instructions

1. Heat the olive oil in a pot over medium-high heat.
2. Add the onion in and sauté it until becomes translucent.
3. Add the broccoli, season with the salt and pepper, and bring to boil.
4. Cover the pot and cook for 6 - 8 minutes.
5. Transfer the broccoli mixture into blender, and blend until smooth.
6. Pour the cream, and blend for further 30 seconds.
7. Return the soup in a pot, and reheat it.
8. Adjust salt and pepper, and serve hot with grated nutmeg.

Nutrition information:

Calories: 205 Carbohydrates: 5g Proteins: 35g Fat: 18g Fiber: 0.4g

Creamy Mushroom Soup with Crumbled Bacon

Serves: 6, Preparation: 15 minutes, Cooking: 55 minutes

Ingredients
- 1 Tbsp of lard
- 2 lbs of white mushrooms
- 1/2 cup of water
- 3 1/2 cups of almond milk
- 2 green onions, finely sliced
- 3 sprigs of fresh rosemary
- 2 cloves garlic, finely chopped
- 6 slices of bacon, fried and crumbled
- Salt and ground black pepper

Instructions
1. Heat the lard in a large skillet and sauté green onions and garlic over medium-high heat.
2. Season with the salt and pepper, and rosemary; pour water and cook for 5 minutes.
3. Add the mushrooms and sauté for 1-2 minutes.
4. Pour the almond milk, stir, cover and simmer for 40 minutes over low heat.
5. Remove the rosemary, and transfer the soup in your blender; blend until creamy and soft.
6. Adjust salt, and if necessary, add some warm water.
7. Chop the bacon and fry in a hot pan until it becomes crisp.
8. Serve your soup in bowls and sprinkle with chopped bacon.

Nutrition information:
Calories: 101 Carbohydrates: 5.5g Proteins: 8g Fat: 6g Fiber: 2g

Delicious Pork Stew

Serves: 4, Preparation: 10 minutes, Cooking: 40 minutes

Ingredients
- 2 Tbsp lard
- 2 spring onions finely chopped
- 1 1/2 lb pork boneless, cut into cubes
- Sea salt and black ground pepper to taste
- 1 red bell pepper (cut into thin strips)
- 1/2 cup water
- 1/2 tsp of cumin
- 1/2 tsp caraway seeds

Instructions
1. Heat the lard in a large skillet over medium-high heat.
2. Sauté the spring onions for 3 - 4 minutes; stir.
3. Add the pork and simmer for about 5 minutes.
4. Add all remaining ingredients and stir well.
5. Lower heat, cover and cook for 25 minutes over low heat.
6. Taste and adjust salt and pepper to taste.
7. Serve hot.

Nutrition information:
Calories: \380 Carbohydrates: 3g Proteins: 30g Fat: 27g Fiber: 1g

Fragrant "Greenery" Soup

Serves: 6, Preparation: 10 minutes, Cooking: 25 minutes

Ingredients

- 1/3 cup olive oil
- 1 leek, the white and tender green part, cut into slices
- 2 fresh onions, white and tender green part, finely chopped
- 1 lb of various greens (spinach, lettuce, chard, etc.), coarsely chopped
- Salt and ground pepper to taste
- 1/4 tsp of nutmeg
- 6 cups of water
- 1/2 cup of fresh dill, finely chopped

Instructions

1. Pout the oil in a pot, and sauté the leek, fresh onions and greens for 5 minutes; stir.
2. Season with the salt and pepper, grated nutmeg and pour water; bring to boil.
3. Cover and cook for 8 - 10 minutes over medium-low heat.
4. When the vegetables softened, transfer them in a blender; blend until soft.
5. Serve in a bowl, and sprinkle each serving with fresh dill and freshly ground pepper.

Nutrition information:

Calories: 140 Carbohydrates: 6g Proteins: 4g Fat: 13g Fiber: 1g

Hungarian Tokany Turkey Stew (Keto adapted)

Serves: 6, Preparation: 15 minutes, Cooking: 1 hour 55 minutes

Ingredients

- 1/3 cup almond flour
- 1 tsp salt and ground pepper
- 2-1/2 lbs turkey thighs skinned & boned; cut into 1-inch cubes
- 2 Tbsp olive oil
- 1 cup green onions finely chopped
- 1/2 cup mushrooms sliced
- 1 grated tomato
- 1 cup dry white wine
- 1 Tbsp of ground paprika
- 1/2 tsp marjoram
- 1 cup water or bone broth
- 1/2 cup of fresh cream
- 3 slices of turkey bacon cooked and crumbled (optional)

Instructions

1. In plastic bag, combine almond flour, salt and pepper. Add the turkey meat in batches, and coat well with almond flour mixture.
2. Heat the oil in a large frying skillet and sauté turkey cubes for 4 - 5 minutes over medium heat; stir.
3. In Dutch oven, sauté green onions with a pinch of salt until translucent.
4. Add mushrooms, carrot, grated tomato and wine. Bring mixture to boil, reduce heat to low and simmer for 10 -12 minutes. Stir in paprika, marjoram, water or bone broth and turkey; bring mixture to boil.
5. Reduce heat, cover and simmer 1 1/2 hours or until turkey are totally tender.
6. Serve in a bowls with fresh cream and crumbled bacon.

Nutrition information:

Calories: 315 Carbohydrates: 6g Proteins: 34g Fat: 13g Fiber: 2g

Light Grouper Soup with Celery

Ingredients

- 5 celery stalks, cut into three pieces each
- 1 Tbsp of dried oregano
- 7 -8 saffron fiber
- 1 carrot preferably organic, sliced
- 8 cups of water
- 2 small grouper fish, about 3 1/2 - 4 lbs, washed and cleaned
- 3/4 cup of olive oil
- 2 Tbsp of lemon juice
- Salt and ground black pepper

Instructions

1. Add celery and carrot in a large and wide pot, and sprinkle with oregano and saffron.
2. Place the fish pieces, and pour the olive oil.
3. Pour water and bring to boil over medium-high heat; cover and simmer for 15 minutes.
4. Season with the salt and pepper.
5. Remove the fish from the pot, and place on a large plate.
6. Strain the broth, return to pot, and cook for further 10 minutes.
7. Remove soup from heat and pour the lemon juice.
8. Taste and adjust salt to taste.
9. Clean carefully the fish and serve immediately with hot soup.

Nutrition information:

Calories: 166 Carbohydrates: 3g Proteins: 27g Fat: 19g Fiber: 1g

Perfect Pork Stew

Serves: 6, Preparation: 15 minutes, Cooking: 1 hour 45 minutes

Ingredients

- 1/2 cup olive oil
- 2 lbs of pork [cut into cubes]
- 1 cup of red wine
- 1 small carrot, cut into slices
- 1 cup of white mushrooms, sliced
- 1 green onion, finely chopped
- 1 small grated tomato
- 1 cup of bone broth or water
- 1/2 tsp oregano
- 1 bay leaf
- Salt and ground black pepper to taste

Instructions

1. In a large pan, pour the oil and sauté the pork for 2 - 3 minutes.
2. Add the onion and sauté for 2 - 3 minutes; season with the salt and pepper.
3. Pour wine and stir for two minutes.
4. Add carrots, mushrooms, green onion, grated tomato, broth or water, oregano and bay leaf.
5. Bring to boil, lower heat, cover and cook for 1 1/2 hours on very low heat.
6. Taste and adjust salt and pepper to taste.
7. Serve hot.

Nutrition information:

Calories: 695 Carbohydrates: 3g Proteins: 18g Fat: 73g Fiber: 1g

Spicy Ground Bison Meat Stew

Serves: 6, Preparation: 10 minutes, Cooking: 35 minutes

Ingredients

- 2 Tbsp of lard
- 1 1/2 lb grass-fed bison, ground
- 2 spring onions, finely chopped
- 2 cloves of garlic, minced
- 1 grated tomato
- 2 Tbsp mustard (Dijon, English, ground stone)
- 1 Tbsp chili powder
- 2 bay leaves
- 2 tsp cumin
- 1 tsp cinnamon
- 2 tsp salt and ground black pepper
- 1 1 cups bone broth
- Fresh cilantro and lime wedges to garnish

Instructions

1. Heat the lard in a large frying skillet over medium-high heat.
2. Add ground bison meat and sauté for 3 - 4 minutes; stir.
3. Add sliced onions and garlic and sauté until translucent.
4. Add grated tomato and tomato paste and cook for 5 minutes.
5. Add all remaining ingredients and bring to boil.
6. Cover, lower heat to low, and cook for 20 minutes.
7. Adjust seasonings and serve hot with fresh cilantro and a squeeze of lime.

Nutrition information:

Calories: 282 Carbohydrates: 4g Proteins: 38g Fat: 16g Fiber: 2g

Swiss chard Soup with Fresh Herbs

Serves: 6, Preparation: 10 minutes, Cooking: 25 minutes

Ingredients

- 1/4 cup extra virgin olive oil
- 2 spring onions (only green parts finely chopped)
- 1 clove of garlic minced
- 2 lbs Swiss chard, tender stems and leaves cur into pieces
- 3 cups bone broth (or water)
- 1 Tbsp of fresh dill, parsley and thyme, chopped
- Salt and black ground pepper to taste

Instructions

1. Heat the oil in a large pot over medium-high heat.
2. Sauté the green parts of spring onions and garlic with a pinch of salt for 3 - 4 minutes.
3. Add chopped Swiss chard and bone broth; bring to the boil and let simmer for 10 minutes. Add chopped dill and parsley and cook for further 5 minutes.
4. Transfer your soup in a food processor. Blend into a very smooth soup.
5. Adjust seasonings and serve hot.

Nutrition information:

Calories: 66 Carbohydrates: 6g Proteins: 6g Fat: 3g Fiber: 3g

Chapter 8 Poultry Recipes

Chicken Breast Stuffed with Asparagus

Serves: 4, Preparation: 15 minutes, Cooking: 30 minutes

Ingredients

- 2 large skinless, boneless chicken breast halves
- 8 asparagus spears, trimmed
- 1/2 cup shredded parmesan cheese
- 1/4 cup ground almonds or Macadamia nuts
- Salt and black pepper to taste

Instructions

1. Preheat oven to 375 F/190 C. Grease the baking dish; set aside.
2. Place each chicken breast between two sheets freezer bags on a solid surface.
3. Sprinkle each side with salt and pepper.
4. Place 4 spears of asparagus down the center of a chicken breast, and spread about 1/4 cup of parmesan cheese over the asparagus.
5. Repeat with the other chicken breast, and roll the chicken around the asparagus and cheese to make a compact roll.
6. Place the rolls seam sides down in the prepared baking dish, and sprinkle each with about 2 tablespoons of ground almonds.
7. Bake for about 25 - 30 minutes.
8. Allow to cool for 10 minutes.
9. Serve warm.

Nutrition information:

Calories: 236 Carbohydrates: 3.8g Proteins: Fat: 32g Fiber: 2g

Roasted Emmental Chicken

Serves: 6, Preparation: 10 minutes, Cooking: 50 minutes

Ingredients

- 1/4 lb mushrooms
- 2 lbs boneless skinless chicken breasts
- 6 oz Emmental cheese
- 1 cup bone broth (preferable homemade)
- 1/2 cup dry white wine
- 1 cup of almond flour or finely ground almonds
- 1/2 cup of butter grass-fed melted

Instructions

1. Preheat oven to 350 F/175 C.
2. Slice cheese and mushrooms.
3. Place chicken in a greased 9X13X2-inch baking dish.
4. Top each piece with a slice of Emmental cheese, and arrange mushrooms over the chicken and cheese.
5. Combine the bone broth with wine and pour over chicken. Sprinkle with ground almonds.
6. Drizzle melted butter over the top of ground almonds.
7. Bake 45-50 minutes or until chicken is cooked through.

Nutrition information:

Calories: 175 Carbohydrates: 2.6g Proteins: 19g Fat: 11g Fiber: 0.2g

Spiced and Creamy Chicken in Oven

Serves: 8, Preparation: 10 minutes, Cooking: 50 minutes

Ingredients

- 2 tsp of chicken fat
- 1 fresh whole chicken, cut up
- 1/2 cup ground almonds
- 1/4 tsp cayenne pepper
- 1/2 tsp onion powder
- 1/8 tsp ground ginger
- 1/2 tsp garlic powder
- 1/3 cup plain yogurt

Instructions

1. Preheat oven to 360 F/180 C.
2. Grease large baking tray with the chicken fat; set aside.
3. Cut the chicken in large parts.
4. Rinse chicken pieces and pat dry.
5. In a large bowl, combine ground almonds, onion powder, garlic powder, cayenne pepper and ginger.
6. Dip chicken pieces in yogurt, and then roll in a ground almond mixture.
7. Place breaded chicken in prepared baking dish.
8. Bake, uncovered, for 45 to 50 minutes or until chicken is tender.

Nutrition information:

Calories: 420 Carbohydrates: 2.8g Proteins: 31g Fat: 321g Fiber: 1g

White Mushroom and Chicken Stew

Serves: 4, Preparation: 5 minutes, Cooking: 20 minutes

Ingredients

- 1 Tbsp of olive oil
- 1 lb chicken breasts, skinless, boneless
- 1 lb fresh white mushrooms
- 2 green onions
- 1 cup diced celery
- 1 tsp minced garlic
- 1 grated tomato
- 1/2 tsp salt
- 2 cups fresh green beans, trimmed and halved

Instructions

1. Heat the oil in a large frying skillet until hot.
2. Add chicken; cook until brown, 3 to 4 minutes a side; remove from skillet.
3. Add mushrooms, green onion, celery and garlic; cook, stirring frequently, for about 6 to 8 minutes or until tender.
4. Add the grated tomato, salt and chicken; top with green beans.
5. Cover and simmer until chicken is cooked through, for about 5 to 6 minutes.
6. Serve hot.

Nutrition information:

Calories: 102 Carbohydrates: 8.4g Proteins: 8.5g Fat: 4.5g Fiber: 3g

Cold Shredded Chicken and Cabbage Salad

Serves: 4, Preparation: 15 minutes, Cooking: 30 minutes

Ingredients

- 1 lb red cabbage, shredded
- 2 cloves garlic finely chopped
- 1 lb cooked chicken, shredded
- 4 Tbsp olive oil
- 3 Tbsp lemon juice (freshly squeezed)
- Salt to taste
- 3 Tbsp mustard (Dijon, English, or whole grain)

Instructions

1. Shred the cabbage and place in a large salad bowl; season with the salt and toss.
2. Add garlic over the cabbage.
3. Add shredded chicken and pour with olive oil; toss.
4. Add the mustard and gently stir with wooden spoon.
5. Refrigerate for 30 minutes, sprinkle with the fresh lemon juice and serve.

Nutrition information:

Calories: 209 Carbohydrates: 7.3g Proteins: 23.5g Fat: 9.5g Fiber: 3.3g

Crunchy Chicken Nuggets with Coconut Aminos

Serves: 5, Preparation: 15 minutes, Cooking: 10 minutes

Ingredients

- 2 egg whites (from pastured or organic eggs)
- Salt and ground black pepper to taste
- 2 1/2 cups ground almonds
- 2 lbs skinless, boneless chicken breasts cut into 20 pieces
- 1/4 cup garlic-infused olive oil
- 3 Tbsp of coconut aminos (from coconut sap)
- 1/4 cup water

Instructions

1. Whisk the egg whites, salt and pepper in a bowl.
2. Add the ground almonds into a separate bowl.
3. Dip the chicken pieces in egg mixture.
4. Roll the chicken pieces into almonds flour until coated.
5. Heat the olive oil in a skillet at medium-high heat; cook for about 5 - 6 chicken or until golden brown.
6. Whisk the coconut aminos and water and pour over the chicken.
7. Cook for 2 - 3 minutes and remove from the heat.
8. Serve hot.

Nutrition information:

Calories: 564 Carbohydrates: 6.4g Proteins: 54g Fat: 46g Fiber: 6g

Roasted Frozen Parmesan Chicken Wings

Serves: 4, Preparation: 5 minutes, Cooking: 1 hour

Ingredients

- 2 Tbsp olive oil
- 20 frozen wings
- 1 cup grated parmesan cheese
- 1 tsp chives, chopped
- 2 tsp dried oregano
- Salt and ground pepper to taste
- Lemon wedges for serving

Instructions

1. Preheat oven to 440 F/220 C. Grease a roasting pan with the olive oil.
2. Place frozen chicken wings on a baking pan. Sprinkle with chives, oregano and salt.
3. Bake for 40 minutes.
4. Remove from the oven and sprinkle with the parmesan cheese.
5. Bake for further 20 minutes.
6. Serve hot with lemon wedges.

Nutrition information:

Calories: 646 Carbohydrates: 1.5g Proteins: 55g Fat: 53g Fiber: 0.4g

Roasted Turkey Breast with Garlic-Parsley Sauce

Serves: 6, Preparation: 10 minutes, Cooking: 1 ½ hours

Ingredients

- 1/3 cup fresh parsley finely chopped
- 3 garlic cloves, minced
- 1/2 cup lemon juice
- 1/2 cup garlic-infused olive oil
- 1 tsp hot ground paprika (optional)
- 1 tsp cumin
- 2 turkey breast (4-5 pounds)

Instructions

1. Preheat oven to 350 F/175 degrees C.
2. Stir the chopped parsley, garlic, lemon juice, olive oil, ground paprika and cumin in a bowl.
3. Season turkey breast with the salt and pepper, and generously brush with prepared mixture.
4. Place turkey breasts in a greased roasting dish and cook for 1 hour.
5. Baste turkey breast with remaining mixture, and roast for further 30 minutes or until the internal temperature reaches 165 F/80 C.
6. Remove from the oven, and let turkey breast rest for 10 minutes before slicing and serving.

Nutrition information:

Calories: 481 Carbohydrates: 7.3g Proteins: 52g Fat: 23g Fiber: 2g

Slow Cooked Chicken Salad with Spinach

Serves: 4, Preparation: 10 minutes, Cooking: 5 hours

Ingredients

- 2 Tbsp of garlic-infused olive oil
- 1 1/2 lb chicken breast fillet
- 1 lb fresh spinach
- 1 red peppers cut into thin strips
- 1 red hot chilli peppers (optional)
- 2 Tbsp mustard
- 1 Tbsp of fresh basil finely chopped
- 1 Tbsp of fresh mint finely chopped
- 1 tsp of coriander
- Sea salt to taste
- 3 Tbs lemon juice (freshly squeezed)

Instructions

1. Pour the olive oil to the inner stainless steel pot of Slow Cooker; place the spinach on the bottom.
2. Cut the chicken fillets into small cubes and place over spinach.
3. Add the bell pepper and red hot chili pepper (if used).
4. Combine all remaining ingredients in a bowl and pour over chicken; gently stir with wooden spoon.
5. Cover and cook on LOW for 4-5 hours.
6. Adjust salt to taste and serve hot with lemon juice.

Nutrition information:

Calories: 281 Carbohydrates: 4.7g Proteins: 37.5g
Fat: 12g Fiber: 2g

Almond Breaded Chicken Patties

Serves: 8, Preparation: 15 minutes, Cooking: 10 minutes

Ingredients

- 2 lbs of minced chicken
- 4 eggs from free-range chickens
- 1 cup of parmesan cheese
- 1 cup fresh parsley finely chopped
- 3 slices of bacon, fried and crumbled
- 2 cloves of garlic, finely sliced
- Salt and black pepper freshly ground
- Olive oil for frying

For breading

- Almond flour
- 2 large eggs, beaten
- Ground almonds

Instructions

1. In a non-stick frying pan, fry bacon slices until crispy; allow to cool, crumble, and set aside.
2. Combine minced chicken, cheese, eggs, parsley, bacon, garlic melted and the salt and freshly ground pepper.
3. Using your hands, knead the mixture until combined well.
4. Shape from the mixture small patties.
5. Heat the olive oil in a large frying pan at medium-high heat.
6. Coat chicken patties with almond flour, dip in beaten eggs and cover with ground almonds.
7. Fry the chicken patties in hot oil for about 5 minutes or until golden brown.
8. Place on a serving plate lined with absorbent paper.
9. Serve hot.

Nutrition information:

Calories: 279 Carbohydrates: 4.6g Proteins: 16g
Fat: 23g Fiber: 1.7g

Roasted Stone-Ground Mustard Chicken in Foil

Serves: , Preparation: 10 minutes, Cooking: 40 minutes

Ingredients

- 4 chicken breasts, boneless and skinless
- 4 garlic cloves, minced
- 3 Tbsp stone-ground mustard
- 1 Tbsp olive oil
- 1 Tbsp of Italian seasoning
- Sea salt and ground black pepper to taste

Instructions

1. Preheat oven to 450 F/220 C.
2. Line one baking dish with aluminum foil and sprinkle little oil.
3. Heat the oil in a frying pan at medium heat and sauté garlic until soft.
4. Stir in stone-ground mustard, Italian seasoning to your preference.
5. Place chicken breasts on prepared baking dish, season the salt and pepper and cover with aluminum foil.
6. Bake uncovered for 25-30 minutes.
7. Allow to cool, slice and serve.

Nutrition information:

Calories: 315 Carbohydrates: 1.9g Proteins: 51g Fat: 10.5g Fiber: 1g

Asian Style Ginger Chicken

Serves: 6, Preparation: 15 minutes, Cooking: 30 minutes

Ingredients

- 1/2 whole chicken, roughly chopped
- Salt, to taste
- 1/4 cup ginger, grated
- 1 Tbsp of coconut aminos (from coconut sap)
- 2 Tbsp red wine
- 1/2 cup of sesame oil
- 2 Tbsp of chopped spring onion

Instructions

1. Rub the chicken with the salt.
2. Place the chicken in a pot fitted with the steamer basket over water. Steam chicken over medium high heat for about 30 minutes, or until chicken cooked through.
3. Drain chicken; reserve 1/2 cup of chicken soup.
4. In a frying skillet, heat up sesame, add ginger, coconut aminos, wine, and reserved chicken soup; stir for two minutes.
5. Remove the chicken on platter, pour sauce and garnish with spring onions; serve.

Nutrition information:

Calories: 468 Carbohydrates: 1g Proteins: 49g Fat: 28g Fiber: 0.2g

Broiled Coconut Aminos - Glazed Chicken Drumsticks

Serves: 4, Preparation: 1 hour 10 minutes, Cooking: 35 minutes

Ingredients

- 8 chicken drumsticks, skin-on or skinless
- 2 Tbsp of peanut butter
- 1/4 cup of coconut aminos (from coconut sap)
- 1/2 tsp ground ginger
- 1/2 tsp salt and freshly ground black pepper

Instructions

1. Preheat the oven's broiler, and line a broiler pan with aluminum foil.
2. In a large bowl, stir together peanut butter, coconut aminos, ginger, salt and pepper.
3. Add the chicken drumsticks and toss to coat. Refrigerate and marinate for one hour.
4. Remove the drumsticks from the fridge and place them in a prepared broiler pan.
5. Broil 13 to 15 minutes, turn the drumsticks and broil for additional 5 minutes.
6. Serve hot.

Nutrition information:

Calories: 351 Carbohydrates: 2g Proteins: 55g Fat: 13g Fiber: 0.6g

Chicken Breast with Dark Sauce

Serves: 4, Preparation: 5 minutes, Cooking: 35 minutes

Ingredients

- 2 Tbsp olive oil
- 2 lbs of chicken breasts, boneless, cut into bite-size pieces
- 1 garlic clove, crushed
- 1/4 tsp ginger
- 3/4 tsp crushed red pepper flakes
- 1/4 cup white wine
- 2 Tbsp stevia granulated sweetener
- 1/3 cup coconut aminos (from coconut sap)
- 1 Tbsp apple cider vinegar (preferably non-pasteurized)
- 1/2 cup water

Instructions

1. Heat the olive oil in a large frying skillet.
2. Add the chicken pieces and cook until lightly browned.
3. Remove chicken, and place on a plate: set aside.
4. Add all remaining ingredients in a skillet, and stir for 3 - 4 minutes over medium heat.
5. Add chicken, stir well, cover and simmer for 20 minutes over low heat.
6. Serve hot.

Nutrition information:

Calories: 347 Carbohydrates: 2g Proteins: 50g Fat: 13g Fiber: 0.3g

Oven Baked "Buffalo" Turkey Wings

Serves: 6, Preparation: 10 minutes, Cooking: 1 hour and 10 minutes

Ingredients

- 3 1/2 lbs turkey wings, cut in half
- 3/4 cup almond flour
- 1/2 tsp salt to taste
- 1 tsp cayenne pepper
- Olive oil for frying
- 1/4 cup almond butter melted
- 2 Tbsp of white vinegar
- 2 Tbsp hot red pepper sauce
- 2 Tbsp of fresh celery chopped

Instructions

1. Preheat the oven on 375 F/180 C.
2. Combine the almond flour, salt and cayenne pepper on a plate. Dust wings in almond flour mixture, shaking off excess.
3. Heat olive oil in a large heavy skillet over medium heat. Fry chicken for 10 minutes, turning once. Remove from heat, and drain on kitchen paper towels.
4. Combine the almond butter, vinegar and hot pepper sauce in a small bowl. Place wings in a large baking pan; drizzle sauce over wings.
5. Bake wings for 1 hour, turning once.
6. Serve hot with fresh chopped celery.

Nutrition information:

Calories: 549 Carbohydrates: 2.5g Proteins: 63g Fat: 31g Fiber: 1.2g

Oven Baked Creamy Chicken Thighs

Serves: 6, Preparation: 10 minutes, Cooking: 40 minutes

Ingredients

- 3/4 cup mayonnaise
- 1/4 cup yellow mustard
- 1/2 cup Parmesan cheese freshly grated
- 1 tsp Italian seasoning
- 1/4 tsp of coriander
- 1/4 tsp of marjoram
- 2 lbs chicken thighs (boneless and skinless)
- 1/2 tsp salt and ground black pepper

Instructions

1. Preheat oven to 400 F/200 C.
2. Oil one 8-inch square baking dish.
3. In a bowl combine together the mayonnaise, mustard, Parmesan cheese, coriander, marjoram and Italian seasoning.
4. Season generously chicken thigh with salt and pepper and place in a prepared baking dish.
5. Spread with mayo-mustard sauce and bake for 35 - 40 minutes. Serve warm.

Nutrition information:

Calories: 335 Carbohydrates: 7g Proteins: 34g Fat: 18g Fiber: 0.3g

Roasted Turkey - Mushrooms Loaf

Serves: 6, Preparation: 15 minutes, Cooking: 1 hour

Ingredients

- 1/2 cup ground almonds
- 1 Tbsp of dried parsley
- 1/4 tsp ground allspice
- 1/2 tsp dried thyme leaves
- 1/2 tsp salt and pepper to taste
- 1 1/2 lb ground turkey
- 8 oz turkey ham cut into 1/4-inch cubes
- 1/2 lb mushrooms coarsely chopped
- 1/2 cup spring onion chopped
- 2 cloves garlic minced
- 1 large egg beaten
- Olive oil cooking spray

Instructions

1. Preheat the oven to 350 F/175 C.
2. In large bowl combine ground almonds, parsley, allspice, thyme, salt and pepper.
3. Add ground turkey, turkey ham, mushrooms, spring onions, garlic and beaten egg; knead with your hands to get a compact mixture.
4. Coat one 9-inch pie plate with olive oil cooking spray, shape turkey mixture into round loaf.
5. Bake for 50 to 60 minutes or until inserted thermometer reaches 160 degrees F.
6. Serve hot.

Nutrition information:

Calories: 310 Carbohydrates: 5.5g Proteins: 34g
Fat: 18g Fiber: 2g

Chicken - Artichokes Casserole

Serves: 4, Preparation: 10 minutes, Cooking: 25 minutes

Ingredients

- 2 Tbsp butter
- 1 can (11 oz) of artichoke hearts, drained
- 2 green onions, green and white parts included, chopped
- 1 chicken breast cut in cubes
- 1/2 cup dry white wine
- 1 Tbsp almond flour
- 1/2 cup bone broth (or water)
- 1/2 cup cream
- 1 tsp salt and ground black pepper
- 1/4 tsp tarragon leaves
- 2 Tbsp chopped parsley for serving

Instructions

1. Preheat oven to 350 F/175 C.
2. Grease one deep casserole dish with the butter.
3. Cut artichokes and place on the bottom of casserole dish.
4. Add the green onion, and the chicken cubes over the artichokes.
5. In a bowl, combine together wine, bone broth, cream and almond flour; stir until almond flour is completely dissolved.
6. Pour the mixture evenly in a casserole dish.
7. Place in the oven and bake for 20 - 25 minutes. Serve hot.

Nutrition information:

Calories: 101 Carbohydrates: 8.5g Proteins: 22g
Fat: 29g Fiber: 6g

Chicken Liver and Pancetta Casserole

Serves: 4, Preparation: 5 minutes, Cooking: 50 minutes

Ingredients

- 1/4 cup of olive oil
- 1 onion finely chopped
- 2 cloves of garlic
- 1 1/2 lb of chicken liver
- 1/2 tsp smoked red ground pepper
- 7 oz of pancetta (cut into strips)
- 1 tsp of dried thyme
- 1/2 cup of red wine
- 1 bunch of parsley finely chopped
- Salt and freshly ground black pepper

Instructions

1. Preheat oven to 350 F/175 C.
2. Grease a casserole with olive oil; set aside.
3. Heat the olive oil in a skillet over medium-high heat.
4. Sauté the onion and the garlic for 3 - 4 minutes,
5. Add chopped pancetta and stir for 1 - 2 minutes.
6. Add chicken liver, smoked pepper, thyme, salt and pepper and cook for 3-4 minutes.
7. Pour the red wine, and add chopped parsley; stir.
8. Transfer the mixture in a prepared casserole dish.
9. Bake for 35 - 45 minutes. Serve hot.

Nutrition information:

Calories: 340 Carbohydrates: 4g Proteins: 29g Fat: 22g Fiber: 1g

Chicken Pandemonio Casserole

Serves: 6, Preparation: 15 minutes, Cooking: 35 minutes

Ingredients

- 1 Tbsp of chicken fat
- 2 lb of chicken, cubed
- Salt and ground pepper to taste
- 12 oz of frozen or fresh spinach
- 1/4 cup bacon crumbled
- 1 cup of cream cheese softened
- 1/2 cup of mayonnaise
- 1 tsp garlic powder
- 1 cup grated parmesan cheese

Instructions

1. Preheat oven to 350F/ 175 C
2. Grease one 9 x13 baking dish with chicken fat.
3. Season the chicken generously with the salt and pepper, and place into baking dish.
4. Add the spinach over chicken, and sprinkle with crumbled bacon.
5. In a bowl, combine together the cream cheese, mayo, garlic, and grated parmesan cheese.
6. Pour the mixture in a casserole.
7. Place in oven and bake for 30 - 35 minutes.
8. Serve hot.

Nutrition information:

Calories: 374 Carbohydrates: 8.5g Proteins: 15g Fat: 32g Fiber: 2g

Chicken with Curry and Coriander Casserole

Serves: 4, Preparation: 10 minutes, Cooking: 25 minutes

Ingredients

- 1 lb of chicken breast cut in cubes
- 1 Tbsp of chicken fat
- 1 onion finely sliced
- 1 carrot
- 2 tsp of curry powder
- 1 pinch of saffron
- 1/2 cup of wine
- 1/2 cup of bone broth
- 1 Tbsp of fresh coriander
- Salt to taste

Instructions

1. Cut the chicken breasts into large cubes.
2. Heat the chicken fat in a casserole and sauté the onion.
3. Add the chicken cubes and brown them on all sides; stir for 2 - 3 minutes.
4. Sprinkle with curry and saffron, stir in the carrots and stir well.
5. Pour the wine and bone broth and stir.
6. Season with the salt, cover and let simmer for 20 minutes.
7. Sprinkle with fresh chopped coriander leaves and serve.

Nutrition information:

Calories: 186 Carbohydrates: 6g Proteins: 26g Fat: 8g Fiber: 2g

Asiago Chicken Wings

Serves: 6, Preparation: 10 minutes, Cooking: 20 minutes

Ingredients

- 2 Tbsp olive oil
- 20 frozen chicken wings
- 1 tsp salt
- 1/2 Tbsp garlic powder
- 2 tsp dried oregano
- 1 cup of grated Asiago cheese (or Parmesan)
- 1/2 can water

Instructions

1. Pour the oil to the inner stainless steel pot in the Instant Pot.
2. Season frozen chicken legs with salt, garlic powder and oregano.
3. Place the seasoned chicken wings in your Instant Pot and pour water.
4. Lock lid into place and set on the POULTRY setting for 20 minutes.
5. Use Quick Release - turn the valve from sealing to venting to release the pressure.
6. Transfer chicken wings to serving platter and generously sprinkle with grated cheese.
7. Let rest for 10 minutes and serve.

Nutrition information:

Calories: 438 Carbohydrates: 2g Proteins: 37g Fat: 35g Fiber: 0.5g

Chicken Cilantro Wraps

Serves: 4, Preparation: 10 minutes, Cooking: 12 minutes

Ingredients

- 2 chicken breasts boneless, skinless
- 1 cup bone broth (or water)
- Juice of 1 lemon freshly squeezed
- 1 green onion finely chopped
- 1 cup cilantro, chopped
- 1 tsp chili powder
- 1 tsp cumin
- 1 tsp garlic powder
- Sea salt and pepper to taste
- 12 lettuce leaves

Instructions

1. Season chicken breast with the salt and pepper and place in your Instant Pot.
2. Add all remaining ingredients (except lettuce leaves; lock lid into place and set on the POULTRY setting for 12 minutes.
3. When the timer beeps, press "Cancel" and carefully flip the Quick Release valve to let the pressure out.
4. Open lid and transfer chicken in a bowl; Shred chicken with two forks.
5. Combine shredded chicken with juices from Instant Pot.
6. Add one spoon of shredded chicken in each lettuce leaf and wrap. Serve immediately.

Nutrition information:

Calories: 7163 Carbohydrates: 4g Proteins: 34g Fat: 5g Fiber: 1g

Perfect Braised Turkey Breast

Serves: 8, Preparation: 10 minutes, Cooking: 30 minutes

Ingredients

- 2 Tbsp butter softened on room temperature
- 4 lbs turkey breast boneless
- 1 cup water
- 1/2 cup coconut aminos (from coconut sap)
- 1/2 tsp fresh rosemary, finely chopped
- 1/2 tsp fresh sage, finely chopped
- 1/2 tsp fresh rosemary finely chopped
- 1 tsp salt and ground red pepper to taste

Instructions

1. Season turkey breasts with salt and pepper.
2. Press SAUTÉ button on your Instant Pot.
3. When the word "hot" appears on the display, add butter and sear turkey breasts for 3 minutes.
4. Pour water and coconut aminos and stir for 2 minutes.
5. Sprinkle with herbs, and the salt and pepper and stir again. Turn off the SAUTÉ button.
6. Lock lid into place and set on the MANUAL high pressure setting for 28 - 30 minutes (turkey meat is ready when meat thermometer shows 161 F/80 C).
7. When the timer beeps, press "Cancel" and carefully flip the Natural Release for 15 minutes.
8. Remove turkey breast on a plate, and allow it to cool for 10 minutes.
9. Slice and serve.

Nutrition information:

Calories: 357 Carbohydrates: 1.5g Proteins: 62g Fat: 10g Fiber: 0.5g

Roasted Whole Chicken

Serves: 6, Preparation: 10 minutes, Cooking: 35 minutes

Ingredients

- 2 cups water
- 4 lb whole chickens
- 1/4 cup olive oil
- Seasoned salt and black ground pepper to taste
- 1/4 tsp dry thyme
- 1/4 tsp dry rosemary
- 1/4 tsp dry marjoram
- 1/4 tsp of dry sage

Instructions

1. Pour water to the inner stainless steel pot in the Instant Pot, and place the trivet inside (steam rack or a steamer basket).
2. Rinse well the turkey and pat dry. Rub with olive oil and season to taste with salt and pepper, thyme, rosemary, marjoram and sage.
3. Put the turkey on the trivet into Instant Pot.
4. Press MANUAL mode and set time for 35 minutes.
5. Use Natural Release - it takes 15 - 20 minutes to depressurize naturally.
6. Remove the chicken on a serving plate and allow cool for 15 minutes before serving.

Nutrition information:

Calories: 589 Carbohydrates: 0.1g Proteins: 54g Fat: 47g Fiber: 1g

Serrano Chicken Stir Fry

Serves: 6, Preparation: 10 minutes, Cooking: 15 minutes

Ingredients

- 2 lbs chicken breasts cut small pieces
- 1 tsp sea salt
- 1 Tbsp sesame oil
- 1 Tbsp ginger, minced
- 1 Tbsp lemon juice
- 2 Tbsp coconut oil
- 1 green onion, minced
- 2 cloves garlic, minced
- 8 Serrano peppers cut in half
- 1 cup water

Instructions

1. In a bowl, whisk the salt, sesame oil, ginger and lemon juice.
2. Season chicken breast with the mixture.
3. Turn on the Instant Pot and press SAUTÉ button.
4. When the word "hot" appears on the display, add the coconut oil and sauté the green onion and garlic about 3 minutes. Add halved peppers and sauté for about 2 minutes.
5. Turn off SAUTÉ button; add seasoned chicken, pour water and stir.
6. Lock lid into place and set on the POULTRY setting on HIGH pressure for 10 minutes.
7. When the timer beeps, press "Cancel" and carefully flip the Quick Release valve to let the pressure out. Serve hot.

Nutrition information:

Calories: 359.55 Carbohydrates: 2.5g Proteins: 48g Fat: 17g Fiber: 1g

Tasty Chicken Curry

Serves: 4, Preparation: 10 minutes, Cooking: 10 minutes

Ingredients

- 2 Tbsp olive oil
- 1 lb chicken breast boneless, skinless, cut in small cubes
- Salt and ground black pepper
- 1/2 tsp onion powder
- 1/2 tsp garlic powder
- 1 tsp of curry powder
- 1 1/2 cup coconut cream
- 1/2 cup water
- 1 Tbsp of chopped parsley for serving

Instructions

1. Pour the oil to the inner stainless steel pot in the Instant Pot.
2. Season salt and pepper the chicken breast and place in Instant Pot.
3. In a bowl, combine together all remaining ingredients and pour over chicken.
4. Lock lid into place and set on the MANUAL setting for 10 minutes.
5. Use Natural Release for 15 minutes.
6. Serve hot with chopped parsley.

Nutrition information:

Calories: 304 Carbohydrates: 2g Proteins: 25g Fat: 22g Fiber: 0.3g

Chicken Thighs in Coconut Sauce

Serves: 6, Preparation: 10 minutes, Cooking: 4 hours and 20 minutes

Ingredients

- 1 1/2 lbs of chicken thighs boneless and skinless
- 1 red bell pepper finely chopped
- 1 green onion chopped
- 1 chili pepper (peeled and finely chopped)
- 2 cloves garlic (minced)
- 1 cup of bone broth
- 1/2 cup of coconut flakes
- 2 Tbsp of curry powder
- Salt and ground pepper to taste
- 1/4 tsp of ground cinnamon
- 1/2 cup of coconut milk unsweetened
- 1 Tbsp of coconut flour
- Fresh cilantro for serving

Instructions

1. Place the chicken thighs, bell pepper, onions, chili pepper and garlic in Crock Pot.
2. Pour broth, and add the coconut flakes, curry powder, salt and pepper, and cinnamon.
3. Cover and cook on LOW for 8 - 9 hours or HIGH for 4 hours.
4. In a small bowl, dissolve the coconut flour in coconut milk.
5. Open lid and pour the coconut mixture; stir.
6. Cover again and cook on HIGH for further 20 minutes.
7. Serve hot with fresh chopped cilantro.

Nutrition information:

Calories: 359 Carbohydrates: 5g Proteins: 24g Fat: 28g Fiber: 1.5g

Delicious Chicken Breast with Turmeric

Serves: 4, Preparation: 15 minutes, Cooking: 4 hours

Ingredients

- 1/2 cup chicken fat
- 4 chicken breasts, boneless, skinless
- Table salt and ground white pepper to taste
- 4 cloves garlic, finely sliced
- 1 Tbsp ground turmeric
- 1 cup of bone broth

Instructions

1. Season the salt and pepper chicken breast and cut into pieces.
2. Add tallow in inner pot of your Slow Cooker, and place the chicken breasts.
3. Add the turmeric, garlic and chicken broth.
4. Cover and cook on LOW for 3 - 4 hours.
5. Transfer the chicken breasts on a serving plate.
6. Serve hot with cooking juice.

Nutrition information:

Calories: 488 Carbohydrates: 2.5g Proteins: 52g Fat: 32g Fiber: 0.5g

Chicken Cutlets with Spinach Stir-Fry

Serves: 4, Preparation: 5 minutes, Cooking: 15 minutes

Ingredients

- 2 Tbsp chicken fat
- 1 spring onion (only green parts), finely chopped
- 2 medium cloves garlic, thinly sliced
- 8 boneless, skinless, chicken breast cutlets cut in pieces
- Salt and freshly ground black pepper
- 3 Tbsp capers, rinsed and chopped
- 1 lb of fresh spinach, steamed
- 1/2 cup water
- 2 Tbsp fresh lemon juice

Instructions

1. Heat the chicken fat in a deep pot, and sauté spring onion and garlic for 3 - 4 minutes.
2. Add chicken cutlets, and stir for 4 - 5 minutes.
3. Season with the salt and pepper,
4. Reduce the heat to medium and add the capers and spinach leaves. Cook stirring, until the spinach softens, about 3 minutes.
5. Pour water and lemon juice, and cook for further 2 - 3 minutes.
6. Serve hot.

Nutrition information:

Calories: 347 Carbohydrates: 5g Proteins: 57g Fat: 15g Fiber: 3g

Chicken with Zucchini Spaghetti Stir Fry

Serves: 4, Preparation: 15 minutes, Cooking: 7 - 10 minutes

Ingredients

- 1 lb chicken breasts, boneless, skinless, cut in slices
- 2 Tbsp of chicken fat
- 2 cups zucchini, spiralized (or made into ribbons with a vegetable peeler)

Marinade

- 1 spring onion finely chopped
- 2 cloves garlic, minced
- 1 cup water
- 1 cup fresh lemon juice
- 1/3 cup coconut aminos
- 1/3 cup olive oil
- 4 green onion, sliced
- 1" piece of ginger, grated
- Salt and ground black pepper to taste

Instructions

1. Place the chicken slices in a container and season with the salt and pepper.
2. In a deep bowl, combine all ingredients for marinade; stir until well combined.
3. Pour the marinade evenly over the chicken; cover and refrigerate for 2 hours.
4. Heat the chicken fat in a large and deep frying skillet over medium-high heat.
5. Add the chicken to the skillet and stir-fry about 5 - 7 minutes. Toss in the zucchini ribbons and cook only for 2 minutes. Serve hot.

Nutrition information:

Calories: 327 Carbohydrates: 6g Proteins: 27g Fat: 22g Fiber: 2g

Hungarian Chicken Fillet Stir-fry

Serves: 4, Preparation: 5 minutes, Cooking: 30 minutes

Ingredients

- 1 Tbsp of chicken fat
- 1 lb of chicken fillet cut in strips
- 2 - 3 spring onions, finely chopped
- 2 cloves garlic
- 1 green pepper, chopped
- 1 tomato grated
- Salt and black ground pepper to taste
- 1 Tbsp of fresh parsley, chopped
- 1 egg, beaten

Instructions

1. Heat the chicken fat in a large pan.
2. Sauté the onion and garlic with a pinch of salt for 4 - 5 minutes.
3. Add chicken strips and stir for 5 - 6 minutes.
4. Add chopped pepper and grated tomato; season with the salt and pepper.
5. Cover and cook for 12 - 15 minutes over low-medium heat.
6. Crack one egg in a pan and stir well.
7. Sprinkle with fresh parsley and serve hot.

Nutrition information:

Calories: 67 Carbohydrates: 6.5g Proteins: 6g Fat: 3g Fiber: 2g

Serrano Pepper - Chicken Stir-Fry

Serves: 4, Preparation: 10 minutes, Cooking: 20 minutes

Ingredients

- 2 lbs chicken breasts, boneless skinless, cut in pieces
- 1 tsp sea salt
- 2 cloves garlic, minced
- 1 Tbsp almond flour
- 1 cup water
- 1 Tbsp sesame oil
- 1 Tbsp ginger, minced
- 4 - 5 Serrano peppers, sliced
- 3 Tbsp olive oil
- 2 green onions cut into thin slices

Instructions

1. Place chicken in a large container, and rub with the mixture of salt, garlic, sesame oil, ginger, almond flour and water.
2. Refrigerate for 1 hour.
3. Heat the olive oil in a large skillet over a high heat.
4. Add Serrano peppers and fry for about 2 minutes.
5. Add the chicken, stir, reduce the heat and stir-fry for 5 - 6 minutes.
6. Add chopped green onion, some water, and cook for further 6-7 minutes.
7. Adjust salt, stir and serve hot.

Nutrition information:

Calories: 388 Carbohydrates: 2g Proteins: 48g Fat: 20g Fiber: 0.5g

Shredded Turkey with Asparagus Stir-fry

Serves: 4, Preparation: 5 minutes, Cooking: 30 minutes

Ingredients

- 2 Tbsp of chicken fat
- 2 spring onions, diced
- 1 tsp minced garlic
- 1 red pepper finely chopped
- 1/4 lb button mushrooms sliced thin
- 1 cup cooked asparagus cut into small pieces
- 1/2 tsp dried rosemary
- Salt and ground black pepper to taste
- 1 1/2 lbs turkey breast meat, boneless, shredded
- 1 cup bone broth

Instructions

1. In a large frying skillet heat the chicken fat over medium-high heat.
2. Sauté the onion, garlic and red pepper with a little salt for 4 to 5 minutes.
3. Add mushrooms and asparagus; sauté for 2 - 3 minutes.
4. Stir in rosemary, pepper, and season with the salt to taste.
5. Add shredded turkey meat, and stir well.
6. Pour the bone broth, cover and cook for 13 -15 minutes over medium heat.
7. Taste and adjust seasonings. Serve hot.

Nutrition information:

Calories: 210 Carbohydrates: 8g Proteins: 35g Fat: 4g Fiber: 2.5g

Squash Spaghetti and Chicken Mince Stir-fry

Serves: 4, Preparation: 5 minutes, Cooking: 25 minutes

Ingredients

- 1/4 cup olive oil
- 1 1/4 lb squash, spiralized
- 1 lb chicken mince
- 1 Tbsp fresh lemon juice (about 2 lemons)
- 1/2 Tbsp fresh herbs mixture (tarragon, marjoram, oregano)
- Salt and freshly ground pepper to taste
- 1/2 cup shredded Mozzarella cheese for garnish

Instructions

1. Heat the olive oil in a skillet over medium-high heat.
2. Sauté the squash spaghetti with a pinch of salt for about 8 minutes.
3. Add the ground chicken, fresh lemon juice, fresh herbs and season salt and pepper to taste.
4. Stir, and stir-fry for 8 - 10 minutes over medium heat.
5. Taste and adjust seasonings; cook for further 5 minutes; gently stir.
6. Serve hot with shredded cheese.

Nutrition information:

Calories: 338 Carbohydrates: 6g Proteins: 32g
Fat: 21g Fiber: 2g

Turkey Mince and Green Beans Stir-fry

Serves: 4, Preparation: 5 minutes, Cooking: 15 minutes

Ingredients

- 1 Tbsp chicken fat
- 1 lb turkey mince
- 2 cloves garlic, minced
- 2 spring onions, sliced
- 1 piece ginger, finely grated
- 1/2 lb of green beans, boiled
- 2 zucchini, cut into slices
- 2 Tbsp yellow mustard
- 1/2 cup fresh basil leaves
- Salt and ground black pepper

Instructions

1. Heat the chicken fat in a large frying pan.
2. Add turkey mince and stir-fry for 2 - 3 minutes,
3. Stir the garlic, spring onions and ginger; season with the salt and pepper and stir-fry for 3 -4 minutes.
4. Add green beans and zucchini, and stir-fry for 3 minutes; stir well.
5. At the end, add mustard and gently toss.
6. Serve hot with fresh basil leaves.

Nutrition information:

Calories: 193 Carbohydrates: 9g Proteins: 23g
Fat: 6g Fiber: 4g

Chapter 9 Pork, Beef & Lamb Recipes

Baked Juicy Pork Chunks with Mushrooms
Serves: 8, Preparation: 10 minutes, Cooking: 45 minutes

Ingredients
- 8 pork chunks
- 4 oz of mushrooms
- Salt and ground black pepper to taste
- 1 cup of white wine
- 1/2 cup of bone broth

Instructions
1. Preheat oven to 425 F/210 C.
2. Season pork chunks with the salt and pepper.
3. Place the pork chunks in a large baking sheet.
4. Sprinkle mushrooms over pork evenly.
5. Pour white wine and bone broth over mushrooms and pork.
6. Place in oven and bake for 40 - 45 minutes.
7. The pork chunks are ready when internal temperature reaches 160 F.
8. Serve hot.

Nutrition information:
Calories: 173 Carbohydrates: 1.2g Proteins: 26g Fat: 4g Fiber: 0.2g

Baked Pork Chops with Mozzarella and Bacon Gravy
Serves: 4, Preparation: 10 minutes, Cooking: 40 minutes

Ingredients
- 4 pork chops
- 1 tsp of nutmeg
- Salt and ground pepper to taste
- 2 Tbsp of olive oil
- 4 slices of bacon cut in thin strips
- 1 cup of cream
- 1 egg beaten
- 1 cup of shredded mozzarella

Instructions
1. Preheat your oven to 350 F/180 C. Brush the pork chops with oil, and place them in a baking dish.
2. Generously, season the pork chops with salt and ground pepper. Grill your pork chops for about 25 - 30 minutes, turning once.
3. In a meantime, fry bacon in a skillet strip until crisp.
4. Add cream, pepper, nutmeg and shredded mozzarella. Stir mixture for 5 minutes stirring continuously.
5. When mozzarella melts, remove skillet from the heat.
6. Add beaten egg and stir for 2 - 3 minutes.
7. Remove pork chops from the oven and place on serving platter.
8. Pour with bacon/mozzarella gravy and serve.

Nutrition information:
Calories: 581 Carbohydrates: 3.2g Proteins: 36g Fat: 56g Fiber: 0.1g

Pork with Celery in Egg-Lemon Sauce

Serves: 6, Preparation: 10 minutes, Cooking: 35 minutes

Ingredients

- 1 lb of fresh celery root and leaves
- Salt and ground white pepper to taste
- 2 lbs of pork, boneless, cut into cubes
- 2 scallions finely chopped
- 3 cups of warm water
- 1/2 cup of olive oil
- 2 eggs from free-range chickens
- 1 lemon

Instructions

1. Rinse the celery root, clean it and cut it into pieces. Wash the celery leaves and chop.
2. Bring water and salt to boil in a large pot, and add celery root and leaves.
3. Reduce the temperature to medium-low and cook for 30 minutes or until soft and tender.
4. Drain and discard cooking liquid.
5. Rinse the meat well, and dry on the kitchen pepper towel.
6. Heat the olive oil in a large skillet and sauté the pork meat with chopped scallions.
7. Add 3 cups warm water, cover and cook until meat softened.
8. Add cooked celery, and shake the pot (do not stir) to combine well.
9. In a small bowl, whisk the egg with the lemon juice.
10. Pour the lemon-egg mixture to the pot and gently stir.
11. Remove from the heat and let sit for 5 minutes.
12. Taste and adjust salt and pepper to taste.
13. Serve hot.

Nutrition information:

Calories: 699 Carbohydrates: 4.3g Proteins: 19.5g Fat: 79g Fiber: 1.5g

Breaded Triple Pork Rolls

Serves: 4, Preparation: 15 minutes, Cooking: 35 minutes

Ingredients

- 6 slices pork loin
- 6 bacon slices
- 6 cheese slices
- Almond flour for coating
- 2 large eggs, beaten
- Extra virgin olive oil

Instructions

1. Place a slice of bacon and a slice of cheese on top of each pork loin slice.
2. Roll up into a cylinder and secure with toothpicks.
3. Dip bacon in the beaten egg mixture, and then in almond flour.
4. Fry in the large skillet for 6 - 7 minutes or until golden browned on all sides.
5. Drain and serve hot.

Nutrition information:

Calories: 674 Carbohydrates: 1g Proteins: 53g Fat: 50g Fiber: 0g

Cypriot Sheftalia - Traditional Dish

Serves: 6, Preparation: 20 minutes, Cooking: 15 minutes

Ingredients

For the sheftalia
- 1 1/2 lb ground pork
- 1/3 cup of green onions finely chopped
- 3 Tbsp fresh parsley finely chopped
- 1 clove garlic, minced
- 1 Tbsp fresh lemon juice
- 1 tsp dried oregano
- 1 tsp dried mint
- 1 tsp salt and freshly ground black pepper

For the tahini sauce
- 1/4 cup sesame paste
- 1/4 cup extra-virgin olive oil
- 1 Tbsp fresh lemon juice
- 1 clove garlic, minced
- 1/2 tsp salt to taste
- 1/8 tsp cayenne pepper (or to taste)
- Olive oil

Instructions
1. Combine all of the ingredients from seftalia in a large bowl; using your hands, combine the mixture well.
2. Divide the pork mixture into 6 portions.
3. Wrap each portion of the pork tightly around a skewer to form a long cylinder.
4. Transfer to a baking sheet, cover, and refrigerate for 4 hours.

Make the tahini sauce
1. Place all ingredients for tahini sauce in your blender, and blend until smooth. Refrigerate until serving.

Grilling
1. Preheat your grill (pellet, gas, charcoal) to 350F/175 C.
2. Brush the sheftalia with oil and grill for 8 to 12 minutes, turning occasional.
3. Serve hot with tahini sauce.

Nutrition information:
Calories: 409 Carbohydrates: 3.4g Proteins: 21g
Fat: 35g Fiber: 1.3g

Keto Barbecue Pork Skillet

Serves: 4, Preparation: 5 minutes, Cooking: 15 minutes

Ingredients
- 1 tsp sesame oil
- 1/4 cup Italian dressing
- 1/4 cup Worcestershire sauce
- 1 tsp smoked paprika
- 1 tsp apple cider vinegar (preferably non-pasteurized)
- 6 pork chops, 3/4-inch thick

Instructions
1. In a large skillet, combine together sesame oil, Italian dressing, Worcestershire sauce and smoked paprika and vinegar for two minutes over moderate heat.
2. Add the pork chops, cover with the sauce and simmer for 10 minutes or until chops are tender.
3. Serve hot.

Nutrition information:
Calories: 246 Carbohydrates: 5g Proteins: 31g
Fat: 10g Fiber: 0.3g

Easy Pork Roast Casserole

Serves: 5, Preparation: 10 minutes, Cooking: 1 hour

Ingredients

- 2 Tbsp butter
- 2 lbs of pork roast
- 1 green onion chopped
- 1 Tbsp of almond flour
- 1/2 cup of white wine
- 1 cup of bone broth
- 1/2 cup of cream
- 3 fresh tarragon sprigs
- 3 slices of Cheddar cheese
- Salt and ground pepper to taste

Instructions

1. Heat the butter in a casserole over medium heat.
2. Brown the roast for 5 - 6 minutes, and add chopped green onion.
3. Pour the wine and let simmer for 2 - 3 minutes.
4. Season with the salt and pepper, pour the bone broth, cover and cook for 30 minutes.
5. Add the cream and chopped tarragon and gently stir.
6. Place cheddar slices on the top of meat, cover and cook for further 15 minutes.
7. Serve hot.

Nutrition information:

Calories: 549 Carbohydrates: 2g Proteins: 43.5g Fat: 40g Fiber: 0.1g

Pork and Bacon Baked Casserole

Serves: , Preparation: 10 minutes, Cooking: 25 minutes

Ingredients

- 2 lbs pork loin cut large strips
- Salt and pepper to taste
- 1 Tbsp of lard
- 1/2 lb of bacon, finely chopped
- 1 spring onion finely chopped
- 2 cloves of garlic finely chopped
- 1 cup of white wine
- 3 bay leaves

Instructions

1. Preheat oven to 350 degrees F/170 C.
2. Season the pork strips with the salt and pepper.
3. In a deep and heavy frying skillet, heat the lard over medium - high heat.
4. Fry the bacon for 2 minutes.
5. Add the green onion and garlic, and sauté for 2 - 3 minutes; stir.
6. Add the pork meat and season with the salt and pepper; stir for 2 minutes.
7. Pour wine, sprinkle with crumbled bay leaves, and season with the salt and pepper.
8. Transfer the mixture in the casserole pan.
9. Place in oven and bake for 20 - 25 minutes. Serve hot.

Nutrition information:

Calories: 412 Carbohydrates: 2g Proteins: 38g Fat: 24g Fiber: 0.2g

Pork with Button Mushrooms Casserole

Serves: 4, Preparation: 10 minutes, Cooking: 30 minutes

Ingredients

- 1 Tbsp of almond flour
- Salt and freshly ground black pepper
- 1 1/2 lbs of pork loin chops, cut in strips
- 2 Tbsp of butter
- 1 green onion, chopped
- 2 cloves of garlic, finely sliced
- 1 cup of button mushrooms
- 1 cup red wine
- 1/2 cup of water
- 1 tsp of fresh thyme
- 1 Tbsp of mustard grain

Instructions

1. In a large container, combine the almond flour with thyme and the salt and pepper, and roll the pork strips.
2. Heat the butter in a large casserole dish over medium heat and sauté the pork for 2 - 3 minutes.
3. Add all remaining ingredients and sprinkle with the salt and pepper; stir only for 2 - 3 minutes.
4. Bake in a oven for about 20 minutes
5. Serve hot.

Nutrition information:

Calories: 341 Carbohydrates: 5.5g Proteins: 40g Fat: 17g Fiber: 1g

"Kaula" Pork with Cabbage

Serves: 6, Preparation: 15 minutes, Cooking: 5 minutes

Ingredients

- 3 lbs pork tenderloin
- 2 tsp garlic powder
- 1 Tbsp kosher salt
- 1/2 cup bone broth (preferable homemade)
- 1/2 cup of water
- 1 small head of cabbage cut in chunks

Instructions

1. Season salt and garlic powder over pork.
2. Place the pork in your Instant Pot; pour bone broth and water.
3. Lock lid into place and set on the MANUAL setting on HIGH pressure for 85 minutes.
4. After the pressure cooking time has finished, use Natural Release - it takes 10 - 25 minutes to depressurize naturally.
5. Open lid and remove the pork to a large bowl.
6. Add the cabbage wedges in your Instant Pot and sprinkle with the salt.
7. Lock lid into place and set on the MANUAL setting on HIGH for 3 minutes.
8. Use Quick Release - turn the valve from sealing to venting to release the pressure.
9. Place cabbage wedges on a large serving platter.
10. Use two forks and shred the pork. Spoon the pork over the cabbage, and pour with juice from the Pot.

Nutrition information:

Calories: 282 Carbohydrates: 6g Proteins: 50g Fat: 6g Fiber: 3g

Mouth-watering Shredded BBQ Roast

Serves: 8, Preparation: 10 minutes, Cooking: 30 minutes

Ingredients

- 4 lbs pork roast
- 1 tsp garlic powder
- Salt and pepper to taste
- 1/2 cup water
- 2 can (11 oz) of barbecue sauce, keto unsweetened

Instructions

1. Season the pork with garlic powder, salt and pepper; place in your Instant Pot.
2. Pour water and lock lid into place; set on the MEAT/STEW, high pressure setting for 30 minutes.
3. When ready, use Quick Release - turn the valve from sealing to venting to release the pressure.
4. Remove pork in a bowl, and with two fork shred the meat.
5. Pour BBQ sauce and stir to combine well.
6. Serve.

Nutrition information:

Calories: 373 Carbohydrates: 2.5g Proteins: 34g Fat: 24g Fiber: 3g

Sour and Spicy Spareribs

Serves: 10, Preparation: 15 minutes, Cooking: 35 minutes

Ingredients

- 5 lbs spare spareribs
- Salt and pepper to taste
- 2 Tbsp of tallow
- 1/2 cup coconut aminos (from coconut sap)
- 1/2 cup vinegar
- 2 Tbsp Worcestershire sauce, to taste
- 1 tsp chili powder
- 1 tsp garlic powder
- 1 tsp celery seeds

Instructions

1. Cut the rack of ribs into equal portions.
2. Season salt and ground pepper your spare ribs from all sides.
3. Add tallow in your Instant Pot and place spare ribs.
4. In a bowl, combine together all remaining ingredients and pour over spareribs.
5. Lock lid into place and set on the MANUAL setting on HIGH heat for 35 minutes.
6. When the timer beeps, press "Cancel" and carefully flip the Natural Release for 20 minutes.
7. Open the lid and transfer ribs on a serving platter.
8. Serve hot.

Nutrition information:

Calories: 598 Carbohydrates: 2g Proteins: 36g Fat: 54g Fiber: 0.2g

Tender Pork Shoulder with Hot Peppers

Serves: 8, Preparation: 10 minutes, Cooking: 30 minutes

Ingredients

- 3 lbs pork shoulder boneless
- Salt and ground black pepper to taste
- 3 Tbsp of olive oil
- 1 large onion, chopped
- 2 cloves garlic minced
- 2 - 3 chili peppers, chopped
- 1 tsp ground coriander
- 1 tsp ground cumin
- 1 ½ cups of bone broth (preferable homemade)
- 1/2 cup water

Instructions

1. Season salt and pepper the pork meat.
2. Turn on the Instant Pot and press SAUTÉ button. When the word "hot" appears on the display, add the oil and sauté the onions and garlic about 5 minutes.
3. Add pork and sear for 1 - 2 minutes from all sides; turn off the SAUTÉ button.
4. Add all remaining ingredients into Instant Pot.
5. Lock lid into place and set on the MEAT/STEW setting on HIGH heat for 30 minutes.
6. When the timer beeps, press "Cancel" and carefully flip the Natural Release button for 15 minutes. Serve hot.

Nutrition information:

Calories: 389 Carbohydrates: 2.5g Proteins: 36g Fat: 27g Fiber: 0.5g

Braised Sour Pork Filet

Serves: 6, Preparation: 10 minutes, Cooking: 8 hours

Ingredients

- 1/2 tsp of dry thyme
- 1/2 tsp of sage
- Salt and ground black pepper to taste
- 2 Tbs of olive oil
- 3 lbs of pork fillet
- 1/3 cup of shallots (chopped)
- 3 cloves of garlic (minced)
- 3/4 cup of bone broth
- 1/3 cup of apple cider vinegar

Instructions

1. In a small bowl, combine together thyme, sage, salt and black ground pepper.
2. Rub generously pork from all sides.
3. Heat the olive oil in a large frying pan, and sear pork for 2 - 3 minutes.
4. Place pork in your Crock Pot and add shallots and garlic.
5. Pour broth and apple cider vinegar / juice.
6. Cover and cook on SLOW for 8 hours or on HIGH for 4-5 hours.
7. Remove pork on a plate, adjust salt and pepper, slice and serve with cooking juice.

Nutrition information:

Calories: 348 Carbohydrates: 3g Proteins: 51g Fat: 12.5g Fiber: 0.1g

Pork with Anise and Cumin Stir-fry

Serves: 4, Preparation: 5 minutes, Cooking: 30 minutes

Ingredients

- 2 Tbsp lard
- 2 spring onions finely chopped (only green part)
- 2 cloves garlic, finely chopped
- 2 lbs pork loin, boneless, cut into cubes
- Sea salt and black ground pepper to taste
- 1 green bell pepper (cut into thin strips)
- 1/2 cup water
- 1/2 tsp dill seeds
- 1/2 anise seeds
- 1/2 tsp cumin

Instructions

1. Heat the lard n a large frying pot over medium-high heat.
2. Sauté the spring onions and garlic with a pinch of salt for 3 - 4 minutes.
3. Add the pork and simmer for about 5 - 6 minutes.
4. Add all remaining ingredients and stir well.
5. Cover and let simmer for 15 - 20 minutes
6. Taste and adjust seasoning to taste. Serve.

Nutrition information:

Calories: 351 Carbohydrates: 3g Proteins: 1g Fat: 51.5g Fiber: 1g

Baked Meatballs with Goat Cheese

Serves: 8, Preparation: 15 minutes, Cooking: 35 minutes

Ingredients

- 1 Tbsp of tallow
- 2 lbs of ground beef
- 1 organic egg
- 1 grated onion
- 1/2 cup of almond milk (unsweetened)
- 1 cup of red wine
- 1/2 bunch of chopped parsley
- 1/2 cup of almond flour
- Salt and ground pepper to taste
- 1/2 Tbsp of dry oregano
- 4 oz of hard goat cheese cut in cubes

Instructions

1. Preheat oven to 400 F/200 C.
2. Grease a baking pan with tallow.
3. In a large bowl, combine all ingredients except goat cheese.
4. Knead the mixture until ingredients are evenly combined.
5. Make small meatballs and place in a prepared baking dish.
6. Place one cube of cheese on each meatball.
7. Bake for 30 - 35 minutes.
8. Serve hot.

Nutrition information:

Calories: 404 Carbohydrates: 2.2g Proteins: 25.5g Fat: 31g Fiber: 0.5g

Parisian Schnitzel

Serves: 4, Preparation: 15 minutes, Cooking: 10 minutes

Ingredients

- 4 veal steaks; thin schnitzel
- Salt and ground black pepper
- 2 Tbsp of butter
- 3 eggs from free-range chickens
- 4 Tbsp of almond flour

Instructions

1. Season steaks with the salt and pepper.
2. Heat butter in a large non-stick frying pan at medium heat.
3. In a bowl, beat the eggs.
4. Add almond flour in a bowl.
5. Roll each steak in almond flour, add then, dip in beaten eggs.
6. Fry about 3 minutes per side.
7. Serve immediately.

Nutrition information:

Calories: 355 Carbohydrates: 0.3g Proteins: 54g
Fat: 15g Fiber: 0g

Keto Beef Stroganoff

Serves: 6, Preparation: 5 minutes, Cooking: 30 minutes

Ingredients

- 2 lbs of rump or round steak or stewing steak
- 4 Tbsp of olive oil
- 2 green onions, finely chopped
- 1 grated tomato
- 2 Tbsp ketchup (without sugar)
- 1 cup of button mushrooms
- 1/2 cup of bone broth
- 1 cup of sour cream
- Salt and black pepper to taste

Instructions

1. Cut the meat into strips and sauté in large frying skillet.
2. Add chopped onion and a pinch of salt, and cook meat for about 20 minutes at medium temperature.
3. Add mushrooms and ketchup and stir for 3 - 5 minutes.
4. Pour the bone broth and sour cream, and cook for 3 - 4 minutes.
5. Remove from the heat, taste and adjust salt and pepper to taste.
6. Serve hot.

Nutrition information:

Calories: 348 Carbohydrates: 4,2g Proteins: 37g
Fat: 21g Fiber: 1g

Meatloaf with Gruyere

Serves: 6, Preparation: 15 minutes, Cooking: 40 minutes

Ingredients

- 1 1/2 lbs ground beef
- 1 cup ground almonds
- 1 large egg from free-range chickens
- 1/2 cup grated Gruyere cheese
- 1 tsp fresh parsley finely chopped
- 1 scallion finely chopped
- 1/2 tsp ground cumin
- 3 eggs boiled
- 2 Tbsp of fresh grass-fed butter, melted

Instructions

1. Preheat oven to 350 F175 C.
2. Combine all ingredients (except eggs and butter) in a large bowl.
3. Using your hands, combine well the mixture.
4. Shape the mixture into a roll and place in the middle sliced hard-boiled eggs.
5. Transfer the meatloaf to a 5x9 inch loaf pan greased with melted butter.
6. Place in oven and bake for 40 minutes or until internal temperature of 160 degrees F.
7. Remove from the oven and allow rest for 10 minutes.
8. Slice and serve.

Nutrition information:

Calories: 598 Carbohydrates: 5,3g Proteins: 28g Fat: 63g Fiber: 2.6g

Roasted Filet Mignon in Foil

Serves: 6, Preparation: 15 minutes, Cooking: 45 minutes

Ingredients

- 3 lbs filet mignon in one piece
- Salt to taste and ground black pepper
- 1 tsp of garlic powder
- 1 tsp of onion powder
- 1 tsp of cumin
- 4 Tbsp of olive oil

Instructions

1. Preheat the oven to 425 F/210 C.
2. Rinse and clean the filet mignon, removing all fats, or ask your butcher to do it for you.
3. Season with the salt and pepper, garlic powder, onion powder and cumin.
4. Wrap filet mignon in foil and place in a roasting pan; drizzle with the olive oil.
5. Roast for 15 minutes per pound for medium-rare or to desired doneness.
6. Remove from the oven and allow to rest for 10 -15 minutes before serving.

Nutrition information:

Calories: 350 Carbohydrates: 0.8g Proteins: 52.5g Fat: 12.2g Fiber: 0.2g

Stewed Beef with Green Beans

Serves: 6, Preparation: 10 minutes, Cooking: 50 minutes

Ingredients
- 1/2 cup olive oil
- 1 1/2 lbs beef cut into cubes
- 2 scallions, finely chopped
- 2 cups water
- 1 lb fresh green beans - trimmed and cut diagonally in half
- 1 bay leaf
- 1 grated tomato
- 1/2 cup fresh mint leaves, finely chopped
- 1 tsp fresh or dry rosemary
- Salt and freshly ground pepper to taste

Instructions
1. Chop the beef into 1-inch thick cubes.
2. Heat the olive oil in a large pot at high heat. Sauté the beef for about 4 - 5 minutes; sprinkle with a pinch of salt and pepper.
3. Add the scallions, and stir and sauté for about another 3 - 4 minutes until softened. Pour water and cook for 2-3 minutes.
4. Add the bay leaf and grated tomato. Cook for about 5 minutes; lower the heat at medium-low. Cover and simmer for about 15 minutes.
5. Add the green beans, rosemary, salt, fresh ground pepper and water enough to cover all ingredients. Gently simmer for 15 - 20 minutes until the green beans are tender.
6. Sprinkle with the mint and rosemary, gently mix and remove from the heat. Serve hot.

Nutrition information:
Calories: 354 Carbohydrates: 6g Proteins: 23g Fat: 26.5g Fiber: 2.7g

Beef and Chicken Meatballs with Curry Sauce

Serves: 8, Preparation: 15 minutes, Cooking: 30 minutes

Ingredients
- 1 lb of ground beef
- 3/4 lb of chicken mince
- 1 hot pepper finely chopped
- 2 fresh onions finely chopped
- 1 tsp of fresh grated ginger
- 3 Tbsp of fresh coriander chopped
- Ground almonds
- Salt and ground black pepper

For curry sauce
- 3 Tbsp of sesame oil
- 2 spring onions finely chopped
- 2 cloves garlic finely sliced
- 1 Tbsp of curry paste
- 1 Tbsp of cumin
- 1 grated tomato
- 2 cups of canned coconut milk
- 2 Tbsp of fresh coriander

Instructions
1. Combine all the ingredients in a bowl; with your hand knead until combine well.
2. Form from the mixture fine meatballs.
3. Heat the oil in a large wok or in a frying skillet.
4. Fry the meatballs for about 10 minutes in total.
5. Remove the meatballs on a plate lined with absorbent paper.

Curry sauce
1. In the wok or frying skillet, sauté the green onions for 3 - 4 minutes; add the garlic, ginger and curry paste and stir.
2. Add the ground cumin and grated tomato, and cook for 5 minutes, stirring occasionally.
3. Add the coconut milk, season with the salt and bring to boil.
4. Cook, stirring, for 4 - 5 minutes.
5. Add the meatballs and cook for 5 minutes at medium-low heat.
6. Add fresh coriander and stir well.
7. Adjust salt and pepper, stir and serve.

Nutrition information:
Calories: 389 Carbohydrates: 7.1g Proteins: 19g Fat: 32g Fiber: 2.7g

Creamy and Peppery Beef Fillets

Serves: 6, Preparation: 10 minutes, Cooking: 15 minutes

Ingredients

- 4 beef fillets (about 2 lbs)
- 1 small red bell pepper, thinly chopped
- 1 red hot chili pepper, finely chopped
- 2 cloves garlic, finely sliced
- 2 Tbsp olive oil
- 1/3 cup of brandy
- 2 Tbsp of butter
- 1 cup of fresh cream
- 1/2 cup of bone broth
- Salt and ground black pepper

Instructions

1. Sprinkle the beef fillets with the chopped bell pepper, garlic and red hot chili pepper; press deep into the meat. Wrap fillets with a foil and refrigerate for 30 minutes.
2. Heat the oil in a wok or in a large frying pan, and fry the fillets for 6 minutes in total for medium-rare.
3. Transfer them on a plate lined with absorbent paper; sprinkle with a pinch of the salt and pepper.
4. In the same wok or the frying pan add brandy, butter, cream and bone broth; stir and cook for 5 minutes, stirring periodically.
5. Return your fillets in a work or skillet and cover with the sauce. Serve.

Nutrition information:

Calories: 587 Carbohydrates: 2.7g Proteins: 31g
Fat: 55g Fiber: 0.7g

Perfect Oven Roasted Spare Ribs

Serves: 6, Preparation: 10 minutes, Cooking: 1 hour 25 minutes

Ingredients

- 3 lbs beef spare ribs with the bone
- 1 Tbsp fresh butter
- 2 Tbsp of olive oil
- 2 green onions, finely chopped
- 2 cloves garlic
- 3 Tbsp of fresh celery, chopped
- 1 Tbsp of grated tomato
- 2 Tbsp of fresh thyme, chopped
- 1 cup of white dry wine
- 1/2 cup of bone broth
- Salt and freshly ground black pepper

Instructions

1. Preheat the oven to 360 F/180 C.
2. Grease one large baking dish with the butter.
3. Season beef spare ribs with the salt and pepper.
4. Place meat in a baking dish with the fat side down.
5. Heat the oil in a frying pan and sauté the onions, garlic for 3 - 4 minutes.
6. Add fresh celery, grated tomato and fresh thyme; stir well and cook for 2 - 3 minutes.
7. Pour the wine and bone broth and stir for 3 minutes.
8. Pour the sauce over the meat.
9. Cover with aluminum foil and bake for 1 1/2 hours.
10. Uncover and baste meat with the sauce and roast for further 30 minutes.
11. 1Allow the meat to cool for 10 - 15 minutes and serve.

Nutrition information:
Calories: 554 Carbohydrates: 2g Proteins: 33.5g Fat: 88g Fiber: 0.8g

Baked Ground Beef and Eggplant Casserole

Serves: 6, Preparation: 15 minutes, Cooking: 35 minutes

Ingredients

- 1 Tbsp of tallow
- 1 lb ground beef
- 1 spring onion, finely chopped
- 1 eggplant, diced
- 1 grated tomato
- 1/2 tsp dried parsley flakes
- 1/2 tsp dried celery flakes
- 1 tsp seasoned salt
- 1/2 cup water
- 1 cup cheddar cheese, grated

Instructions

1. Preheat oven to 350 F/286 C.
2. In a large casserole dish, heat the tallow and sauté the ground beef, chopped onion for two minutes; stir.
3. Add eggplant and stir for two minutes.
4. Add all remaining ingredients and give a good stir.
5. Sprinkle with grated cheese and bake for 15 minutes. Serve hot.

Nutrition information:
Calories: 477 Carbohydrates: 8g Proteins: 29g Fat: 36g Fiber: 4.5g

Festive Rosemary Flavored Beef Fillet

Serves: 6, Preparation: 15 minutes, Cooking: 15 minutes

Ingredients

- 1/4 cup olive oil
- 3 1/2 lb center-cut beef tenderloin roast
- Kosher salt and ground black pepper to taste
- 2 cloves garlic finely chopped
- 2 - 3 Tbsp fresh rosemary (chopped)

Instructions

1. Preheat oven to 350 F/175 C.
2. Grease one roasting pan with olive oil; set aside.
3. Pat beef roast dry, and generously coat with the salt, pepper, garlic and rosemary.
4. Place meat in a prepared roasting pan.
5. Bake for 25 - 30 minutes per pound or until inserted thermometer for internal temperature reaches 175 F/85 C.
6. Remove from oven and allow to cool for 10 -15 minutes.
7. Slice and serve.

Nutrition information:

Calories: 549 Carbohydrates: 0.3g Proteins: 40g Fat: 42g Fiber: 0.3g

Grilled Fillet Mignon with Peppercorn

Serves: 6, Preparation: 10 minutes, Cooking: 15 minutes

Ingredients

- 8 beef filet mignon steaks 1-inch cut
- Sea salt to taste
- 2 Tbsp of olive oil
- Cracked black peppercorn, to taste

Instructions

1. Preheat your grill (pellet, gas, charcoal) to HIGH according to manufacturer instructions.
2. Season each fillet with the sea salt.
3. Brush each filet with oil, and press some peppercorns in the top side of each steak.
4. Place your fillets in a grill racks, close the lid, and grill for 10 to 12 minutes for medium-rare turning once.
5. Serve hot.

Nutrition information:

Calories: 569 Carbohydrates: 0 g Proteins: 43g Fat: 46g Fiber: 0 g

Keto Beef Satay

Serves: 4, Preparation: 15 minutes, Cooking: 5 minutes

Ingredients

- 1 lb beef strips, sliced
- 1 tsp turmeric
- 1/2 tsp dried chili flakes
- 1 Tbsp of coconut aminos
- 1 tsp of stevia granulated sweetener
- 1/2 tsp salt
- 1/2 cup coconut milk
- 1 Tbsp of tallow

Instructions

1. Cut beef in strips about 1/4" thick. In a container, combine all remaining ingredients, add the beef strips and marinate for 2 hours.
2. Remove the beef strips from fridge, and drain on a kitchen paper towel: reserve marinade.
3. Heat the tallow in a skillet, and fry the chicken strips for 5 minutes in total over medium heat.
4. Pour the marinade over the pork and simmer for two minutes.
5. Serve hot.

Nutrition information:

Calories: 579 Carbohydrates: 2g Proteins: 64g Fat: 34g Fiber: 0.2g

Keto Beef Stroganoff

Serves: 6, Preparation: 10 minutes, Cooking: 30 minutes

Ingredients

- 2 Tbsp of fresh butter
- 1/2 cup green onions (scallions) finely chopped
- 1/2 cup cream cheese, at room temperature
- 1/2 tsp of ground garlic
- 1/2 tsp dried sage
- 1 tsp celery
- 2 lbs of beef tenderloin cut into 2-inch strips
- 1 cup sliced mushrooms
- Salt and ground pepper to taste

Instructions

1. Melt butter in medium skillet over medium heat; add green onion and sauté for 3 minutes. Add cream cheese, ground garlic, sage and celery; stir until combined well. Remove skillet from heat; set aside.
2. Place beef strips with mushrooms in a large frying skillet. Cover and cook for 3 minutes on high heat. Uncover; add the cream cheese mixture and stir well.
3. Cover and cook for 20 -25 minutes over low heat.
4. Remove from the heat, and let sit for 10 minutes before serving.

Nutrition information:

Calories: 506 Carbohydrates: 2g Proteins: 29g Fat: 42g Fiber: 0.4g

Tasty Veal Roast with Herb Crust

Serves: 6, Preparation: 12 minutes, Cooking: 2 hours and 15 minutes

Ingredients

- 3 lb veal leg round roast, boneless
- 1/4 cup ground almonds
- 2 Tbsp water
- 1 Tbsp mustard (Dijon, English, or whole grain)
- 1 Tbsp lemon juice
- 1/2 tsp ground pepper
- 1 tsp dried thyme
- 1 tsp dried basil
- 1 cup bone broth (or water)
- 2 Tbsp almond flour
- 1/4 cup sour cream

Instructions

1. Heat the oven to 350 F/175 C.
2. Place meat in a roasting pan.
3. In a bowl, stir together ground almonds, water, mustard, lemon juice, basil, thyme, and pepper.
4. Generously spread mixture over the meat.
5. Place a pan in oven and bake for 2-1/2 hours or until inserted thermometer reaches 160 F/ 80 C.
6. Transfer meat to a platter; cover and set aside.
7. In a saucepan stir bone broth or water with the flour. Cook and stir until thickened and bubbly, about two minutes.
8. Stir in the sour cream and just heat through.
9. Serve meat with the sauce, and Bon appetite!

Nutrition information:

Calories: 515 Carbohydrates: 2g Proteins: 83g Fat: 15g Fiber: 1g

Beef "Satare in Booca" Casserole

Serves: 8, Preparation: 35 minutes ,Cooking: 10 minutes

Ingredients

- 8 beef steaks
- 1 cup of white wine
- 8 slices prosciutto
- 8 leaves of sage
- 2 Tbsp of capers
- Salt and freshly ground black pepper
- 2 Tbsp of butter

Instructions

1. Put the steaks in the container; season generously with the salt and pepper, and pour the wine; marinate for 30 minutes; drain and reserve the wine.
2. Preheat the oven to 350 F/ 175 C.
3. Place the prosciutto slice and sage leave on each beef steak, and fasten with a toothpick or slice into a roll, and then fasten.
4. Grease the casserole dish with the butter and place the steaks.
5. Sprinkle with capers, little fresh pepper, and pour with reserved wine.
6. Bake for 7 - 10 minutes per side.
7. Remove from the oven, and let the meat rest before serving.

Nutrition information:

Calories: 432 Carbohydrates: 1.5g Proteins: 34g Fat: 53g Fiber: 0.2g

Ground Beef and Baby Spinach Casserole

Serves: 4, Preparation: 10 minutes, Cooking: 45 minutes

Ingredients

- 1 lb of ground beef (turkey, beef, lamb, bison)
- Salt and freshly ground black pepper
- 1 grated tomato
- 2 cups of baby spinach
- 1 cup sliced black olives
- 1 Tbsp of fresh cilantro, finely chopped
- 8 eggs
- 1/2 cup grated cheese (Cheddar or Parmesan)

Instructions

1. Preheat oven to 350 F/175 C.
2. Place the ground beef in a greased casserole and sprinkle with a pinch of salt and pepper.
3. Add grated tomato, olives and baby spinach over the meat; sprinkle with the little salt and fresh cilantro.
4. In a bowl, whisk the eggs until frothy; add grated cheese and stir. Season it with the salt and pepper, and stir.
5. Pour the egg mixture in casserole.
6. Place in the oven, and bake for 40 - 45 minutes. Serve hot.

Nutrition information:

Calories: 484 Carbohydrates: 3.5g Proteins: 35g Fat: 36g Fiber: 2g

Tangy Beef Chuck Roast (Instant Pot)

Serves: 6, Preparation: 10 minutes, Cooking: 1 hour and 5 minutes

Ingredients

- 2 Tbsp olive oil
- 3 lbs beef chuck roast, boneless
- Seasoned salt and ground black pepper to taste
- 1 pinch garlic powder
- 2 spring onions finely chopped
- 1 carrot, sliced
- 1 1/2 cup bone broth (preferable homemade)
- 1 1/2 Tbsp Worcestershire sauce

Instructions

1. Season generously the beef roast with seasoned salt and ground black pepper and garlic powder.
2. Press SAUTÉ button on your Instant Pot
3. When the word "hot" appears on the display, add beef and sear from all sides.
4. Add onions and sliced carrot, turn-off the SAUTÉ button.
5. Pour bone broth and Worcestershire sauce
6. Lock lid into place and set on the MANUAL setting for 60 minutes.
7. Naturally release pressure for 5 minutes and quick release remaining pressure.
8. Remove lid, transfer roast to the large plate and shred the roast. Serve hot.

Nutrition information:

Calories: 654 Carbohydrates: 5g Proteins: 49g Fat: 60g Fiber: 1g

Fresh Herbs and Mustard Beef (Slow Cooker)

Serves: 6, Preparation: 10 minutes, Cooking: 8 hours

Ingredients

- 2 Tbsp tallow
- 2 lbs grass-feed beef roast, any kind
- Salt and black ground pepper to taste
- 2 Tbsp yellow ground mustard seeds
- 1 Tbsp fresh parsley, finely chopped
- 1 tsp fresh thyme, finely chopped
- 1 tsp fresh cilantro (chopped)
- 1 Tbsp fresh butter grass-fed
- 1 1/2 cup water

Instructions

1. Grease the inner steel pot in the Slow Cooker.
2. Season the beef with the salt and pepper from all sides.
3. Place the beef roast in Slow Cooker and sprinkle with mustard seeds and fresh herbs.
4. Pour the water, add the mustard and sprinkle with parsley-cilantro mix; stir.
5. Cover and cook on LOW for 6 - 8 hours.
6. Remove roast from Slow Cooker on a platter; allow to cool, slice and serve.

Nutrition information:

Calories: 466 Carbohydrates: 0.5g Proteins: 27g Fat: 38g Fiber: 0.3g

Ground Beef with Swiss chard Stir-fry

Serves: 4, Preparation: 10 minutes, Cooking: 20 minutes

Ingredients

- 1 Tbsp lard or butter
- 2 green onions (only green parts finely chopped)
- 1 lb ground beef
- 1 tsp garlic powder
- 1 tsp ground cumin
- 1 tsp oregano
- Salt and ground pepper to taste
- 1 lb Swiss chard, tender stems and leaves finely chopped

Instructions

1. In a large pot boil water and cook Swiss chard for 5 - 7 minutes or until soft; transfer in colander to drain.
2. Heat the lard in a large and deep frying pan.
3. Add the green onions with a pinch of salt, and sauté for 3 - 4 minutes over medium heat.
4. Add ground beef and stir for 4 -5 minutes.
5. Season with the garlic powder, cumin and oregano; stir well.
6. Add steamed Swish Card and gently stir to combine all ingredients; cover and cook for further 2 - 3 minutes. Serve hot.

Nutrition information:

Calories: 351 Carbohydrates: 5g Proteins: 23g Fat: 21g Fiber: 3g

Ground Beef, Kale Stew and Almonds Stir-fry

Serves: 4, Preparation: 5 minutes, Cooking: 25 minutes

Ingredients

- 1 lb kale (chopped, tough stems discarded)
- 2 Tbsp olive oil
- 1 lb of ground beef
- 1/4 tsp of cinnamon
- 1 tsp cumin
- 1 tsp oregano
- 1 tsp garlic powder
- Salt and freshly ground black pepper, to taste
- 1 cup almonds, finely chopped or ground

Instructions

1. Boil water in a large pot; submerge kale and boil for 5 - 6 minutes; transfer kale in a colander to drain.
2. Heat the oil in a large and deep frying skillet, and sauté ground meat for 6 - 7 minutes.
3. Season with the cinnamon, cumin, oregano, garlic powder, and the ground pepper and salt; stir well.
4. Add streamed kale, stir gently, cover and cook for 3 - 4 minutes over low heat.
5. Taste and adjust seasonings. Sprinkle with ground almonds and serve hot.

Nutrition information:

Calories: 481 Carbohydrates: 8g Proteins: 28g Fat: 38g Fiber: 3.5g

Perfect Keto Beef and Broccoli Stir-Fry

Serves: 4, Preparation: 10 minutes, Cooking: 15 minutes

Ingredients

- 1 lb pre-cut beef strips or beef for stir-fry
- 2 Tbsp almond flour
- 1/2 cup water
- 1/2 tsp garlic powder
- 2 Tbsp olive oil, divided
- 4 cups broccoli florets
- 1 small onion, cut into wedges
- 1 tsp ground of fresh ginger

Instructions

1. In a bowl, combine 2 tablespoons of almond flour, 2 tablespoons water and garlic powder until smooth.
2. Pour the mixture over the beef, and toss to combine well.
3. In a large skillet heat the oil over medium-high heat, stir-fry the beef strips for 4 - 5 minutes, or 1 until beef reaches desired doneness. Remove the beef on a plate.
4. Heat some more oil in the same skillet and sauté the onion for 3 -4 minutes.
5. Add the broccoli; season with the salt and pepper and sauté for about 2 - 3 minutes.
6. Add the chicken again in a skillet, stir and cook along with remaining ingredients for 2 minutes. Serve hot.

Nutrition information:

Calories: 228 Carbohydrates: 1.5g Proteins: 29g Fat: 11g Fiber: 0.5g

Toothsome Grilled Lamb Skewers

Serves: 6, Preparation: 15 minutes, Cooking: 10 minutes

Ingredients

- 2 lbs of lamb fillet cut in cubes
- Salt to taste
- 1/2 cup of olive oil
- 1 Tbsp of grated ginger
- 1 cup of white wine
- 2 Tbsp of wine vinegar
- 1/4 tsp of freshly ground black pepper

Instructions

1. Rinse and trim your lamb fillet; cut lamb fillet into 1 1/2-inch cubes. Season the lamb meat generously with salt.
2. In a bowl, whisk the olive oil, ginger, wine, vinegar, and pepper to make the marinade.
3. Add the lamb cube and combine with marinade. Cover and refrigerate for 2-3 hours or overnight.
4. Preheat your grill (pellet, gas, charcoal) to HIGH according to manufacturer instructions.
5. Remove the lamb from the fridge and pat dry on kitchen paper towel. Thread the meat onto skewers and place on grill.
6. Grill for about 10 minutes in total for medium-rare, turning every 1-2 minutes, until lamb is cooked to desired doneness.
7. Remove skewers from the grill and let sit for 5 minutes. Serve.

Nutrition information:

Calories: 487 Carbohydrates: 1.3g Proteins: 28g Fat: 38.5g Fiber: 0.05g

Grilled Lamb Patties

Serves: 6, Preparation: 15 minutes, Cooking: 10 minutes

Ingredients

- 1 3/4 lbs of minced lamb meat
- 1/4 cup ground almonds
- 1 tsp dried oregano
- 1 large egg at room temperature
- 1/2 tsp garlic powder
- 1/2 tsp of onion powder
- 1 tsp cumin
- 2 tsp chopped fresh rosemary
- Cayenne pepper (more or less to taste)
- Sea salt to taste

Instructions

1. Combine all ingredients in a large bowl.
2. Using your hands, combine and knead the mixture until combine well.
3. Wet your hands and form mixture into 6 patties, and place on a plate lined with parchment paper.
4. Place the lamb patties in a fridge for one hour.
5. Preheat your grill (pellet, gas, charcoal) to HIGH according to manufacturer instructions.
6. Arrange lamb patties on grill rack and cook for about 4 - 5 minutes per side for medium-rare.
7. Transfer lamb patties to serving plate and let rest for 10 minutes.
8. Serve.

Nutrition information:

Calories: 270 Carbohydrates: 4g Proteins: 39g Fat: 10g Fiber: 1g

Roasted Lamb Loin with Yogurt Sauce

Serves: 6, Preparation: 15 minutes, Cooking: 35 minutes

Ingredients

- 2 Tbsp olive oil
- 1 cup of yogurt
- 1 Tbsp of tomato paste
- 2 Tbsp of fresh thyme, chopped
- 3 cloves garlic finely chopped
- 2 lbs lamb loin
- Salt and black pepper freshly ground
- 1 bunch of parsley, chopped

Instructions

1. Preheat the oven at 325 F/160 C.
2. Combine olive oil, yogurt, tomato paste, thyme and garlic in a bowl and pour in a large baking pan.
3. Season the lamb loin with the salt and pepper and place in a baking pan.
4. Baste the lamb with sauce.
5. Cover with aluminum foil and place in oven.
6. Bake for 1 hour, and then uncover and bake for further 40 minutes.
7. Sprinkle with chopped parsley and remove from the oven.
8. Before serving, allow to cool for 10 minutes.

Nutrition information:

Calories: 389 Carbohydrates: 4.8g Proteins: 30g Fat: 27g Fiber: 0.8g

Grilled Baby Lamb Chops on Spanish Way

Serves: 4, Preparation: 20 minutes, Cooking: 10 minutes

Ingredients

- 16 baby lamb chops
- Roasted red peppers
- 1 garlic clove, minced
- 1 tsp parsley, chopped
- 3 Tbsp Spanish extra virgin olive oil
- Pinch of salt
- Black pepper

Instructions

1. Preheat your grill (pellet, gas, charcoal) to HIGH according to manufacturer instructions.
2. Season the lamb chops with the salt and pepper, and drizzle with the olive oil.
3. Place the lamb chops on grill and cook for 3 – 4 minutes per side for medium-rare.
4. Meanwhile cut the red peppers into strips and add the garlic clove, parsley, Spanish olive oil, salt and black pepper.
5. Season the lamb chops with salt and serve immediately along with the peppers.

Nutrition information:

Calories: 285 Carbohydrates: 1g Proteins: 38g Fat: 13g Fiber: 0.4g

Grilled Lamb Chops with "Sweet" Marinade

Serves: 4, Preparation: 15 minutes, Cooking: 15 minutes

Ingredients

- 3 Tbsp of olive oil
- 1/4 cup stevia granulate sweetener
- 1 tsp garlic powder
- 2 tsp ground ginger
- 2 tsp dried tarragon
- 1 tsp ground cinnamon
- Salt and ground black pepper to taste
- 4 lamb chops

Ingredients

1. In a bowl, combine the olive oil, stevia, garlic, ginger, tarragon, cinnamon and salt and pepper. Rub lamb chops with mixture, and place in a deep container. Cover, and refrigerate for 2 hours (preferable overnight).
2. Preheat your grill (pellet, gas, charcoal) to HIGH (on 450 F) according to manufacturer instructions.
3. Remove the lamb chops from marinade and place directly on grill grate.
4. Grill for 4 to 6 minutes per side or until inserted thermometer reaches135F internal temperature. Serve hot.

Nutrition information:

Calories: 407 Carbohydrates: 0.3g Proteins: 28g Fat: 32g Fiber: 0.5g

Lamb Chops with Greens

Serves: 8, Preparation: 10 minutes, Cooking: 35 minutes

Ingredients

- 1/4 cup olive oil
- 2 spring onions finely chopped
- 2 can (11 oz) garlic, finely sliced
- 3 lbs lamb chops
- 2 lbs wild greens such Chicory, Dandelions...etc.
- 1 tsp dry rosemary
- 1 cup water
- Salt and ground pepper to taste
- Lemon wedges for serving

Instructions

1. Rinse and clean wild greens from any dirt.
2. Press SAUTÉ button on your Instant Pot.
3. When the word "hot" appears on the display, add the oil and sauté green onions and garlic for about 2 - 3 minutes.
4. Add lamb meat and sear for 2 - 3 minutes.
5. Lock lid into place and set on the MANUAL setting for 25 minutes.
6. Use Quick Release - turn the valve from sealing to venting to release the pressure.
7. Add greens, season with the salt and pepper and sprinkle with rosemary. Pour one cup of water and cover.
8. Lock lid into place and set on the MANUAL setting for 3 minutes.
9. When the timer beeps, press "Cancel" and carefully flip the Quick Release valve to let the pressure out.
10. Serve hot with lemon wedges.

Nutrition information:

Calories: 322 Carbohydrates: 8g Proteins: 35g Fat: 16g Fiber: 5g

Chapter 10 Fish & Seafood

Oven Baked Fish-balls with Red Sauce
Serves: 6, Preparation: 10 minutes, Cooking: 35 minutes

Ingredients
- 1 lb of white fish filet
- 1 scallion chopped
- 1 egg
- 2 Tbsp of almond flour
- Sea salt and ground white pepper to taste
- 2 cloves garlic, finely sliced
- 1 grated tomato
- 2 Tbsp of white wine
- 1/2 cup of olive oil
- 1/2 cup of fresh chopped parsley
- 1 lemon

Instructions
1. Preheat your oven to 360 F/180C.
2. In a bowl combine minced fish filet, scallion finely chopped, almond flour, egg, garlic and season with the salt and white pepper.
3. Shape a fish mixture in small balls.
4. Place the fish-balls in a greased baking dish.
5. In a bowl, combine grated tomato, white wine, olive oil, fresh parsley and lemon juice.
6. Pour prepared sauce evenly over fish-balls.
7. Bake for 25 - 35 minutes and until golden brown. Serve hot.

Nutrition information:
Calories: 298 Carbohydrates: 3.8g Proteins: 18g Fat: 24g Fiber: 1.4g

"Inebriated" Salmon Carpaccio
Serves: 6, Preparation: 15 minutes, Cooking:

Ingredients
- 2 lbs of sushi-grade salmon fillet
- 1 cup of fresh parsley, finely chopped
- 1 cup of arugula finely chopped
- Sea salt to taste
- 2 Tbsp of extra-virgin olive oil
- 2 Tbsp of natural granulated sweetener stevia
- 3 Tbsp of brandy
- White pepper to taste

Instructions
1. Rinse and remove the spine from the salmon.
2. Cut wafer-thin slices and arrange on a platter.
3. Add chopped parsley and arugula on salmon.
4. In bowl, combine the olive oil, sweetener, brandy and the salt and ground pepper to taste.
5. Pour dressing over the salmon and greens.
6. Serve or refrigerate until serving.

Nutrition information:
Calories: 253 Carbohydrates: 0.8g Proteins: 30.5g Fat: 10g Fiber: 0.4g

Delicious Tartar Salmon

Serves: 4, Preparation: 10 minutes

Ingredients

- 1 1/2 lb of salmon fillet, skinless
- 1 1/2 Tbsp of lemon juice
- Zest of 1 lemon
- 2 Tbsp olive oil
- Handful of fresh dill
- Salt and black pepper to taste

Instructions

1. Remove the salmon bones.
2. Once cleaned, cut into small cubes with a sharp knife.
3. In a bowl, combine salmon with olive oil, dill, lemon juice, lemon zest, and salt and pepper to taste.;
4. Put the mixture in a round shape and refrigerate for 2 - 3 hours.
5. Serve cold.

Nutrition information:

Calories: 328 Carbohydrates: 0.6g Proteins: 37.3g Fat: 19g Fiber: 0.2g

Keto Hake Fish "Torte"

Serves: 6, Preparation: 10 minutes, Cooking: 5 minutes

Ingredients

- 2 lbs minced hake fish
- Salt and ground pepper to taste
- 2 Tbsp lemon juice
- 1/2 cup cream cheese (full-fat)
- 2 Tbsp of mayonnaise
- 2 Tbsp mustard (Dijon, English, or whole grain)
- 1 Tbsp chopped chives
- 1 Tbsp chopped fresh parsley
- 1 small red pepper very thin sliced
- 1 lettuce salad
- 1 tomato

Instructions

1. Marinate the fish with salt and lemon juice for at least 1 hour.
2. Then, steam the fish with salt and freshly ground black pepper for 3 - 4 minutes.
3. Place the fish on a plate and allow it to cool; mince the fish.
4. In a large bowl, combine the minced fish with the cream cheese, mayonnaise, chives, parsley, and red pepper.
5. Season the salt and pepper and stir.
6. Add the fish mixture in separate molds and refrigerate until serving.

Nutrition information:

Calories: 410 Carbohydrates: 4,6g Proteins: 30g Fat: 30g Fiber: 1.5g

Roasted Herbed Sunchokes

Serves: 6, Preparation: 10 minutes, Cooking: 45 minutes

Ingredients

- 2 lbs sunchokes (Jerusalem Artichokes)
- 2 Tbsp of olive oil
- 2 cloves garlic finely chopped
- 1 Tbsp fresh lime juice
- 2 Tbsp of fresh parsley chopped
- 1 Tbsp of fresh mint leaves finely chopped
- Salt and freshly black pepper to taste

Instructions

1. Pre-heat oven to 375 F/190 C.
2. Just scrub the sunchokes, clean, rinse and chop into chunks.
3. Arrange on a baking sheet together with olive oil, garlic and lime juice.
4. Bake sunchokes for 35-45 minutes or until soft completely.
5. Season with the salt and pepper to taste.
6. Sprinkle with parsley and mint and serve warm.

Nutrition information:

Calories:121 Carbohydrates: 10.1g Proteins: 6g
Fat: 13g Fiber: 10g

Salmon Feta Casserole

Serves: 4, Preparation: 15 minutes, Cooking: 15 minutes

Ingredients

- 1 Tbsp butter softened on room temperature
- 4 Tbsp of grated parmesan cheese
- 2 salmon fillets
- 2 large eggs from free-range chickens
- Salt and black pepper to taste
- 3/4 cup feta cheese, crumbled

Instructions

1. Preheat oven to 400 F/200 C.
2. Grease a refractory dish with the butter and sprinkle with the parmesan.
3. Spread the salmon in the baking pan.
4. Divide the egg whites from the egg yolks.
5. Beat the egg whites with a pinch of salt until stiff.
6. In another bowl, whisk the egg yolk with feta cheese, salt and pepper and some parmesan cheese.
7. Combine the egg whites with egg yolk/Feta mixture and mix well.
8. Pour the mixture over the salmon and bake for 15 minutes or until golden brown. Serve immediately.

Nutrition information:

Calories: 438 Carbohydrates: 1.5g Proteins: 48.4g
Fat: 26g Fiber: 1g

Wrapped and Grilled Salmon with Saffron

Serves: 4, Preparation: 10 minutes, Cooking: 10 minutes

Ingredients

- 3/4 cup black olives, pitted and cut into quarters
- 1 grated tomato
- 1/4 cup olive oil
- 2 cloves fresh garlic minced
- 1/2 tsp sea salt and freshly ground black pepper to taste
- 1 tsp fresh thyme finely chopped
- Pinch of saffron (15 to 20 threads)
- 4 salmon fillets

Instructions

1. Preheat your grill (pellet, gas, charcoal) to HIGH according to manufacturer instructions.
2. In a medium bowl, combine all ingredients (except salmon).
3. Set one piece of salmon on foil and sprinkle lightly with salt and pepper. Spoon a quarter of the mixture over the fish and seal the foil tightly. Repeat to make four packets.
4. Place on the grill, cover the lid and cook for about 8-10 minutes. Transfer fish packets on a serving plate, and allow it to cool before serving.

Nutrition information:

Calories: 361 Carbohydrates: 4.6g 32g Proteins: Fat: 4g Fiber: 1.4g

Creamy Tuna and Mushrooms Casserole

Serves: 5, Preparation: 10 minutes, Cooking: 15 minutes

Ingredients

- 1/4 cup of olive oil
- 15 white mushrooms sliced
- 2 can (15 oz) tuna fish
- 1 1/4 cups of cream
- 1 1/4 cups of grated cheddar cheese

Instructions

1. Preheat the oven to 400 F/200 C.
2. Heat the oil in a large skillet over high heat.
3. Add the mushrooms and sauté for two minutes.
4. Add the tuna fish and cream; gently stir.
5. Pour the tuna mixture in a heat-proof dish and sprinkle with grated cheese.
6. Bake for 15 minutes or until bubbling. Serve hot.

Nutrition information:

Calories: 551 Carbohydrates: 3g Proteins: 51g Fat: 38g Fiber: 0.5g

Lemon Salmon and Broccoli Casserole
Serves: 4, Preparation: 10 minutes, Cooking: 15 minutes

Ingredients
- 1 Tbsp of olive oil
- 1 onion finely chopped
- 1 cup of mushrooms
- 1 large broccoli
- 2 cloves garlic
- 1 lb smoked salmon
- 1 cup of cream
- 3/4 cup of water
- Lemon juices of 2 lemons
- Capers, to taste
- 1 cup of grated cheese

Instructions
1. Heat the olive oil in a large over-proof saucepan over medium heat and sauté the onions and mushrooms for 2 - 3 minutes.
2. Add the garlic and broccoli, cook, stirring occasionally, for a total of 5 minutes.
3. Add water and cream, and season with the salt and pepper.
4. Add the lemon juice and mix.
5. Add the cream, smoked salmon and capers and mix again.
6. Cover with the grated cheese and put in the oven, broil about 3 minutes, while the cheese is melted.

Nutrition information:
Calories: 503 Carbohydrates: 8.5g Proteins: 34g Fat: 38g Fiber: 1g

Herbed Shrimp with Cilantro
Serves: 6, Preparation: 15 minutes, Cooking: 4 minutes

Ingredients
- 1 cup water
- 1 1/2 lb large shrimp, peeled
- 1 bunch cilantro, finely chopped
- 1/4 cup olive oil
- 1 cup grated tomato
- 2 cloves garlic, minced
- 1 tsp cumin
- 1 tsp coriander
- 1 tsp turmeric
- 3 Tbsp of lime juice, freshly squeezed

Instructions
1. Pour water to the inner stainless steel pot in the Instant Pot.
2. Add shrimp and sprinkle with chopped cilantro and pinch of salt.
3. In a bowl, stir together the olive oil, grated tomato, garlic, cumin, coriander and turmeric.
4. Pour the mixture over shrimp and cilantro; toss to combine well.
5. Lock lid into place and set on the MANUAL setting for 3 -4 minutes.
6. When the timer beeps, press "Cancel" and carefully flip the Quick Release valve to let the pressure out.
7. Serve hot shrimp with sauce.

Nutrition information:
Calories: 168 Carbohydrates: 2.5g Proteins: 16g Fat: 13g Fiber: 0.5g

Seafood - Coconut Stew

Serves: 8, Preparation: 10 minutes, Cooking: 2 minutes

Ingredients

- 1 lb white fish fillet
- 2 pinch of sea salt
- 2 cloves garlic, finely chopped
- 1 Tbsp coriander fresh, finely chopped
- 1 lemon juice, freshly squeezed
- 2 Tbsp olive oil
- 2 spring onions finely chopped
- 1 grated tomato
- 1 lb of shrimp
- 2 cups of coconut milk
- 1 cup water

Instructions

1. Season the fish with salt, garlic, coriander and lemon juice.
2. Pour olive oil in your Instant Pot and layer the fish fillets.
3. Put chopped onions, tomatoes and peppers and sprinkle with a coriander on top.
4. Pour 1/2 cup water.
5. Lock lid into place and set on the MANUAL setting for 2 minutes.
6. When the timer beeps, press "Cancel" and carefully flip the Quick Release valve to let the pressure out.
7. Open the lid and add shrimps and coconut milk: stir to combine well.
8. Lock lid into place and set on the MANUAL setting for 1 minute.
9. Use Quick Release - turn the valve from sealing to venting to release the pressure.
10. Serve hot.

Nutrition information:

Calories: 221 Carbohydrates: 4g Proteins: 21g Fat: 15g Fiber: 0.5g

Simple "Grilled" Shrimp

Serves: 4, Preparation: 10 minutes, Cooking: 2 minutes

Ingredients

- 2 Tbsp fresh butter softened
- 1 1/2 lb shrimp (21-25 size, peeled, deveined)
- Sea-salt flakes
- 1 Tbsp fresh tarragon and chervil finely chopped
- 1 cup water
- Lemon wedges for serving

Instructions

1. Add the butter to the inner stainless steel pot in the Instant Pot.
2. Add shrimp into Instant Pot, and sprinkle with sea-salt flakes and chopped tarragon and chervil.
3. Lock lid into place and set on the MANUAL setting for 2 minutes.
4. When the timer beeps, press "Cancel" and carefully flip the Quick Release valve to let the pressure out.
5. Ready! Serve with lemon wedges.

Nutrition information:

Calories: 62 Carbohydrates: 4g Proteins: 1g Fat: 6g Fiber: 3g

Mussels ala Marinera

Serves: 6, Preparation: 15 minutes, Cooking: 3 hours

Ingredients

- 4 lbs of mussels, cleaned
- 1 small onions, chopped
- 1 Tbsp of ground paprika
- 2 Tbsp of almond flour
- 1 glass of white wine
- 1 cup of bone broth
- A bunch of chopped fresh parsley
- Salt to taste
- 2 Tbsp of extra virgin olive oil
- 6 bay leaves

Instructions

1. Place the mussels in your Slow Cooker along with all remaining ingredients.
2. Cover and cook on HIGH for 2 hours.
3. Open lid, remove mussels; debeard and clean them.
4. Place mussels in a Slow Cooker, cover and cook on HIGH for further 1 hour.
5. Serve.

Nutrition information:

Calories: 310 Carbohydrates: 7g Proteins: 42g Fat: 8g Fiber: 0.2g

Temptation Shrimp in Sauce

Serves: 6, Preparation: 5 minutes ,Cooking: 3 hours and 40 minutes

Ingredients

- 3 cloves garlic, pressed
- 1/2 cup olive oil
- 2 bay leaves
- 1 1/2 cup white wine
- 1/4 tsp Salt
- 1/2 tsp of cayenne powder
- 1/4 cup Tabasco sauce (optional)
- 1 fresh lemon juice
- 3 Tbsp Worcester sauce
- 1 Tbsp Fresh parsley, chopped
- 1 Tbsp of fresh rosemary leaves
- 3 lbs fresh whole shrimps

Instructions

1. Combine all ingredients (except shrimp) in your 6- or 8-quart Slow Cooker.
2. Cover and cook on LOW for 2 - 3 hours.
3. Open lid and add shrimp in Slow Cooker; toss to combine well with the sauce.
4. Cover and cook on HIGH heat for 30 - 40 minutes or until shrimp are pink.
5. Serve shrimp with cooking sauce.

Nutrition information:

Calories: 165 Carbohydrates: 5g Proteins: 3g Fat: 12g Fiber: 0.5g

Coconut Aminos Shrimps Stir-fry

Serves: 4, Preparation: 10 minutes, Cooking: 15 minutes

Ingredients

- 2 lbs medium shrimp
- 3 Tbsp coconut aminos (from coconut sap)
- 1 lemon zest
- 1/2 cup lemon juice (freshly squeezed)
- 2 Tbsp of olive oil
- 2 green onions (finely chopped)
- Salt and freshly ground pepper
- 2 Tbsp fresh coriander leaves finely chopped for garnish

Instructions

1. In a bowl, whisk the coconut aminos, lemon juice and zest, and the salt and pepper.
2. Place shrimp in a large container and cover with coconut aminos sauce; cover and refrigerate for 2 hours.
3. Heat the oil in a large frying skillet.
4. When hot, sauté the green onion for 5 - 6 minutes.
5. Add marinated shrimps and stir-fry for 3 - 3 1/2 minutes (for large 3 - 4 minutes).
6. Garnish with coriander and serve hot.

Nutrition information:
Calories: 245 Carbohydrates: 5g Proteins: 32g Fat: 10g Fiber: 1.5g

Grouper Fish and Celery Casserole

Serves: 8, Preparation: 10 minutes, Cooking: 15 minutes

Ingredients

- 3 1/2 lbs of grouper fish (or swords, sea bass)
- 1 1/2 lb of fresh celery chopped
- 1/2 cup white wine
- 1 cup of olive oil
- Salt and black pepper freshly ground
- Juice of 1 lemon juice

Instructions

1. Season the fish with the salt and pepper.
2. Rinse and clean the celery and finely cut.
3. Place the celery in a large saucepan.
4. Place the fish slices over celery.
5. Pour the olive oil, lemon juice and wine; cook over high heat until boil.
6. Reduce the heat to medium, cover and cook for 5-6 minutes.
7. Taste and adjust salt and pepper to taste.
8. Serve hot.

Nutrition information:
Calories: 371 Carbohydrates: 3.4g Proteins: 23g Fat: 29g Fiber: 1.55g

Shrimp, Fish, and Fennel Soup

Serves: 6, Preparation: 10 minutes, Cooking: 15 minutes

Ingredients

- 2 Tbsp garlic-infused olive oil
- 1 scallion, green parts only, chopped
- 1 fennel bulb, finely sliced
- Salt and ground white pepper
- 1 tomato, peeled and grated
- 1/4 cup fresh parsley, finely chopped
- 1 Tbsp fresh coriander leaves, finely chopped
- 4 cups water
- 12 oz of medium shrimp
- 12 oz of cod fillets
- 2 Tbsp lemon zest

Instructions

1. Heat the oil in a large pot over medium-high heat.
2. Sauté the scallion and sliced fennel until softened.
3. Season the scallion with the salt and ground white pepper.
4. Add the parsley and coriander; pour the water and bring to boil; cook for 5 minutes.
5. Add grated tomato and cook for 2 - 3 minutes; stir.
6. Add the cod fish and shrimp, and simmer for further 4 - 5 minutes.
7. Taste and adjust seasonings.
8. Serve hot.

Nutrition information:

Calories: 112 Carbohydrates: 4g Proteins: 12g Fat: 6g Fiber: 2.2g

Baked Sea Bass with Fresh Herbs

Serves: 4, Preparation: 10 minutes, Cooking: 20 minutes

Ingredients

- 2 Tbsp extra virgin olive oil
- 1 tsp fresh thyme chopped
- 1 tsp garlic, finely chopped
- 1 tsp fresh mint finely chopped
- 1/2 Tbsp fresh basil chopped
- 1/2 tsp sea salt and ground black pepper to taste
- 4 fillets Sea bass skinless
- Lemon slices for serving
- Olive oil for greasing

Instructions

1. Preheat the oven to 400F/200C. Grease with the olive one baking dish; set aside.
2. In a small bowl, combine together a thyme, mint, basil, garlic, salt and pepper and stir well.
3. Apply the herb mixture and rub on both sides of fish fillets.
4. Place the fish fillets in prepared baking dish.
5. Bake for 20 minutes or until done.
6. Serve warm and garnish with lemon slices.

Nutrition information:

Calories: 308 Carbohydrates: 1g Proteins: 46g Fat: 12g Fiber: 1g

Baked Sole Fish with in Aluminum Foil

Serves: 4, Preparation: 10 minutes, Cooking: 30 minutes

Ingredients

- 1/4 cup olive oil
- 8 sole fish fillets
- 2 lemons (slices and juice)
- 1 Tbsp fresh dill finely chopped
- 1 Tbsp of fresh parsley finely chopped
- 1 tsp fresh mint finely chopped
- Sea salt to taste

Instructions

1. Preheat the oven to 400F/200C.
2. Season fish with sea salt evenly.
3. Grease the baking pan with the olive oil and arrange the fish.
4. Place the lemon slices on each fish fillet.
5. Sprinkle fish with fresh parsley, dill and mint.
6. Pour some oil and lemon juice over the fish.
7. Cover the baking pan with aluminum foil, and bake in over for 30 minutes.
8. Then, remove the foil and continue to bake for about 10 minutes.
9. Serve hot.

Nutrition information:

Calories: 237 Carbohydrates: 2.5g Proteins: 41g Fat: 7g Fiber: 0.2g

Fried Fish "Burgers"

Serves: 3, Preparation: 15 minutes, Cooking: 15 minutes

Ingredients

- 1 1/2 lbs fish (sea bream, hammer, etc.) ground or finely chopped
- 1/4 cup olive oil
- 1 green onion finely chopped
- 1/2 onion, chopped
- 1 Tbsp of garlic, finely chopped
- 1 Tbsp of fresh ginger, finely chopped
- 1/4 cup almonds, ground
- 1 large egg at room temperature
- 1/2 tsp fresh mint, chopped
- 1/2 tsp freshly ground coriander
- Salt to taste

Instructions

1. Heat 2 tablespoon of oil in a frying pan over medium heat.
2. Sauté the onions and garlic with a pinch of salt until soft.
3. Add the garlic and ginger and sauté for 2 minutes. Remove the mixture from the heat and allow to cool.
4. Combine the onion mixture with the remaining ingredients and knead well.
5. Form mixture in patties or balls.
6. Heat the oil in a frying skillet on a high heat; fry burgers until they get good color from both sides.
7. Serve hot with lemon slices.

Nutrition information:

Calories: 424 Carbohydrates: 4g Proteins: 45g Fat: 25g Fiber: 1.5g

Fried Sea bream in Wine Sauce

Serves: 4, Preparation: 15 minutes, Cooking: 10 minutes

Ingredients

- 2 lbs of sea bream
- 3 Tbsp of almond flour
- Salt and ground pepper
- 1/4 cup of olive oil
- 3 green onions finely chopped
- 2 cloves of garlic, sliced
- 1/2 cup of white wine
- 1 bunch of parsley
- 1/2 cup of sliced radishes (optional)

Instructions

1. Clean and wash well the fish, and put in colander to strain.
2. Combine the almond flour with the salt and pepper; roll in the fish from all sides.
3. Heat the oil in large frying skillet on high heat.
4. Put the fish in the skillet and add chopped onions and garlic and cook for 2 minutes (depending on size) per side.
5. Pour the wine, and leave for 1-2 minutes to evaporate; remove from the heat.
6. Serve the fish with chopped parsley and thin radish slices.

Nutrition information:

Calories: 371 Carbohydrates: 2.5g Proteins: 42g Fat: 18g Fiber: 0.5g

Grilled Lemon Marinated Halibut Fillets

Serves: 6, Preparation: 10 minutes, Cooking: 2 hours

Ingredients

- 1 cup of virgin olive oil
- 1 Tbsp fresh rosemary (chopped)
- 1 Tbsp fresh parsley and cilantro, finely chopped
- 1/2 cup white vinegar
- 2 Tbsp lemon juice (freshly squeezed)
- 4 halibut fillets

Instructions

1. Whisk the olive oil, fresh herbs and white vinegar in a container.
2. Add halibut fillets and toss to combine well.
3. Cover and marinate in refrigerator preferably overnight.
4. Remove halibut fillets from marinade and dry on paper towels for 30 minutes.
5. Preheat your grill (pellet, gas, charcoal) to HIGH according to manufacturer instructions.
6. Smoke the fish for about 2 hours or more, until the internal temperature reaches 140 degrees F.
7. Place the fish on a grill, and cook for 5 minutes per side.
8. Serve hot with lemon juice.

Nutrition information:

Calories: 250 Carbohydrates: 0.5g Proteins: 51g Fat: 4g Fiber: 0.1g

Grilled Salmon with Mustard and Herbs

Serves: 4, Preparation: 10 minutes, Cooking: 8 minutes

Ingredients
- 3 Tbsp of olive oil
- 20 -30 sprigs of finely chopped fresh herb mixture (dill, parsley, thyme, mint...)
- 1 clove of garlic minced
- 1/4 tsp of salt
- 2 Tbsp of mustard
- 2 lbs of salmon fillets
- 2 lemons for serving

Instructions
1. Preheat the grill to moderate - high temperature.
2. In a ball, combine the olive oil, chopped herbs, minced garlic, salt and mustard.
3. Apply the mixture over the salmon fillets.
4. Place the fish on the grill grate directly over the fire, and cook for 8 minutes in total.
5. Serve hot with lemon slices.

Nutrition information:
Calories: 374 Carbohydrates: 6g Proteins: 43g Fat: 20g Fiber: 3g

Grilled Salmon with Saffron

Serves: 4, Preparation: 10 minutes, Cooking: 10 minutes

Ingredients
- 6 skin-on salmon fillets
- 1/2 cup of olive oil
- 1/2 tsp chopped fresh thyme
- 1/2 tsp kosher salt and freshly ground black pepper
- 20 pinch saffron threads
- 1 Tbsp fresh basil and thyme to taste for garnish

Instructions
1. Combine the olive oil, thyme, salt, pepper and saffron.
2. Generously rub the spice mix all over the fish.
3. Preheat your grill (pellet, gas, charcoal) to HIGH according to manufacturer instructions.
4. Place the salmon on a grill, and cook for 8 - 10 minutes in total, turning once.
5. Serve hot with fresh basil and thyme to taste.

Nutrition information:
Calories: 599 Carbohydrates: 0.3g Proteins: 59g Fat: 46g Fiber: 0.05g

Mackerel in Vinegar Sauce

Serves: 6, Preparation: 10 minutes, Cooking: 10 minutes

Ingredients

- 1 1/4 cups of olive oil
- 1 1/2 cups of wine vinegar
- 3 cloves of garlic, finely sliced
- 1 tsp of oregano
- 1 tsp of rosemary
- Salt and ground black pepper
- 6 mackerel, cleaned

Instructions

1. Heat the olive oil over medium-high heat,
2. Add the garlic, oregano, rosemary, little salt and half of vinegar; stir and cook for 2 - 3 minutes.
3. Add the fish, stir and cook for 3 - 4 minutes.
4. Pour the remaining vinegar, cover and cook for further 5 minutes on low heat.
5. Serve hot.

Nutrition information:

Calories: 537 Carbohydrates: 0.8g Proteins: 34g Fat: 48g Fiber: 0.2g

Monkfish Casserole

Serves: 4, Preparation: 20 minutes, Cooking: 15 minutes

Ingredients

- 2 lbs monkfish, cubed
- Sea salt
- 2 Tbsp almond flour
- 1/4 cup olive oil
- 20 almonds, blanched, ground
- 2 garlic cloves, peeled
- 1 Tbsp of fresh parsley finely chopped
- 3 Tbsp white wine
- 1 green onion, chopped (or scallions)
- 1 grated tomato
- 1/2 cup water
- Black pepper

Instructions

1. Preheat the oven to 350 F/180 C.
2. Season the fish cubes with the salt, and dust them with almond flour.
3. Heat the olive oil in a frying pan and fry the monkfish quickly on both sides.
4. Remove the fish into ovenproof casserole.
5. In the same olive oil, fry the almonds, garlic until crisped and then remove. In a mortar or blender, grind the almonds, garlic, parsley and wine to make a paste.
6. In the remaining olive oil, fry the onion until softened.
7. Add the tomato and cook for two minutes.
8. Add the almond paste and water and stir. Let it simmer for one minute.
9. Season with the salt and black pepper and pour over the fish.
10. Cover and bake in the oven for about 15 minutes. Serve hot.

Nutrition information:

Calories: 221 Carbohydrates: 3.5g Proteins: 34g Fat: 6g Fiber: 1g

Oven Baked Almond Coated Cod

Serves: 6, Preparation: 15 minutes, Cooking: 13 minutes

Ingredients

- 3 lbs cod fillet boneless
- 1 cup of almond flour or finely chopped almonds
- 3/4 cup of olive oil
- Salt and ground pepper
- 2 Tbsp of fresh parsley finely chopped
- Lemon slices for serving

Instructions

1. Heat the oven to 400 F/200 C.
2. Rinse well the fish and pat dry on the kitchen towel.
3. Cut the fish in small pieces.
4. In a bowl, combine together almond flour, and the salt and pepper.
5. Roll each fish piece in almond flour mixture.
6. Oil one large baking dish and place the fish; sprinkle with fresh parsley.
7. Bake for 10 - 13 minutes or until fish is well baked.
8. Serve hot with lemon slices.

Nutrition information:

Calories: 432 Carbohydrates: 4g Proteins: 41g Fat: 29g Fiber: 2g

Oven Baked Breaded Fish Sticks

Serves: 4, Preparation: 15 minutes, Cooking: 30 minutes

Ingredients

- 1 lb white fish such as tilapia or haddock cut into strips the size of a finger
- 1/2 cup almond flour
- 2 Tbsp grated Romano cheese
- 1 tsp dried parsley
- 2 large eggs at room temperature
- Salt and ground black pepper to taste

Instructions

1. Preheat oven to 400F.
2. Cut the fish in fingers shape sticks and salt to taste.
3. Mix in a bowl the almond flour with cheese and parsley.
4. Beat the eggs in a separate bowl.
5. Dip the fish fingers in egg mixture, and then in almond/cheese mixture. Place the fish on oiled baking dish.
6. Bake for 30 minutes.
7. Serve hot or cold.

Nutrition information:

Calories: 131 Carbohydrates: 0.4g Proteins: 23g Fat: 4g Fiber: 0.3g

Perch with Lemony Butter in Oven
Serves: 4, Preparation: 10 minutes, Cooking: 20 minutes

Ingredients
- 3 Tbsp olive oil
- 2 Tbsp butter, grass-fed unsalted
- 1 lemon sliced
- 2 Tbsp lemon juice
- 1 lemon zest
- 6 perk fillets
- Sea salt and black ground pepper
- 2 Tbsp fresh parsley finely chopped

Instructions
1. Preheat oven to 360F/180C.
2. Grease the baking dish with olive oil.
3. Mix the oil, butter, lemon juice and lemon zest in a bowl; stir well.
4. Season fish fillets with the salt and pepper and arrange them in a baking dish.
5. Pour the butter/lemon mixture evenly over the fish.
6. Cover fish with lemon slices.
7. Bake in oven for 15 - 20 minutes.
8. Serve hot with chopped parsley.

Nutrition information:
Calories: 297 Carbohydrates: 2g Proteins: 47g Fat: 10g Fiber: 20.3g

Sea Bass with Spinach and Dill
Serves: 6, Preparation: 10 minutes, Cooking: 15 minutes

Ingredients
- 1/4 cup of olive oil
- 1 onion finely chopped
- 1 green onion, sliced
- 2 cloves of garlic
- Salt and ground pepper
- 1/2 cup of white wine
- Zest and juice from 2 lemons
- 1 lb of fresh spinach
- 1/2 cup of water
- 4 sea bass fillets
- For serving
- Lemon slices
- 1/3 bunch of dill
- 1 Tbsp of olive oil

Instructions
1. Heat the olive oil in a large skillet on high heat.
2. Chop the onion, leek and garlic, and sauté them for 3 - 4 minutes.
3. Season with the salt and pepper, and stir for one minute.
4. Pour the wine and leave for 1-2 minutes to evaporate. Add the lemon zest and juice and stir.
5. Add chopped spinach and water; stir and leave to cook for 5 minutes.
6. Add the fish fillets, pepper, olive oil; cover and cook for 4 minutes on medium heat.
7. Serve hot with finely chopped dill and olive oil.

Nutrition information:
Calories: 312 Carbohydrates: 8g Proteins: 34g Fat: 15g Fiber: 4g

Sea Bream with Chili and Basil

Serves: 6, Preparation: 10 minutes, Cooking: 15 minutes

Ingredients

- 4 lbs of sea bream, cleaned
- Sea salt and ground black pepper
- 2 Tbsp olive oil for frying
- 1 Tbsp of ginger, fresh
- 1 clove of garlic, chopped
- 1 onion finely chopped
- 1 chili pepper, chopped
- 1 cup of white wine
- 1 bunch of fresh basil leaves
- 1 tsp of fresh thyme, chopped
- Zest from 1 lemon
- 1 lemon, for serving

Instructions

1. Season fish with the salt and pepper.
2. Heat the olive oil in a large skillet on high heat.
3. Once the oil is warm enough, place the fish on one side and leave it for 3-4 minutes.
4. With a spatula, turn the fish over and fry on the other side for 3-4 minutes.
5. Transfer fish on a serving platter.
6. In the same skillet, add ginger, chopped garlic, onion, chill pepper and sauté for 2-3 minutes.
7. Pour the wine and cook for 2-3 minutes.
8. Add the half of basil, thyme and the lemon zest; stir and remove from the fire.
9. Pour the sauce over the fish and garnish with the remaining basil leaves and sliced.
10. Serve immediately.

Nutrition information:

Calories: 355 Carbohydrates: 3.5g Proteins: 56g
Fat: 11g Fiber: 2g

Sesame Breaded Fish Patties

Serves: 6, Preparation: 15 minutes, Cooking: 10 minutes

Ingredients

- 1 lb cooked white fish fillets, without skin
- 1 tsp of grated fresh ginger
- 1 Tbsp of curry powder
- 1/2 cup of ground almonds
- 2 green onions finely chopped
- 2 eggs from free-range chicken
- 3 Tbsp of sesame
- Olive oil for frying
- Salt to taste
- Lemon slices for serving

Instructions

1. In a large bowl, combine chopped fish fillets, ginger, curry, and ground almond, salt and chopped green onions.
2. Knead the mixture until combined well.
3. Form mixture in patties or balls.
4. Heat the oil in a large skillet over high heat.
5. Dip fish patties/balls in beaten egg and then roll into sesame seeds.
6. Fry the fish patties/balls for 3 minutes per side or until golden brown.
7. Serve hot with lemon slices.

Nutrition information:

Calories: 291 Carbohydrates: 6g Proteins: 22g
Fat: 21g Fiber: 3g

Skewers with Marinated Salmon and Lemon

Serves: 6, Preparation: 15 minutes, Cooking: 10 minutes

Ingredients

For salmon
- 16 wooden skewers
- 1 1/2 lbs of salmon fillet cut into cubes
- 3 lemons cut into thin slices, seedless

For the marinade
- 2 Tbsp of fresh chopped parsley
- 2 cloves of garlic chopped
- 1/2 Tbsp of mustard
- 1/2 Tbsp of coconut aminos
- Salt and ground pepper
- 2 Tbsp of olive oil
- 2 Tbsp of lemon juice

Instructions
1. In a bowl, combine together all ingredients for the marinade.
2. At the same time place the skewers in water - or even better in white wine - and let them soak for at least 30 minutes.
3. Thread salmon pieces alternately with the lemon slices on skewers.
4. Preheat the grill (any) on HIGH. Put the skewers on grill, and brush well with the marinade.
5. Cook for about 7 - 10 minutes, turning several times.
6. Serve hot with the remaining marinade.

Nutrition information:
Calories: 331 Carbohydrates: 4g Proteins: 34g Fat: 20g Fiber: 0.3g

Smoked Creamy Fish Fat Bombs

Serves: 6, Preparation: 15 minutes

Ingredients
- 1/4 cup of mayonnaise
- 1 cup cream cheese
- 1 Tbsp of mustard
- 1 filet smoked fish, boneless, crumbled
- 2 Tbsp grated cheese
- 1 tsp fresh parsley, chopped

Instructions
1. Combine all ingredients and beat in a food processor.
2. Make 6 balls and place them on a lined pan with parchment paper.
3. Refrigerate for 3 hours.
4. Serve cold.

Nutrition information:
Calories: 221 Carbohydrates: 2g Proteins: 20g Fat: 15g Fiber: 0.1g

Steamed Bream with Fennel

Serves: 4, Preparation: 10 minutes, Cooking: 20 minutes

Ingredients

- 2 Tbsp of olive oil
- 4 Tbsp of water
- 2 large spring onion, sliced
- 1 sprig of fresh rosemary, only the leaves, chopped
- 1 clove of garlic, crushed
- 4 fillets of sea bream (about 1 1/2 lbs.)
- Juice of 1 lemon
- 4 Tbsp of fresh fennel
- Salt and ground pepper

Instructions

1. Heat the olive oil in a large skillet.
2. Add the spring onions, cover and cook for 7 - 8 minutes on medium heat.
3. Next, add the garlic, water rosemary, salt, pepper, stir and cook for 2 - 3 minutes.
4. In a large pot heat water and set a steamer with the fish.
5. Cover the pot and steam the fish for 8 minutes.
6. Remove fish on a plate, and cover with the spring onion sauce.
7. Sprinkle with chopped fennel, and drizzle with fresh lemon juice.

Nutrition information:

Calories: 281 Carbohydrates: 5g Proteins: 38g Fat: 12g Fiber: 3g

The Eggs Fish Fry

Serves: 3, Preparation: 15 minutes, Cooking: 15 minutes

Ingredients

- 1 lb Fish fillet- skinless and boneless (Tilapia, Cat Fish or any white fish)
- 1/2 Lime juice
- Sea salt
- 1 green onion
- 1/2 inch ginger
- 3 cloves garlic
- 1/2 cup cilantro
- 2 green chilies
- 1 egg
- 1 cup ground almonds
- Oil for frying

Instructions

1. Cut the fish fillet into pieces, rinse and pat dry.
2. Put the fish fillets in a plastic bag, and marinate with lime juice and the salt.
3. Make a fine paste with onion, ginger, garlic, green chilies and cilantro.
4. Add the paste to the marinade and shake to combine well.
5. Remove the fish pieces only, and discard the excess marinate.
6. Whisk the egg with 2-3 tbsp of water to have a smooth consistency.
7. Spread the ground almonds on a flat surface.
8. Dip the fish piece in the egg mixture, and then roll into ground almonds.
9. Heat the oil in deep frying skillet.
10. Fry the fish fillets until get a nice golden brown color.
11. Remove from the skillet and place on a paper towel to absorb the excess oil.
12. Serve hot.

Nutrition information:

Calories: 381 Carbohydrates: 9g Proteins: 44g Fat: 19g Fiber: 2g

Tuna Salad with Avocado, Sesame and Mint

Serves: 6, Preparation: 15 minutes, Cooking: 15 minutes

Ingredients

- 1 cucumber, sliced
- 1 pepper green, hot
- 1 avocado
- 1 zucchini, sliced
- Juice and zest of 2 limes
- 1/4 cup of olive oil
- Salt and ground pepper
- 1 lb of tuna, fresh
- 2 Tbsp of sesame seeds
- 2 - 3 Tbsp of fresh mint, finely chopped

Instructions

1. Cut the cucumber in the middle and then at 4 slices.
2. Clean and slice the pepper, avocado, zucchini and place in a large bowl.
3. Pour with fresh lime juice and drizzle with olive oil.
4. Cut the tuna fish into large pieces, and season with the salt and pepper.
5. Heat some oil in a skillet at high heat, and fry tuna slices for 2-3 minutes.
6. Remove the tuna from the pan and transfer in a salad bowl; gently stir.
7. Sprinkle with sesame seeds and fresh mint, and serve immediately.

Nutrition information:

Calories: 331 Carbohydrates: 9g Proteins: 24g Fat: 23g Fiber: 4.5g

Almond Breaded Crayfish with Herbs

Serves: 6, Preparation: 15 minutes, Cooking: 5 minutes

Ingredients

- 1 cup of grated almonds
- Orange zest
- 1 bunch of parsley
- 3/4 cup of olive oil
- Salt and ground pepper
- 30 crayfish, cleaned
- 2 lemons for serving

Instructions

1. Place grated almonds, orange zest, parsley, 3 tablespoon of oil, and the salt and ground pepper in a blender.
2. Pour the almond mixture to the deep plate, and roll on each crayfish.
3. Heat the oil in a large skillet over high heat.
4. Cook crayfish for 5 minutes turning 2 - 3 times.
5. Serve hot with lemon wedges.

Nutrition information:

Calories: 489 Carbohydrates: 9g Proteins: 12g Fat: 40g Fiber: 2g

Aromatic Cuttlefish with Spinach

Serves: 6, Preparation: 10 minutes, Cooking: 1 hour

Ingredients

- 2 lbs of cuttlefish
- 3/4 cup of olive oil
- 3 cups of water
- 3/4 cup of fresh anis
- 1 lb of fresh spinach
- 2 spring onions cut into thin slices
- 1 small tomato grated
- Juice of 1 large lemon
- Salt and pepper to taste

Instructions

1. Clean and rinse thoroughly the cuttlefish.
2. Heat the oil in a large skillet and sauté the onion for 1-2 minutes over medium heat.
3. Add the cuttlefish and cook until get the color.
4. Pour 3 cups of water, close the pot lid and simmer for at least 40-45 minutes.
5. Add the spinach, anis, grated tomato, salt and ground pepper.
6. Close the lid again and continue cooking at low temperature until the herbs soften.
7. Pour in the lemon juice and mix well. Serve warm.

Nutrition information:

Calories: 378 Carbohydrates: 5.5g Proteins: 27g Fat: 28g Fiber: 2g

Baked Shrimp Saganaki with Feta

Serves: 6, Preparation: 10 minutes, Cooking: 15 minutes

Ingredients

- 1 cup of olive oil
- 1 large grated tomato
- 1 green onion, sliced
- 2 lbs of large shrimp
- 2 cups of feta cheese, crumbled
- Salt and ground pepper to taste
- 1 cup of fresh parsley, chopped for serving

Instructions

1. Preheat the oven to 350 F/175 C.
2. In a large skillet heat the olive oil, and cook the green onion and tomato.
3. Season with the salt and pepper, and cook for 2 minutes.
4. Add shrimp and stir for 2 minutes.
5. Finally, sprinkle feta cheese evenly over the shrimp.
6. Place in oven and bake for 6 -8 minutes.
7. Serve hot with chopped parsley.

Nutrition information:

Calories: 516 Carbohydrates: 5g Proteins: 28g Fat: 48g Fiber: 1g

Breaded Catfish Fillets

Serves: 4, Preparation: 15 minutes, Cooking: 10 minutes

Ingredients

- 1/2 cup ground almonds
- 1/2 tsp sea salt
- 1/8 tsp freshly-ground black pepper
- 1/2 tsp of garlic powder
- 1 1/2 lb catfish fillets
- 2 eggs, beaten
- Olive oil for frying

Instructions

1. In a bowl, combine ground almonds, salt, garlic powder and pepper. Dip catfish fillets in beaten egg, then coat well with the almond mixture.
2. Heat the oil in a large skillet, and cook breaded fish for 4 minutes from each side over medium heat.
3. Turn only once during cooking.
4. Serve hot.

Nutrition information:

Calories: 410 Carbohydrates: 5.5g Proteins: 32g
Fat: 29g Fiber: 2g

Calamari and Shrimp Stew

Serves: 4, Preparation: 10 minutes, Cooking: 15 minutes

Ingredients

- 3 Tbsp olive oil
- 1 green onion, finely chopped
- 3 cloves garlic, minced
- 3 lbs shrimp cleaned and deveined
- 1 lb of calamari rings, frozen
- 1/4 can of white wine
- 1/2 can fresh parsley finely chopped
- 1 grated tomato
- Salt and freshly ground black pepper

Instructions

1. In a large skillet, heat the olive oil and sauté chopped green onion and garlic for 2-3 minutes or until softened.
2. Add the shrimps and calamari rings.
3. Stir and cook for about 3 - 4 minutes over medium heat.
4. Pour the wine, parsley and grated tomato.
5. Season the salt and pepper to taste.
6. Cover and cook for 4 -5 minutes.
7. Serve hot with chopped parsley.

Nutrition information:

Calories: 184 Carbohydrates: 4.5g Proteins: 24g
Fat: 7g Fiber: 0.7g

Catalonian Shrimp Stew

Serves: 4, Preparation: 5 minutes, Cooking: 15 minutes

Ingredients

- 1/2 cup olive oil
- 1 1/2 lbs shrimp, peeled and deveined
- 36 garlic cloves, minced
- 1/4 cup fresh lemon juice
- 1 tsp red pepper flakes (to taste)
- 4 Tbsp of fresh parsley, chopped
- Salt and fresh ground pepper

Instructions

1. In a large skillet heat the on high heat. Add shrimp and garlic and sauté for about 2-3 minutes.
2. Add the lemon juice, pepper flakes, and salt and pepper to taste. Adjust seasonings to your liking.
3. Serve hot with chopped parsley.

Nutrition information:

Calories: 403 Carbohydrates: 8.5g Proteins: 25g Fat: 29g Fiber: 0.6g

Cuttlefish with Green Olives and Fennel

Serves: 6, Preparation: 10 minutes, Cooking: 20 minutes

Ingredients

- 2/3 glass of olive oil
- 2 green onions finely chopped
- 2 cloves of garlic, minced
- 2 lbs of cuttlefish cleaned
- 2/3 glass of red wine
- 1/2 cup of water
- 11 oz of green olives, pitted
- 1 bunch of fresh fennel chopped
- Salt and ground black pepper

Instructions

1. Wash the cuttlefish very well and cut into thick pieces.
2. Heat the oil in a large skillet over medium-high heat.
3. Add green onion, garlic and cuttlefish; sauté for 2 - 3 minutes.
4. Pour the wine and water and stir for 5 -6 minutes over low heat.
5. In a meantime, in a separate pot, boil the fennel for 3 minutes.
6. Strain the fennel, and add along with olives in a skillet with cuttlefish; stir.
7. Season with the salt and pepper, cover and cook for 2 - 3 minutes. Serve hot.

Nutrition information:

Calories: 433 Carbohydrates: 9g Proteins: 26g Fat: 30g Fiber: 3.5g

Delicious Shrimp with Broccoli

Serves: 4, Preparation: 10 minutes, Cooking: 20 minutes

Ingredients

- 2 Tbsp sesame oil
- 2 large cloves garlic, minced
- 1 cup water
- 2 Tbsp coconut aminos (from coconut sap)
- 2 tsp fresh ginger root, grated
- 2 cups fresh broccoli florets
- 1 1/2 lb shrimp, peeled and deveined
- Lemon wedges for serving

Instructions

1. Heat the oil in a large skillet or wok over medium-high heat.
2. Cook the garlic for about 3 - 4 minutes.
3. Reduce the heat to low; add water, coconut aminos, and ginger.
4. Bring the mixture to a boil, and shrimp; cook and stir until the shrimp turn pink, 3 to 4 minutes.
5. Add broccoli and cook for 10 minutes.
6. Serve hot with lemon wedges.

Nutrition information:

Calories: 220 Carbohydrates: 9g Proteins: 27g Fat: 10g Fiber: 2.7g

Fried Mussels with Mustard and Lemon

Serves: 6, Preparation: 10 minutes, Cooking: 10 minutes

Ingredients

- 1/4 cup garlic-infused olive oil
- 2 spring onions finely chopped
- 1 small green pepper, chopped
- 2 cherry tomatoes
- 1 tsp oregano
- 1 1/2 lb mussels with shells, freshly cleaned
- 1 cup water
- 2 Tbsp mustard (Dijon, English, ground stone)
- Freshly ground pepper to taste
- Pinch of hot pepper (optional)
- 2 lemons, juice, zest and slices

Instructions

1. Heat the oil in a large frying skillet over high heat.
2. Sauté fresh onion, pepper, oregano and chopped tomatoes for 2-3 minutes.
3. Add the mussels and water and cover.
4. Cook for 2-3 minutes on high heat; shake the pan to open the mussels.
5. Combine the mustard with the lemon and pour over mussels. Cook for 1 minute and sprinkle some pepper and hot pepper if used.
6. Serve with lemon juice and lemon juice.

Nutrition information:

Calories: 301 Carbohydrates: 9.5g Proteins: 22g Fat: 19g Fiber: 4g

Fried Wine Octopus Patties

Serves: 6, Preparation: 10 minutes, Cooking: 10 minutes

Ingredients

- 2 lbs octopus fresh or frozen, cleaned and cut in small cubes
- 1 cup of ground almond
- 1 cup of red wine
- 2 spring onions finely chopped
- 1 Tbsp of oregano
- Salt and ground black pepper
- 1 cup of olive oil

Instructions

1. In a deep bowl, combine the octopus cubes, ground almond, red wine, spring onions, oregano, and the salt and the pepper.
2. Knead until combined well.
3. Form the mixture into balls or patties.
4. Heat the oil in a large and deep frying skillet.
5. Fry octopus patties until get a golden color.
6. Transfer the octopus patties on a platter lined with kitchen paper towel.
7. Serve warm.

Nutrition information:

Calories: 526 Carbohydrates: 8g Proteins: 28g Fat: 49.5g Fiber: 3g

Grilled King Prawns with Parsley Sauce

Serves: 4, Preparation: 10 minutes, Cooking: 15 minutes

Ingredients

- 40 king prawns, heads off and unpeeled
- 1/4 cup olive oil
- 2 green onions (scallions) finely chopped
- 2 Tbsp of fresh parsley finely chopped
- 3 Tbsp water
- Salt and pepper to taste

Instructions

1. Cut prawns in half so that the meat is exposed in the shell.
2. In a large skillet heat the olive oil and sauté the green onion for 2 - 3 minutes or until softened.
3. Add chopped parsley, water, salt and pepper; stir for 2 minutes and remove from the heat.
4. Preheat your grill (pellet, gas, charcoal) to HIGH according to manufacturer instructions.
5. Brush prawns with onion - parsley mixture, and grill for 3 - 4 each side.
6. Serve hot.

Nutrition information:

Calories: 209 Carbohydrates: 3g Proteins: 38g Fat: 4g Fiber: 0.3g

Grilled Shrimp with a Lime Base

Serves: 6, Preparation: 10 minutes, Cooking: 15 minutes

Ingredients

- 3 Tbsp Cajun seasoning
- 2 lime, juiced
- 2 Tbsp olive oil
- 1 lb peeled and deveined medium shrimp (30-40 per pound)

Instructions

1. Mix together the Cajun seasoning, lime juice, and olive oil in a resalable plastic bag.
2. Add the shrimp, coat with the marinade, squeeze out excess air, and seal the bag.
3. Marinate in the refrigerator for 20 minutes.
4. Preheat your grill (pellet, gas, charcoal) to HIGH according to manufacturer instructions.
5. Remove the shrimp from the marinade, and shake off excess. Discard the remaining marinade.
6. Grill shrimp until they are bright pink on the outside and the meat is no longer transparent in the center, about 2 minutes per side.
7. Serve hot.

Nutrition information:

Calories: 318 Carbohydrates: 8.7g Proteins: 32g Fat: 17g Fiber: 3g

Iberian Shrimp Fritters

Serves: 4, Preparation: 10 minutes, Cooking: 5 minutes

Ingredients

- 1 green onion, finely diced
- 1 lb raw shrimp, peeled, deveined, and finely chopped
- 1 cup almond flour
- 2 Tbsp fresh parsley (chopped)
- 1 tsp baking powder
- 1 tsp hot paprika
- Salt and freshly ground black pepper, to taste
- 1/4 cup olive oil
- Lemon wedges, for serving

Instructions

1. In a large and deep bowl, combine, green onions, shrimp, almond flour, parsley, baking powder, paprika, and pinch of the salt and pepper.
2. Form mixture in patties/balls/fritters.
3. Heat the oil in a large skillet over high heat.
4. Fry shrimp fritters for about 5 minutes in total turning once or twice.
5. Using a spatula, transfer fritters to plate lined with kitchen paper towels to drain.
6. Serve immediately with lemon wedges.

Nutrition information:

Calories: 271 Carbohydrates: 3.5g Proteins: 16g Fat: 22g Fiber: 1g

Mussels with Herbed Butter on Grill
Serves: 4, Preparation: 15 minutes, Cooking: 10 minutes

Ingredients
- 1/2 cup of butter unsalted, softened
- 2 Tbsp fresh parsley, chopped
- 1 Tbsp of fresh dill
- 2 Tbsp of spring/green onions finely chopped
- 2 tsp lemon juice
- Salt and freshly ground pepper
- 2 lbs of fresh mussels
- Lemon for serving

Instructions
1. In a bowl, combine butter, softened at room temperature, parsley, dill, spring onions and lemon juice.
2. Season with the salt and pepper to taste.
3. Preheat your grill (pellet, gas, charcoal) to HIGH according to manufacturer instructions.
4. Grill mussels for 8 - 10 minutes or until shells open.
5. Remove mussels on serving plate, pour with herbed butter, and serve with lemon.

Nutrition information:
Calories: 401 Carbohydrates: 8g Proteins: 28g Fat: 29g Fiber: 0.3g

Mussels with Saffron
Serves: 4, Preparation: 5 minutes, Cooking: 8 minutes

Ingredients
- 2 lbs of mussels, cleaned
- 1 onion, finely chopped
- 4 Tbsp fresh cream
- 1/2 cup of dry white wine
- Pepper to taste
- 1 pinch of saffron
- 2 Tbsp of fresh parsley finely chopped

Instructions
1. In a large pot, boil the mussels with white wine, chopped onion and two pinch of grated pepper.
2. In a separate saucepot, boil the cream with a pinch of saffron for 2 minutes.
3. Drain the mussels and combine with the cream and saffron.
4. Serve immediately with parsley.

Nutrition information:
Calories: 259 Carbohydrates: 9g Proteins: 28g Fat: 8g Fiber: 0.6g

Mussels with Spinach Stir-fry
Serves: 6, Preparation: 10 minutes, Cooking: 30 minutes

Ingredients
- 1/2 cup of fresh butter
- 2 spring onions, finely sliced
- 2 cloves of garlic, minced
- 1 1/2 lb of fresh mussels
- 2 lb of fresh spinach, roughly chopped
- 1/2 cup of fresh parsley, chopped
- 3 Tbsp of fresh dill
- Salt and ground black pepper
- 1 cup of red wine
- 1 cup of water

Instructions
1. Heat the butter in a large pot or skillet; sauté the green onions and minced garlic for 2 - 3 minutes.
2. Add mussels, spinach, parsley, dill, and the salt and pepper; stir.
3. Pour wine and water, cover and cook for 25 - 30 minutes over medium-low heat.
4. Serve hot.

Nutrition information:
Calories: 277 Carbohydrates: 9g Proteins: 18g Fat: 19g Fiber: 3g

Shrimp and Octopus Soup

Serves: 6, Preparation: 10 minutes, Cooking: 35 minutes

Ingredients

- 2 quarts water
- 2 lbs octopus, cut into 1 inch pieces
- 1 Tbsp olive oil
- 1 small carrot, cut into slices
- 1 cup fresh celery finely chopped
- 1 cup cauliflower floret
- 1/2 cup green onion, or to taste
- 1 Tbsp of coconut aminos
- Salt to taste
- Lemon juice for serving (to taste)

Instructions

1. Place the water in a large soup pot, and bring to a boil over medium-high heat.
2. Add octopus, and continue boiling for about 20 minutes.
3. Add all remaining ingredients and cook for 12 - 15 minutes over medium-low heat.
4. Serve hot with lemon juice.

Nutrition information:

Calories: 98 Carbohydrates: 4g Proteins: 14g Fat: 3g Fiber: 0.7g

Shrimp with Curry and Coconut Milk

Serves: 6, Preparation: 5 minutes, Cooking: 30 minutes

Ingredients

- 1 Tbsp of olive oil
- 2 green onions, finely chopped
- 2 cloves garlic, minced
- 1 hot red pepper, cut into small pieces
- 1 tsp of fresh grated ginger
- 1 Tbsp of curry powder
- 1 grated tomato
- 1 1/2 cups of coconut milk
- Salt and ground black pepper
- 1 1/2 lbs of shrimp, cleaned
- Fresh coriander for serving

Instructions

1. Heat the oil in large skillet over high heat.
2. Sauté the onions, garlic, hot red pepper, and freshly ground ginger; stir.
3. Add curry powder and stir for 1 to 2 minutes.
4. Add grated tomato, coconut milk, the salt and ground pepper, lower the heat, cover and cook for 5 minutes.
5. Add shrimp, cover and cook for about 15 minutes stirring two to three times.
6. Serve hot with chopped coriander.

Nutrition information:

Calories: 227 Carbohydrates: 8.5g Proteins: 21g Fat: 12g Fiber: 2.5g

Spicy Razor Clams

Serves: 6, Preparation: 5 minutes, Cooking: 10 minutes

Ingredients

- 1/2 cup olive oil
- 3 cloves garlic, minced
- 2 hot red chili pepper, finely sliced
- 3 lbs razor clams, cleaned rinsed thoroughly
- 1 cup white wine
- 1 1/2 cups of parsley leaves, finely chopped
- 1 pinch sea salt to taste

Instructions

1. Heat the oil in a large skillet, and sauté garlic and hot red peppers for 4 minutes.
2. Increase heat at high; add razor clams and wine, and cook, covered, until clams are just cooked through, about 3 minutes.
3. Add the parsley and season with the salt; toss razor clams to coat with sauce.
4. Transfer clams to a serving platter and drizzle with remaining sauce.
5. Serve hot.

Nutrition information:

Calories: 198 Carbohydrates: 8g Proteins: 30g Fat: 4g Fiber: 0.3g

Squid with Homemade Pesto Sauce

Serves: 4, Preparation: 10 minutes, Cooking: 10 minutes

Ingredients

- 2 lbs squid fresh, cut in small pieces
- 1 cup of bone broth
- 3 bay leaves
- 2 Tbsp of fresh thyme, finely chopped
- 1 cup of fresh basil, finely chopped
- 4 cloves of garlic, sliced
- 1/3 cup of finely sliced or ground almonds
- 1/3 cup of olive oil
- 2 Tbsp of grated Parmesan cheese

Instructions

1. In a pot, boil the squid with bone broth, bay levers and fresh thyme for about 10 minutes.
2. Remove the squid from the pot, drain and place on a serving platter.
3. Place the basil, garlic, sliced almonds and olive oil in your blender; blend until all ingredients smooth.
4. Add the grated Parmesan, and blend for 30 further seconds.
5. Serve squid pieces with fresh pesto sauce and enjoy your lunch!

Nutrition information:

Calories: 456 Carbohydrates: 9g Proteins: 42g Fat: 28g Fiber: 2g

Chapter 11 Game Recipes

"Tipsy" Quails with Thyme and Oregano

Serves: 4, Preparation: 15 minutes, Cooking: 35 minutes

Ingredients

- 4 quails cleaned
- 2 cloves of garlic minced
- 1 Tbsp of fresh thyme
- 1 Tbsp of oregano fresh or dry
- Freshly ground salt and pepper
- 2 Tbsp of olive oil
- 1 1/2 cups of white wine
- 1 lemon juice

Instructions

1. Rinse the quails well and cut them with kitchen scissors along the spine.
2. Season with the salt and pepper, and place in a deep container.
3. In a separate bowl, combine all remaining ingredients and pour over the quails.
4. Cover with plastic membrane and refrigerate overnight.
5. Remove birds from the marinade, and pat dry on a kitchen paper.
6. Heat some oil in a large frying skillet and sauté the quails for 4 - 5 minutes, or until get a nice color.
7. Pour some wine and lemon juice, lower the heat, and simmer for 20 minutes.
8. If necessary, add some water and continue cooking for another 10 minutes.
9. Serve instantly with cooking sauce.

Nutrition information:

Calories: 353 Carbohydrates: 5g Proteins: 22g
Fat: 20g Fiber: 1g

Antelope Steak on Grill

Serves: 6, Preparation: 10 minutes, Cooking: 25 minutes

Ingredients

- 4 lbs antelope steak (1/2-inch each)
- 1/4 tsp salt and ground pepper
- 1/4 cup Worcestershire sauce, sugar free
- 2 Tbsp of coconut aminos
- 1/4 cup olive oil
- 1/2 cup fresh lemon juice
- 1/4 tsp thyme (optional)
- 1/4 tsp rosemary
- 2 cloves garlic, crushed

Instructions

1. In a large container, combine all ingredients for marinade except meat.
2. Submerge the antelope steak and cover evenly with marinade; refrigerate for 12 - 14 hours.
3. Preheat your grill (any) on HIGH.
4. Place the antelope steaks on the grates.
5. Grill for 5 - 7 minutes per side.
6. Lower the heat, and cook the antelope steak for further 10 minutes.

Nutrition information:

Calories: 422 Carbohydrates: 4g Proteins: 68g
Fat: 16g Fiber: 0.2g

French Marinated Quails

Serves: 4, Preparation: 10 minutes, Cooking: 4 hours

Ingredients

- 2 spring onions finely chopped
- 2 cloves of garlic
- 4 quails cleaned
- 1 carrot
- 1 cup of extra virgin olive oil
- 1 cup of white wine
- 1 1/2 cups of water
- 1/4 cup of fresh rosemary finely chopped
- 1/2 cup of fresh thyme chopped
- 10 -15 grains of black and white pepper
- Salt and ground pepper to taste

Instructions

1. Heat the oil in a large skillet and sauté the onion, carrot and garlic for 2 - 3 minutes.
2. Add quails and sear on both sides.
3. Place quails and all remaining ingredients in Slow Cooker.
4. Cover with liquids (oil, vinegar and water), add sprinkle with the salt and pepper; stir.
5. Cover and cook for on HIGH for 3 - 4 hours.
6. Allow to cool and transfer in a container; refrigerate for 3 - 4 days before consuming.

Nutrition information:

Calories: 276 Carbohydrates: 1.5g Proteins: 22g Fat: 14g Fiber: 1.5g

Bacon Wrapped Pheasant in Wine Sauce

Serves: 4, Preparation: 15 minutes, Cooking: 1 hour and 15 minutes

Ingredients

- 1 pheasant, cleaned
- 8 - 10 slice of bacon
- 1 1/2 cups red wine
- 1 small glass of cognac
- 1 cup of very strong tea
- 3 Tbsp of fresh butter
- Salt and ground pepper

Instructions

1. Season the pheasant with the salt and pepper, and wrap breast and thighs with bacon, and fasten with the string.
2. Place the pheasant in a pot and pour it with the wine, cognac, tea and butter into pieces.
3. Cover and cook for 1 hour over low-medium heat.
4. Remove the pheasant from the pot, cut in a half.
5. Preheat the oven to 360F/180C.
6. Place the pheasant in baking dish, pour the sauce from the pot, and bake for 15 minutes.
7. Serve hot.

Nutrition information:

Calories: 588 Carbohydrates: 3g Proteins: 30g Fat: 46g Fiber: 0g

Fried Quails with Sesame

Serves: 3, Preparation: 10 minutes, Cooking: 25 minutes

Ingredients

- 4 big quail
- 2 Tbsp fresh butter grass fed
- 2 tsp sesame seeds
- 2 Tbsp of white wine vinegar
- 1/4 cup garlic-infused oil
- Salt and freshly ground pepper

Instructions

1. Season the quails with the salt and pepper.
2. Heat the butter in a deep frying pan and sauté quails for 5 minutes or just to take color.
3. Cover and let cook for further 10 minutes over medium heat.
4. In a bowl, stir the vinegar, oil, salt and pepper and sesame seeds.
5. Remove the excess fat from the frying pan with quails.
6. Pour the vinegar over the quails; toss to combine well.
7. Heat the remaining oil in a frying skillet, and fry the quails for 10 minutes from all sides.
8. Serve hot.

Nutrition information:

Calories: 519 Carbohydrates: 1g Proteins: 29g
Fat: 44g Fiber: 0.3g

Gourmet Bison "Chili"

Serves: 4, Preparation: 10 minutes, Cooking: 1 hour

Ingredients

- 1 lb ground bison meat
- 2 Tbsp garlic-infused olive oil
- 1 spring onion (only green parts), diced
- 1 cup bell pepper (red, chopped)
- 2 Tbsp of coconut aminos (from coconut sap)
- 2 Tbsp of chili powder
- 2 tsp cumin
- 2 bay leaves fresh
- 1 tsp cinnamon
- 2 tsp salt and ground pepper or to taste
- 1 ½ cups of water
- Cilantro and lime wedges to garnish

Instructions

1. Heat the oil in a large pot or Dutch oven over medium-high heat.
2. Sauté the spring onion and ground bison meat with a pinch of salt for 10 minutes, or until browned.
3. Add the tomato paste and cook for 5 minutes.
4. Add all remaining ingredients and pour water; bring to boil.
5. Cover, reduce heat to low, and cook for 45 minutes stirring occasional.
6. Serve with fresh cilantro and a squeeze of lime. Enjoy!

Nutrition information:

Calories: 293 Carbohydrates: 4g Proteins: 30g
Fat: 18g Fiber: 2g

Gourmet Smoked Venison

Serves: 8, Preparation: 10 minutes, Cooking: 8 hours

Instructions

- 2 cups water
- 1/3 cup Worcestershire sauce
- 1/4 cup liquid smoke
- 1/4 cup kosher salt and black pepper
- 1/4 cup coconut aminos (from coconut sap)
- 2 tsp paprika
- 5 lbs venison sliced

Instructions

1. In a large and deep and large container, place the venison, and season with the salt and pepper.
2. Combine all remaining ingredients and pour over the meat.
3. Cover and refrigerate overnight.
4. Preheat smoker to 230°F and add Hickory wood chips.
5. Remove the meat from marinade and pat dry on kitchen towel.
6. Place the meat on a grate, and smoke for 6 - 8 hours.
7. Remove the meat from smoker, and allow to cool for 10 -15 minutes before serving.

Nutrition information:

Calories: 259 Carbohydrates: 3.5g Proteins: 47g
Fat: 6g Fiber: 0.5g

Grilled Kangaroo Kebabs

Serves: 4, Preparation: 15 minutes, Cooking: 10 minutes

Ingredients

- 1 lb of ground kangaroo meat, packed
- 3 Tbsp of olive oil
- 1 red onion, finely diced
- 2 garlic, minced
- 1 cup mint, chopped
- 1 cup almonds, roughly chopped
- 1 cup lemon juice
- Zest of 1 lemon
- Sea salt and freshly ground black pepper

Instructions

1. Preheat your grill (any) to HIGH.
2. In a bowl, combine all ingredients and mix well.
3. Arrange the kangaroo meat onto the skewers.
4. Cook for about 10 minutes, turning occasionally and browning all sides.
5. Serve hot.

Nutrition information:

Calories: 456 Carbohydrates: 6g Proteins: 23g
Fat: 38g Fiber: 2g

Instant Wild Venison Roast

Serves: 4, Preparation: 10 minutes, Cooking: 1 hour

Ingredients

- 1 cup of olive oil
- 3 lbs venison roast meat
- 2 sprigs fresh, organic rosemary
- 2 tsp sprigs fresh, summer savory
- 2 cups of bone broth (preferable homemade)

Instructions

1. Season the venison roast with the salt and pepper.
2. Pour the olive oil to the inner stainless steel pot in the Instant Pot.
3. Place deer roast and add all remaining ingredients.
4. Lock lid into place and set on the MEAT setting for 60 minutes.
5. After the pressure cooking time has finished use Natural Release - it takes 10 - 25 minutes to depressurize naturally.
6. Serve hot.

Nutrition information:

Calories: 410 Carbohydrates: 0.5g Proteins: 60g Fat: 20g Fiber: 0.2g

Marinated Venison Tenderloin on Grill

Serves: 4, Preparation: 15 minutes, Cooking: 15 minutes

Ingredients

MARINADE

- 1 tsp salt and freshly ground black pepper
- 1 tsp dried rosemary
- 1 tsp sage leaves finely chopped
- 1 tsp red pepper flakes
- 3 Tbsp fresh lime juice
- 1 Tbsp hot pepper sauce
- 3 Tbsp of Worcestershire sauce sugar free
- 2 Tbsp mustard (Dijon, English, ground stone)

GAME

- 2 lbs venison tenderloin

Instructions

1. In a bowl, whisk all ingredients for marinade.
2. Place the venison tenderloin in a large container, and coat with the marinade evenly.
3. Cover and refrigerate for at least 4 hours (preferably overnight).
4. Preheat your grill (any) on HIGH heat.
5. Remove venison tenderloin from marinade and par dry on kitchen paper.
6. Grill the venison tenderloin for about 7 - 8 minutes per side or until reaches 150 degrees F (65 degrees C).
7. Remove from grill and let sit 10 – 15 minutes before serving.

Nutrition information:

Calories: 291 Carbohydrates: 4g Proteins: 52g Fat: 6g Fiber: 0.3g

Oven Baked Marinated Woodcocks

Serves: 6, Preparation: 15 minutes, Cooking: 2 hours

Ingredients

- 2 spring onions finely chopped
- 2 cloves of garlic
- 8 woodcocks, cleaned
- 3 cups of dry wine
- 1 1/2 cups of olive oil
- 4 medium stalks of celery, chopped
- 2 cinnamon sticks
- 15 allspice grains
- 4 bay leaves
- Salt and ground pepper to taste

Instructions

1. Slice the onions, garlic and celery, and add in a large and deep container.
2. Pour the olive oil, woodcocks, bay leaves, cinnamon sticks, allspice; toss to combine well, and marinade to cover birds well.
3. Cover and refrigerate overnight.
4. Remove birds on a kitchen towel; strain marinade and reserve.
5. We take care of liquids (wine, olive oil) to cover the woodcocks.
6. Heat the oven to 380 F/ 190 C.
7. Place the woodcocks in a greased baking dish, and place birds; pour with reserved marinade.
8. Place in the oven and roast for about 2 hours. Serve hot.

Nutrition information:
Calories: 579 Carbohydrates: 7g Proteins: 50g
Fat: 33g Fiber: 2g

Oven Roasted Marinated Boar

Serves: 6, Preparation: 15 minutes, Cooking: 3 hours

Ingredients

- 1 wild boar leg, skinned, about 2 pounds
- 1 can (6 oz) of beer
- 2 spring onions, in moderate frames
- 2 cloves of garlic in thin slices
- 2 Tbsp of thyme dry, grated
- 1 tsp cumin, powdered
- 1 Tbsp dry coriander, grated
- 1 cup of vinegar
- 1/2 cup of olive oil
- Salt and freshly ground pepper

Instructions

1. In a deep container, put the boar, the vinegar and water to cover the meat.
2. Cover with plastics membrane and leave in the refrigerator for 2 hours.
3. Remove from refrigerator, rinse well and dry on a kitchen towels.
4. Put the boar in the deep pot and add all the other ingredients from the list.
5. Cover with membrane and leave to marinate overnight.
6. Preheat the oven to 360 F/180 C.
7. Transfer the boar meat together with the marinade to the baking dish, cover with lid and bake for 1 ½ hours.
8. Lower the oven temperature to 300 F/150 C and bake for further 1 1/4 - 1 1/2 hours.
9. Remove the boar meat from the oven, let it cool for a while and cut into thin slices. Serve hot.

Nutrition information:
Calories: 388 Carbohydrates: 4.5g Proteins: 33g
Fat: 23g Fiber: 1g

Roasted Gourmet Pheasant

Serves: 4, Preparation: 10 minutes, Cooking: 55 minutes

Ingredients

- 1 pheasant, cleaned, about 3 lbs.
- 1 cup of butter, softened
- Salt and ground pepper to taste
- 1 cup of red wine
- 1 glass of cognac
- 1/2 cup of fresh parsley
- 2 bay leaves

Instructions

1. Preheat oven to 450 F/225 C.
2. Generously season the pheasant with the salt and pepper.
3. Rub the bird with the butter and place in baking dish breast sides up.
4. Pour it with cognac, wine, and sprinkle fresh parsley and crumbled bay leaves.
5. Roast the pheasant for 15 minutes on high temperature.
6. Remove the pheasant on a working surface, and lower the heat to 350 F/175 C. (wait for about 10 -15 minutes).
7. Return the bird in the oven, and bake for 35 -40 minutes or until internal temperature reaches 155 F/75 C to 165 F/80 C.
8. Let the pheasant rest for 10 minutes, cut and serve.

Nutrition information:

Calories: 613 Carbohydrates: 0.7g Proteins: 23g Fat: 49g Fiber: 0.3g

Roasted Partridges with Thyme

Serves: 4, Preparation: 10 minutes, Cooking: 3 hours

Ingredients

- 2 partridges, cleaned
- 1 cup of salted butter
- 6 cloves of garlic
- 1 tsp of nutmeg
- 1 tsp pepper in grains
- 1 1/3 cup of white dry wine
- 1 handful of fresh thyme finely chopped
- Salt and ground pepper to taste

Instructions

1. Preheat the oven to 400 F/200 C.
2. Place the partridges in a baking dish, season with the salt, and rub them with half of butter.
3. Bake for 1 hour in the oven, with the chest down.
4. Combine, and pour the garlic, nutmeg, pepper, wine, and thyme over the birds.
5. Cover them with aluminum foil and bake for further 2 hours on 340 F/ 170 C.
6. Remove partridges from oven and let sit for 15 minutes to cool down.
7. Remove bones and cut meat in pieces.
8. Place meat on a platter, and pour with the melted butter.
9. Sprinkle with a chopped thyme and serve.

Nutrition information:

Calories: 534 Carbohydrates: 4.5g Proteins: 46g Fat: 30g Fiber: 0.5g

Roasted Wild Rabbit

Ingredients

- 2 wild rabbits cut into 8 pieces
- 1/4 cup olive oil
- 6 garlic cloves, unpeeled
- 1 green onion, finely chopped
- 2 sprigs sage
- 2 fresh rosemary leaves
- 2 bay leaves
- 1 green chili pepper
- 1 1/2 cups pitted black olives
- 1 cup white red wine
- Chopped flat-leaf parsley

Instructions

1. Heat the oil in a large frying skillet and sauté the rabbit meat for 5 minutes.
2. Add the garlic and onion, and stir for 5 minutes over a medium heat. Add all remaining ingredients and stir well.
3. Preheat oven to 350F/175 C.
4. Bake rabbits uncovered for 1 ½ hours or until meat is tender and comes away from the bone. Top with chopped parsley and serve.
5. Remove rabbits from oven and let sit for 10 minutes.
6. Serve.

Nutrition information:

Calories: 425 Carbohydrates: 5g Proteins: 53g Fat: 18g Fiber: 1g

Gourmet Rabbit with Rosemary Casserole

Serves: 6, Preparation: 10 minutes, Cooking: 1 hour and 30 minutes

Ingredients

- 1/4 cup olive oil
- 2 rabbits cut into pieces
- Salt and pepper to taste
- 1/2 cup almond flour
- 4 cloves of garlic roughly chopped
- 10 fresh rosemary sprigs
- 2 cup bone broth (preferable homemade)

Instructions

1. Preheat the oven to 350 F/175 C.
2. Season the rabbit generously with the salt and pepper.
3. Toss the rabbit pieces into almond flour, and place them in casserole.
4. Sprinkle the rabbit with garlic and rosemary springs.
5. Pour the bone broth evenly over the rabbits.
6. Place in the oven and bake for about 1 to 1 1/2 hours or until done.
7. Remove from the oven, let sit for 10 minutes and serve hot.

Nutrition information:

Calories: 364 Carbohydrates: 0.8g Proteins: 60g Fat: 16g Fiber: 0.1g

Wild Boar Tenderloin with Avocado

Ingredients

- 2 tsp lard
- 1 medium onion peeled and diced
- 6 boar tenderloin fillets
- 3 ripe avocados peeled, cut in cubes
- 1 Tbsp of Stevia sweetener granulated (optional)
- 1 cup white wine
- Salt and ground black pepper to taste

Instructions

1. Heat 1 teaspoon of lard in a frying skillet over high-moderate heat.
2. Sauté the onion for 3 - 4 minutes until translucent.
3. Add the avocado and sweetener, and stir for 2 minutes.
4. Pour wine, stir and lower the heat to moderate-low.
5. Remove the sauce from the heat and set aside.
6. Heat the remaining lard in a separate frying skillet, and fry the boar fillets for 8 - 10 minutes; season with the salt and pepper and stir.
7. Allow boar to rest 10 minute, and place on a serving plate.
8. Serve warm with the avocado sauce.

Nutrition information:

Calories: 371 Carbohydrates: 9.5g Proteins: 31g
Fat: 19g Fiber: 6g

Chapter 12 Keto Fat Bombs

Absolute Cacao Fat Bombs
Serves: 8, Preparation: 10 minutes

Ingredients
- 1/2 cup of coconut oil, melted
- 3/4 cup heavy cream
- 1/4 cup cacao dry powder, unsweetened
- 3 Tbsp of almond butter
- 1 tsp nutmeg (optional)
- 4 drops of natural sweeter stevia, or to taste

Instructions
1. Melt the coconut oil in a microwave for 10 - 15 seconds.
2. Combine all ingredients in a bowl and stir well.
3. Pour the mixture in a cake moulds and freeze for two hours or until set.
4. Press out of molds and place on a plate or in a container.
5. Keep refrigerated.

Nutrition information:
Calories: 239 Carbohydrates: 3.5g Proteins: 3g Fat: 26g Fiber: 2g

Zucchini Fat Bomb
Serves: 8, Preparation: 15 minutes

Ingredients
- 2 Tbsp almond butter
- 3 large zucchini shredded
- 1 cup fresh basil and chives finely chopped
- 1 cup shredded mozzarella
- 1/2 cup Cheddar cheese
- Pinch of salt (optional)

Instructions
1. Peel zucchini, and shred in a food processor.
2. Line one baking sheet with parchment paper.
3. In a mixing bowl, combine all ingredients in a compact mixture.
4. For mixture into small balls, and place them on a prepared baking sheet.
5. Freeze for 2 - 3 hours in a freezer.
6. Serve. Keep refrigerated.

Nutrition information:
Calories: 108 Carbohydrates: 3g Proteins: 8g Fat: 8g Fiber: 1g

Almonds Gale Fat Bombs

Serves: 12, Preparation: 10 minutes

Ingredients

- 1 cup coconut oil
- 1 cup almond butter (plain, unsalted)
- 1/4 cup ground almonds (without salt)
- 1 tsp vanilla extract
- 1/4 can natural sweetener such Stevia, Erythritol, Truvia,...etc.
- Pinch of salt

Instructions

1. In a microwave safe bowl, softened the coconut butter.
2. Add all ingredients in your fast-speed blender.
3. Blend until thoroughly combined.
4. Make small balls and place on a plate lined with parchment paper.
5. Freeze for about 4 hours or overnight.
6. Serve.

Nutrition information:

Calories: 301 Carbohydrates: 5g Proteins: 6g Fat: 30g Fiber: 2g

Bacon and Basil Fat Bombs

Serves: 8, Preparation: 15 minutes

Ingredients

- 2 cups of cream cheese from refrigerator
- 6 slices of bacon, finely chopped
- 1 small chili pepper, finely chopped
- 1 Tbsp fresh basil (chopped)
- 1/2 tsp onion powder
- 1/4 tsp garlic powder
- Salt and pepper to taste

Instructions

1. Beat the cheese cream in a mixing bowl.
2. Add chopped bacon and stir well with the spoon.
3. Add all remaining ingredients and stir well to combine all ingredients.
4. Make small balls and place on a platter.
5. Refrigerate for 2 - 3 hours and serve.
6. Keep refrigerated.

Nutrition information:

Calories: 265 Carbohydrates: 2g Proteins: 6g Fat: 27g Fiber: 0.03g

Berries and Maca Fat Bombs

Serves: 8, Preparation: 15 minutes

Ingredients

- 2 cups fresh cream
- 2 Tbsp fresh butter, softened
- 1/2 cup of natural granulated sweetener (Stevia, Erythritol...etc.)
- 1/2 cup frozen berries thawed (blueberries, bilberries, raspberries)
- 2 tsp Maca root powder
- 1 Tbsp arrowroot powder (or chia seeds as thickener)
- 1 tsp vanilla extract

Instructions

1. Beat the cream with a hand mixer in a bowl until double in volume and stiff.
2. Add all remaining ingredients and continue to beat until combined completely.
3. Pour the berries mixture in ice cubes tray or in a muffin tray.
4. Freeze for at least 4 hours (preferably overnight).
5. Serve or Keep refrigerated.

Nutrition information:

Calories: 152 Carbohydrates: 6g Proteins: 2g Fat: 15g Fiber: 0.5g

Chilly Tuna Fat Balls

Serves: 8, Preparation: 10 minutes

Ingredients

- 2 cans tuna, drained
- 1 medium avocado, cubed
- 2 Tbsp coconut butter
- 1/2 cup mayonnaise
- 2 Tbsp mustard
- 1 cup Parmesan cheese
- 1/3 cup ground almonds
- 1 tsp garlic powder
- Salt and pepper to taste

Instructions

1. Cut medium avocado in half, remove the pit and skin, and cut the flesh in cubes.
2. Drain and add tuna in a large bawl along with all ingredients; stir well with the spoon.
3. Make the tuna mixture into small bowls
4. Place tuna balls on a plate lined with parchment paper, and refrigerate for 2 hours.
5. Serve or keep refrigerated.

Nutrition information:

Calories: 197 Carbohydrates: 6g Proteins: 9g Fat: 17g Fiber: 2.2g

Choco - Peanut Butter Fat Balls

Serves: 12, Preparation: 15 minutes

Ingredients

- 1/2 cup fresh cream
- 1 cup of dark chocolate chips (60 - 69& cacao solid)
- 1/2 cup of peanut butter, softened
- 1/4 cup of coconut oil, softened
- 1/4 cup of fresh butter, softened
- 2 Tbsp ground peanuts

Instructions

1. In a bowl, beat the cream until stiff peak and double in volume.
2. Melt the chocolate chips in a microwave for about 45 - 60 seconds; stir every 20 seconds.
3. Fold all ingredients in a whipped cream and beat for 2 - 3 minutes.
4. In a meanwhile, whip together peanut butter, coconut oil and butter.
5. Pour the mixture in molds or in cupcakes holders and freeze for 4 hours.
6. Keep refrigerated.

Nutrition information:

Calories: 310 Carbohydrates: 7g Proteins: 5g Fat: 28g Fiber: 2g

Cinnamon - Nutmeg Fat Bombs

Serves: 8, Preparation: 10 minutes

Ingredients

- 1 cup almond butter (plain, unsalted)
- 1/2 cup almond milk (or coconut milk)
- 3/4 cup ground almonds or Macadamia nuts (unsalted)
- 1/2 tsp cinnamon
- 1 tsp vanilla extract
- 1/2 tsp ground nutmeg (optional)
- 2 Tbsp of natural sweetener (Stevia, Truvia, Erythritol...etc.)

Instructions

1. Add all ingredients in your food processor, and process for 45 - 60 seconds.
2. Add more or less sweetener, to taste.
3. Grease your hands with oil and form dough into small balls.
4. Place on a baking pan covered with parchment paper and refrigerate for 2 - 3 hours.
5. Serve.

Nutrition information:

Calories: 274 Carbohydrates: 6.5g Proteins: 11g Fat: 24g Fiber: 3.5g

Creamy Green Olives Fat Bombs

Serves: 8, Preparation: 20 minutes

Ingredients

- 1 lb cold cream cheese
- 1 cup whipped cream
- 1 1/2 cups green olives pitted
- 1/2 cup fresh parsley finely chopped
- 1 pinch of salt (optional)

Instructions

1. Line a platter or baking pan with parchment paper; set aside.
2. Add cream cheese in a bowl and fast whisk with the spoon.
3. In a separate bowl, beat the cream to double in volume.
4. Combine the cream cheese and whipped cream; season with a pinch of salt.
5. Make balls from the cream cheese mixture, and insert one olive in a centre of each ball.
6. Roll each ball in chopped parsley and coat evenly from all sides.
7. Place the balls on prepared platter and refrigerate for 4 hours or overnight
8. Serve.

Nutrition information:

Calories: 131 Carbohydrates: 2g Proteins: 2g Fat: 14g Fiber: 0.5g

Creamy Lime Fat Bombs

Serves: 10, Preparation: 10 minutes

Ingredients

- 3/4 cup coconut oil
- 1/2 cup fresh cream (yields 2 cups whipped)
- 1/2 cup cream cheese
- 1 tsp pure lime extract
- 10 drops natural sweetener (Stevia, Truvia, Erythritol...etc.)

Instructions

1. In a bowl, beat the cream with a hand mixer.
2. Add all remaining ingredients and continue to beat for 45 - 60 seconds.
3. Pour the mixture into a silicone tray and freeze for several hours.
4. When hard enough, remove from the freezer, and from silicone tray and serve.

Nutrition information:

Calories: 223 Carbohydrates: 1g Proteins: 1g Fat: 25g Fiber: 0g

Eggs with Gorgonzola Fat Bombs

Serves: 6, Preparation: 10 minutes

Ingredients

- 2 eggs, boiled
- 1/4 cup fresh butter, softened
- 1 cup cream cheese full-fat
- 3/4 cup Gorgonzola - blue cheese, grated

Instructions

1. First, boil the eggs in a saucepan; remove from heat and set aside for 10 minutes.
2. In a meantime, line a baking pan with parchment paper.
3. Combine cream cheese, butter and grated Gorgonzola. Add the chopped eggs and stir well.
4. Make 6 - 8 balls and place them on a prepared pan.
5. Refrigerate for 2 - 3 hours and serve.

Nutrition information:

Calories: 274 Carbohydrates: 2g Proteins: 8g Fat: 27g Fiber: 0g

Lemon Lilliputian Fat Bombs

Serves: 10, Preparation: 10 minutes

Ingredients

- 1/2 cup coconut oil, melted and cooled
- 1/4 cup heavy cream
- 1/4 cup cream cheese, full-fat
- 1 lemon, freshly squeezed
- 1 lemon zest (finely grated fresh)
- 1 tsp pure lemon extract
- 1/4 cup natural sweetener (Stevia, Erythritol...etc.)
- 1/2 cup coconut shredded, unsweetened

Instructions

1. Melt the coconut oil in a microwave oven for 10 - 15 seconds. Set aside to cool for 2 to 3 minutes.
2. Whisk melted coconut oil with heavy cream, and with the cream cheese.
3. Pour the lemon juice and lemon zest and stir. Add stevia sweetener and stir well until sweetener dissolve completely..
4. At the end, add pure lemon extract and stir.
5. Pour the mixture in a candy molds or ice cube tray.
6. Freeze for two hours, and then remove your fat bombs on a platter.
7. Keep refrigerated.

Nutrition information:

Calories: 165 Carbohydrates: .5g Proteins: 1g Fat: 17g Fiber: 1g

Maca and Vanilla Protein Fat Bombs

Serves: 10, Preparation: 15 minutes

Ingredients

- 1 cup coconut oil (melted)
- 1/2 cup coconut butter
- 1/2 cup coconut shreds
- 1/2 cup raw almonds, peeled and finely chopped
- 2 Tbsp of Maca root powder
- 1 scoop of vanilla protein powder
- 1 tsp vanilla extract
- 1/4 cup of natural sweetener (Stevia, Erythritol...etc.) or to taste

Instructions

1. Melt the coconut butter in a microwave oven for 10 seconds; let it cool for 2 - 3 minutes.
2. Add melted coconut oil along with all other ingredients from the list above in a food processor.
3. Process until the mixture is well combined.
4. Make small balls and place on a platter lined with parchment paper.
5. Freeze for 2 hours, remove from freezer and serve.
6. Keep refrigerated in a container.

Nutrition information:

Calories: 375 Carbohydrates: 7g Proteins: 4g Fat: 38g Fiber: 2g

Minty Chocolate Fat Bombs

Serves: 6, Preparation: 10 minutes

Ingredients

- 1/2 cup coconut oil melted
- 1/4 cup fresh butter, softened
- 2 Tbsp cocoa dry powder
- 1/4 cup natural sweetener (Stevia, Erythritol...etc.)
- 2 Tbsp fresh mint leaves, finely chopped)

Instructions

1. Stir all ingredients in a deep bowl.
2. Pour the mixture into silicon cases or ice cube trays and freeze for 4 hours.
3. Store in a container and keep refrigerated.

Nutrition information:

Calories: 228 Carbohydrates: 2g Proteins: 1g Fat: 26g Fiber: 1g

Monk Fruit Candy Fat Balls

Serves: 10, Preparation: 15 minutes

Ingredients

- 1 cup coconut oil, softened
- 1 cup almond butter
- 2 Tbsp avocado oil
- 1/2 cup cocoa powder, unsweetened
- 1/2 cup coconut shreds
- 2 Tbsp of monk fruit sweetener or to taste

Instructions

1. In a small saucepan over medium-low heat, combine and stir the coconut oil, almond butter and avocado oil.
2. Add cocoa powder, coconut shreds and monk fruit sweetener; stir until all ingredients are combined well.
3. Pour the mixture in a freezer-safe container and freeze for 1 1/2 to 2 hours.
4. Remove the mixture from the freezer, and for into small balls.
5. Place balls on a plate and return in freezer for further 1 hour.
6. Serve immediately or keep balls refrigerated.

Nutrition information:

Calories: 399 Carbohydrates: 3g Proteins: 2g Fat: 44g Fiber: 2g

Piquant Pepperoni Fat Bombs

Serves: 10, Preparation: 15 minutes

Ingredients

- 2 cups of cream cheese from the fridge
- 1 cup of whipped cream, cold from fridge
- 4 slices Pepperoni Sausages** finely chopped
- 3 slices bacon cut into pieces
- 1 chili pepper
- 1 tsp fresh thyme (chopped fine)
- 1/4 tsp hot paprika (or smoked paprika)
- 1 pinch salt and pepper or to taste
- 1/4 tsp garlic powder
- 1/4 tsp onion powder

Instructions

1. Beat the cream cheese in a mixing bowl with the whisker.
2. Add whipped cream and continue to beat for 30 - 45 seconds.
3. Add chopped Pepperoni sausages and bacon and stir well.
4. Add all remaining ingredients and give a good stir.
5. Form the mixture into 12 balls, and place them on a plate lined with parchment paper.
6. Refrigerate balls for 3 hours.
7. Serve immediately or keep refrigerated.

Nutrition information:

Calories: 201 Carbohydrates: 2g Proteins: 5g Fat: 20g Fiber: 0.2g

Rumichino Almond Fat Bombs

Serves: 12, Preparation: 10 minutes

Ingredients

- 1/2 cup coconut oil (refined), melted
- 3/4 cup almond butter
- 3/4 cup fresh butter, softened
- 3 Tbsp of cocoa powder, unsweetened
- 1/2 cup natural sweetener such Stevia, Erythritol, Truvia,...etc.
- 2 Tbsp strong rum

Instructions

1. Melt the coconut butter in a microwave oven for 15 - 20 seconds.
2. Pour the coconut oil in a bowl, and whisk along with almonds butter and fresh butter.
3. Add all remaining ingredients and whisk for 35 - 40 seconds to combine well.
4. Pour the mixture into molds and freeze for 2 hours or more.
5. Serve or store in container and keep refrigerated.

Nutrition information:

Calories: 289 Carbohydrates: 4g Proteins: 4g Fat: 30g Fiber: 2g

Spicy Choco Fat Bombs

Serves: 12, Preparation: 10 minutes

Ingredients

- 3/4 cup fresh butter softened
- 3/4 cup coconut oil softened
- 3/4 cup almond butter
- 1/4 cup cocoa dry powder unsweetened (80% cacao solid)
- 1/4 cup natural sweetener Stevia or Erythritol (or to taste)
- 2 pinch of cayenne pepper or to taste

Instructions

1. Softened coconut oil and fresh butter in a microwave safe bowl; heat in a microwave oven for several seconds.
2. Add all ingredients in a bowl, and stir with the spoon.
3. Pour the mixture into small cupcakes holders, muffin thin, etc).
4. Place in a freezer for 2 hours and serve.
5. Keep refrigerated in a container.

Nutrition information:

Calories: 321 Carbohydrates: 4g Proteins: 4g Fat: 34g Fiber: 2.3g

Strawberry Fat Bombs coated with Ground Nuts

Serves: 8, Preparation: 10 minutes

Ingredients

- 1/3 cup butter softened
- 1/2 cup coconut oil
- 2 Tbsp strawberry extract
- 2 Tbsp cocoa dry powder, unsweetened
- 1/2 cup ground nut mixture (walnuts, hazelnuts, almonds...etc.)

Instructions

1. In a saucepan, heat butter, coconut oil and cocoa powder over moderate heat; stir.
2. Remove from heat, and pour strawberry extract; stir. Set aside to completely cool.
3. Make small balls and roll in ground nut mixture.
4. Place balls on a plate covered with parchment paper and freeze for at least 2 hours.
5. Keep refrigerated.

Nutrition information:

Calories: 245 Carbohydrates: 2g Proteins: 2g Fat: 26g Fiber: 1g

Vanilla Coconut - Nuts Fat Bombs

Serves: 8, Preparation: 10 minutes

Ingredients

- 1/2 cup coconut oil, melted and cooled
- 3 cups coconut shreds, unsweetened
- 1 cup natural sweetener (Stevia, Erythritol...etc.)
- 2 tsp vanilla
- 1 pinch of salt (optional)
- Toppings
- 2 Tbsp shredded coconut
- 2 Tbsp of chopped nuts such Macadamia, almonds, Brazilian...etc.

Instructions

1. Add ingredients from the list above in your food processor.
2. Process until the mixture is compact and blended well.
3. Grease your hands with coconut oil and form balls.
4. Place fat balls on a platter lined with parchment paper and sprinkle with coconut shreds and chopped nuts.
5. Refrigerate for two hours and serve.

Nutrition information:
Calories: 243 Carbohydrates: 4g Proteins: 2g Fat: 25g Fiber: 3g

Cheese Muffin Bombs
Serves: 12, Preparation: 10 minutes

Ingredients

- 1/4 cup coconut butter, softened on room temperature
- 2 cups cream cheese (full fat), softened
- 1 cup heavy whipping cream
- 3/4 cup natural sweetener (Stevia, Truvia, Erythritol...etc.)
- 1 1/2 tsp vanilla extract
- 1 pinch of sea salt

Instructions

1. Prepare two muffin tins with 6 paper liners.
2. Add all ingredients in your blender; blend for 35 -50 seconds.
3. Pour the mixture in a prepared muffin tins evenly.
4. Freeze for 3 - 4 hours and serve.
5. Store in a container and keep refrigerated.

Nutrition information:
Calories: 241 Carbohydrates: 2.5g Proteins: 3g Fat: 25g Fiber: 0g

Chapter 13 Smoothies & Juice

Almonds & Blueberries Smoothie
Serves: 2, Preparation: 5 minutes

Ingredients
- 1/4 cup ground almonds, unsalted
- 1 cup fresh blueberries
- Fresh juice of a 1 lemon
- 1 cup fresh Kale leaves
- 1/2 cup coconut water
- 1 cup water
- 2 Tbsp plain yogurt (optional)

Instructions

1. Dump all ingredients in your high-speed blender, and blend until your smoothie is smooth.
2. Pour the mixture in a chilled glass.
3. Serve and enjoy!

Nutrition information:
Calories: 110 Carbohydrates: 8g Proteins: 2g Fat: 7g Fiber: 2g

Almonds and Zucchini Smoothie
Serves: 2, Preparation: 5 minutes

Ingredients
- 1 cup zucchini, cooked and mashed - unsalted
- 1 1/2 cups almond milk
- 1 Tbsp almond butter (plain, unsalted)
- 1 tsp pure almond extract
- 2 Tbsp ground almonds or Macadamia almonds
- 1/2 cup water
- 1 cup Ice cubes crushed (optional, for serving)

Instructions

1. Dump all ingredients from the list above in your fast-speed blender; blend for 45 - 60 seconds or to taste.
2. Serve with crushed ice.

Nutrition information:
Calories: 322 Carbohydrates: 6g Proteins: 6g Fat: 30g Fiber: 3.5g

Avocado with Walnut Butter Smoothie
Serves: 2, Preparation: 5 minutes

Ingredients
- 1 avocado (fresh diced)
- 1 cup baby spinach
- 1 cup coconut milk (canned)
- 1 Tbsp walnut butter, unsalted
- 2 Tbsp natural sweetener such as Stevia, Erythritol, Truvia...etc.

Instructions

1. Place all ingredients into food processor or a blender; blend until smooth or to taste.
2. Add more or less walnut butter.
3. Drink and enjoy!

Nutrition information:
Calories: 364 Carbohydrates: 7g Proteins: 8g Fat: 35g Fiber: 5.5g

Baby Spinach and Dill Smoothie

Serves: 2, Preparation: 5 minutes

Ingredients

- 1 cup of fresh baby spinach leaves
- 2 Tbsp of fresh dill, chopped
- 1 1/2 cup of water
- 1/2 avocado, chopped into cubes
- 1 Tbsp chia seeds (optional)
- 2 Tbsp of natural sweetener Stevia or Erythritol (optional)

Instructions

1. Place all ingredients into fast-speed blender. Beat until smooth and all ingredients united well.
2. Serve and enjoy!

Nutrition information:

Calories: 136 Carbohydrates: 8g Proteins: 7g Fat: 10g Fiber: 9g

Blueberries and Coconut Smoothie

Serves: 5, Preparation: 5 minutes

Ingredients

- 1 cup of frozen blueberries, unsweetened
- 1 cup Stevia or Erythritol sweetener
- 2 cups coconut milk (canned)
- 1 cup of fresh spinach leaves
- 2 Tbsp shredded coconut (unsweetened)
- 3/4 cup water

Instructions

1. Place all ingredients from the list in food-processor or in your strong blender.
2. Blend for 45 - 60 seconds or to taste.
3. Ready for drink! Serve!

Nutrition information:

Calories: 190 Carbohydrates: 8g Proteins: 3g Fat: 18g Fiber: 2g

Chocolate Lettuce Salad Smoothie

Serves: 2, Preparation: 15 minutes

Ingredients

- 2 cups of fresh lettuce salad
- 1 stalk of celery
- 1 cup almond milk unsweetened
- 1/2 tsp of cocoa powder, unsweetened
- 2 Tbsp dark chocolate chips
- 1/2 tsp cinnamon powder
- 1 tsp pure chocolate extract
- 1 cup of water

Instructions

1. Rinse and carefully clean lettuce salad from any dirt.
2. Place lettuce salad leaves in a blender along with all remaining ingredients from the list above.
3. Blend for 45 - 60 seconds or until done.
4. Serve, drink and enjoy!

Nutrition information:

Calories: 73 Carbohydrates: 5g Proteins: 2g Fat: 6g Fiber: 2g

Collard Greens, Peppermint and Cucumber Smoothie
Serves: 2, Preparation: 15 minutes

Ingredients
- 1 cup Collard greens
- A few fresh peppermint leaves
- 1 big cucumber
- 1 lime, freshly juiced
- 1/2 cups avocado sliced
- 1 1/2 cup water
- 1 cup crushed ice
- 1/4 cup of natural sweetener Erythritol or Stevia (optional)

Instructions

1. Rinse and clean your Collard greens from any dirt.
2. Place all ingredients in a food processor or blender,
3. Blend until all ingredients in your smoothie is combined well.
4. Pour in a glass and drink. Enjoy!

Nutrition information:
Calories: 123 Carbohydrates: 8g Proteins: 4g Fat: 11g Fiber: 6g

Creamy Dandelion Greens and Celery Smoothie
Serves: 2, Preparation: 10 minutes

Ingredients
- 1 handful of raw dandelion greens
- 2 celery sticks
- 2 Tbsp chia seeds
- 1 small piece of ginger, minced
- 1/2 cup almond milk
- 1/2 cup of water
- 1/2 cup plain yogurt

Instructions
1. Rinse and clean dandelion leaves from any dirt; add in a high-speed blender.
2. Clean the ginger; keep only inner part, and cut in small slices; add in a blender.
3. Add all remaining ingredients and blend until smooth.
4. Serve and enjoy!

Nutrition information:
Calories: 58 Carbohydrates: 5g Proteins: 3g Fat: 6g Fiber: 3g

Dark Turnip Greens Smoothie
Serves: 2, Preparation: 10 minutes

Ingredients
- 1 cup of raw turnip greens
- 1 1/2 cup of almond milk
- 1 Tbsp of almond butter
- 1/2 cup of water
- 1/2 tsp of cocoa powder, unsweetened
- 1 Tbsp of dark chocolate chips
- 1/4 tsp of cinnamon
- A pinch of salt
- 1/2 cup of crushed ice

Instructions

1. Rinse and clean turnip greens from any dirt.
2. Place the turnip greens in your blender along with all other ingredients.
3. Blend it for 45 - 60 seconds or until done; smooth and creamy.
4. Serve with or without crushed ice.

Nutrition information:
Calories: 131 Carbohydrates: 6g Proteins: 4g Fat: 10g Fiber: 2.5g

Ever Butter Pecan and Coconut Smoothie

Serves: 2, Preparation: 5 minutes

Ingredients

- 1 cup coconut milk canned
- 1 scoop Butter Pecan powdered creamer
- 2 cups fresh spinach leaves, chopped
- 1/2 banana frozen or fresh
- 2 Tbsp stevia granulated sweetener to taste
- 1/2 cup water
- 1 cup ice cubes crushed

Instructions

1. Place ingredients from the list above in your high-speed blender.
2. Blend for 35 - 50 seconds or until all ingredients combined well.
3. Add less or more crushed ice.
4. Drink and enjoy!

Nutrition information:
Calories: 268 Carbohydrates: 7g Proteins: 6g Fat: 26g Fiber: 1.5g

Fresh Cucumber, Kale and Raspberry Smoothie

Serves: 3, Preparation: 10 minutes

Ingredients

- 1 1/2 cups of cucumber peeled
- 1/2 cup raw kale leaves
- 1 1/2 cups fresh raspberries
- 1 cup of almond milk
- 1 cup of water
- Ice cubes crushed (optional)
- 2 Tbsp natural sweetener (Stevia, Erythritol...etc.)

Instructions

1. Place all ingredients from the list in a food processor or high-speed blender; blend for 35 - 40 seconds.
2. Serve into chilled glasses.
3. Add more natural sweeter if you like. Enjoy!

Nutrition information:
Calories: 70 Carbohydrates: 8g Proteins: 3g Fat: 6g Fiber: 5g

Fresh Lettuce and Cucumber-Lemon Smoothie

Serves: 2, Preparation: 10 minutes

Ingredients

- 2 cups fresh lettuce leaves, chopped
- 1 cup of cucumber
- 1 lemon, cleaned and sliced
- 1/2 avocado
- 2 Tbsp chia seeds
- 1 1/2 cup water or coconut water
- 1/4 cup stevia granulate sweetener (or to taste)

Instructions

1. Add all ingredients from the list above in the high-speed blender; blend until completely smooth.
2. Pour your smoothie into chilled glasses and enjoy!

Nutrition information:

Calories: 51 Carbohydrates: 4g Proteins: 2g Fat: 4g Fiber: 3.5g

Green Coconut Smoothie

Serves: 2, Preparation: 10 minutes

Ingredients

- 1 1/4 cup coconut milk (canned)
- 2 Tbsp chia seeds
- 1 cup of fresh kale leaves
- 1 cup of spinach leaves
- 1 scoop vanilla protein powder
- 1 cup ice cubes
- Granulated stevia sweetener (to taste; optional)
- 1/2 cup water

Instructions

1. Rinse and clean kale and the spinach leaves from any dirt.
2. Add all ingredients in your blender.
3. Blend until you get a nice smoothie.
4. Serve into chilled glass.

Nutrition information:

Calories: 179 Carbohydrates: 5g Proteins: 4g Fat: 18g Fiber: 2.5g

Instant Coffee Smoothie

Serves: 2, Preparation: 20 minutes

Ingredients

- 2 cups of instant coffee
- 1 cup almond milk (or coconut milk)
- 1/4 cup heavy cream
- 2 Tbsp cocoa powder (unsweetened)
- 1 - 2 Handful of fresh spinach leaves
- 10 drops liquid stevia

Instructions

1. Make a coffee; set aside.
2. Place all remaining ingredients in your fast-speed blender; blend for 45 - 60 seconds or until done.
3. Pour your instant coffee in a blender and continue to blend for further 30 - 45 seconds.
4. Serve immediately.

Nutrition information:

Calories: 142 Carbohydrates: 6g Proteins: 5g Fat: 14g Fiber: 3g

Keto Blood Sugar Adjuster Smoothie

Serves: 2, Preparation: 10 minutes

Ingredients

- 2 cups of green cabbage
- 1/2 avocado
- 1 Tbsp Apple cider vinegar
- Juice a 1 lemon
- 1 cup of water
- 1 cup of crushed ice cubes for serving

Instructions

1. Place all ingredients in your high-speed blender or in a food processor and blend until smooth and soft.
2. Serve in chilled glasses with crushed ice.
3. Enjoy!

Nutrition information:

Calories: 74 Carbohydrates: 7g Proteins: 2g Fat: 6g Fiber: 4g

Lime Spinach Smoothie

Serves: 2, Preparation: 5 minutes

Ingredients

- 1 cup water
- 1 lime juice (2 limes)
- 1 green apple cut into chunks, core discarded
- 2 cups fresh spinach, roughly chopped
- 1/2 cup fresh chopped fresh mint
- 1/2 avocado
- Ice crushed
- 1/4 tsp ground cinnamon
- 1 Tbsp natural sweetener of your choice (optional)

Instructions

1. Place all ingredients in your high-speed blender.
2. Blend for 45 - 60 seconds or until your smoothie is smooth and creamy.
3. Serve in a chilled glass.
4. Adjust sweetener to taste.

Nutrition information:

Calories: 112 Carbohydrates: 8g Proteins: 4g Fat: 10g Fiber: 5.5g

Protein Coconut Smoothie

Serves: 2, Preparation: 15 minutes

Ingredients

- 1 1/2 cup of coconut milk canned
- 1 cup of fresh spinach finely chopped
- 1 scoop vanilla protein powder
- 2 Tbsp chia seeds
- 1 cup of ice cubes crushed
- 2 - 3 Tbsp Stevia granulated natural sweetener (optional)

Instructions

1. Rinse and clean your spinach leaves from any dirt.
2. Place all ingredients from the list above in a blender.
3. Blend until you get a smoothie like consistently.
4. Serve into chilled glass and it is ready to drink.

Nutrition information:

Calories: 377 Carbohydrates: 7g Proteins: 10g Fat: 38g Fiber: 2g

Strong Spinach and Hemp Smoothie

Serves: 3, Preparation: 10 minutes

Ingredients

- 1 cup almond milk
- 1 small ripe banana
- 2 Tbsp hemp seeds
- 2 handful fresh spinach leaves
- 1 tsp pure vanilla extract
- 1 cup of water
- 2 Tbsp of natural sweetener such Stevia, Truvia...etc.

Instructions

1. First, rinse and clean your spinach leaves from any dirt.
2. Place the spinach in a blender or food processor along with remaining ingredients.
3. Blend for 45 - 60 seconds or until done.
4. Add more or less sweetener.
5. Serve.

Nutrition information:

Calories: 75 Carbohydrates: 7g Proteins: 4g Fat: 6g Fiber: 3g

Total Almond Smoothie

Serves: 2, Preparation: 15 minutes

Ingredients

- 1 1/2 cups of almond milk
- 2 Tbsp of almond butter
- 2 Tbsp ground almonds
- 1 cup of fresh kale leaves (or to taste)
- 1/2 tsp of cocoa powder
- 1 Tbsp chia seeds
- 1/2 cup of water

Instructions

1. Rinse and carefully clean kale leaves from any dirt.
2. Add almond milk, almond butter and ground almonds in your blender; blend for 45 - 60 seconds.
3. Add kale leaves, cocoa powder and chia seeds; blend for further 45 seconds.
4. If your smoothie is too thick, pour more almond milk or water.
5. Serve.

Nutrition information:

Calories: 228 Carbohydrates: 7g Proteins: 8g Fat: 11g Fiber: 6g

Ultimate Green Mix Smoothie

Serves: 2, Preparation: 15 minutes

Ingredients

- Handful of spinach leaves
- Handful of collards greens
- Handful of lettuce, cos or romain
- 1 1/2 cup of almond milk
- 1/2 cup of water
- 1/4 cup of stevia granulated sweetener
- 1 tsp pure vanilla extract
- 1 cup crushed ice cubes (optional)

Instructions

1. Rinse and carefully clean your greens from any dirt.
2. Place all ingredients from the list above in your blender or food processor.
3. Blend until done or 45 - 30 seconds.
4. Serve with or without crushed ice.

Nutrition information:

Calories: 73 Carbohydrates: 4g Proteins: 5g Fat: 7g Fiber: 1g

Chapter 14 Ice Cream & Dessert

Athletes Matcha & Chia Granita
Serves: 6, Preparation: 10 minutes

Ingredients
- 1/2 cup water
- 1 cup coconut milk unsweetened
- 1-2 tsp chia seeds, soaked for 20 - 30 minutes
- 2 scoops vanilla protein powder
- 2 Tbsp coconut oil
- 1 tsp cinnamon ground
- 1 tsp Matcha powder

Instructions
1. Place all ingredients in your high-speed blender; blend until your mixture gets a smooth consistency.
2. Pour the mixture in a freezer-safe container and freeze for 6 hours.
3. Remove container from the freezer, and stir vigorously to smooth granita.
4. Serve on chilled glasses.

Nutrition information:
Calories: 54 Carbohydrates: 5g Proteins: 2g Fat: 5g Fiber: 2g

Cayenne Strawberry Popsicles
Serves: 8, Preparation: 10 minutes

Ingredients
- 14 oz fresh strawberries, finely chopped
- 1 cup stevia granulate sweetener (or to taste)
- 2 Tbsp lemon juice freshly squeezed
- 1/4 cup water
- Cayenne pepper to taste
- 1 pinch of salt

Instructions
1. Add all ingredients in a blender and blend until smooth.
2. Pour the mango mixture evenly in a Popsicle molds or a cups.
3. Insert sticks into each mold.
4. Place molds in a freezer, and freeze for at least 4 hours.
5. Before serving, place molds under lukewarm water.

Nutrition information:
Calories: 20 Carbohydrates: 4g Proteins: 0.5g Fat: 1g Fiber: 1g

Choco - Strawberry Ice Cream
Serves: 6, Preparation: 15 minutes

Ingredients
- 2 cups almond milk, unsweetened
- 1 cup frozen strawberries
- 1 Tbsp chia seeds, soaked for 10 minutes
- 1 scoop Chocolate Protein Powder
- 1 Tbsp MCT oil
- 1 cup ground Macadamia or Brazilian nuts
- 1 Tbsp raw cocoa powder

Instructions
1. Place all ingredients into your high-speed powered blender; blend on HIGH until all ingredients combined well.
2. Pour the mixture in a safe-freezer container and freeze for 6 hours or overnight.
3. Remove the ice cream from freezer for about 10 - 15 minutes before serving.
4. If you notice the ice crystal, just place the ice cream in a mixing bowl, and beat with a mixer for 3 - 4 minutes.
5. Serve in chilled glasses.

Nutrition information:
Calories: 113 Carbohydrates: 6g Proteins: 5g Fat: 10g Fiber: 3g

Creamy Strawberries Ice Cream
Serves: 10, Preparation: 10 minutes, Cooking: 15 minutes

Ingredients
- 1 lb fresh chopped strawberries
- Juice of 1 lemon
- 1 cup of stevia sweetener
- 1 pinch of salt
- 1 1/2 cup of yogurt
- 1/2 cup of almond milk

Instructions
1. Put the strawberries in a saucepan with lemon juice, sweetener and salt, and heat, stirring, until fruits soften.
2. Remove the saucepan from heat, and allow strawberries to cool.
3. Add yogurt and almond milk and gently stir with wooden spatula.
4. Pour the ice cream mixture in a container, wrap with plastic membrane and freeze for 6 hours.
5. Serve in a chilled glasses or bowls.

Nutrition information:
Calories: 45 Carbohydrates: 4g Proteins: 3g Fat: 7g Fiber: 1g

Dark Parfait Ice Cream

Serves: 10, Preparation: 20 minutes

Ingredients

- 5 egg yolks
- 1/2 cup of stevia granulated sweetener
- 1 US cup of fresh cream
- 3 eggs whites beaten to a meringue
- 2.5 oz of stevia
- 3/4 cup almonds (unsalted) or hazelnuts, Macadamia
- 6 oz of dark chocolate chips (60 - 69% cocoa solid)

Instructions

1. Whisk egg yolks with stevia in a saucepan.
2. Place the saucepan over double boiler (bain-marie), and stir until egg yolks mixture begin to thick.
3. Remove the mixture in a mixing bowl, and let it cool for 5 minutes.
4. Beat with the mixer for 2 - 3 minutes.
5. Add cream and gently stir with wooden spatula.
6. Add meringue and chopped almonds; stir well to combine all ingredients.
7. Melt the chocolate chips and add in a bowl; stir gently to combine well.
8. Pour the mixture in freezer safe bowl or container and freeze overnight.
9. Remove the ice cream from the freezer 10 - 15 minutes before serving.

Nutrition information:

Calories: 160 Carbohydrates: 7g Proteins: 6g Fat: 14g Fiber: 2g

Frozen Keto Chocolate Mousse

Serves: 6, Preparation: 15 minutes

Ingredients

- 2 Tbsp of cocoa powder, unsweetened
- 4 cups of heavy cream
- 1/2 cup stevia granulate sweetener (or to taste)
- 1 Tbsp MCT oil
- 1 pinch of salt
- 1 Tbsp pure vanilla extract
- Shredded coconut, unsweetened

Instructions

1. In a mixing bowl, beat the coconut powder and heavy cream for about 2 - 3 minutes,
2. Add the remaining ingredients and beat with the mixer on low speed for further 3-4 minutes.
3. Pour the mixture in a container and freeze for 6 hours.
4. Remove the ice cream mixture from freeze every hour; place the ice cream in a mixing bowl and beat with the mixer.
5. Remove the ice cream in container and freeze again.
6. This process will avoid making of ice crystals.
7. Serve and enjoy!

Nutrition information:

Calories: 317 Carbohydrates: 4.5g Proteins: 2g Fat: 33g Fiber: 1g

Frozen Red Wine Pops

Serves: 6, Preparation: 15 minutes, Cooking: 10 minutes

Ingredients

- 2 cups of fresh cream
- 1 cup of almond milk (unsweetened)
- 1/2 cup stevia granulated sweetener (or to taste)
- 6 fresh egg yolks
- 1/2 cup red dry wine

Instructions

1. In a saucepan, cook the cream, almond milk and stevia sweetener over low heat; stir.
2. Add egg yolks and stir for 5 minutes.
3. Transfer the mixture in a freezer-safe container and pour the wine; stir well.
4. Freeze the mixture for 2 hours.
5. Remove the ice cream mixture from the freezer and stir well with a hand mixer.
6. Pour the mixture in a Popsicle molds and insert the sticks.
7. Store popsicles in a freezer until froze.
8. Ready! Serve.

Nutrition information:

Calories: 220 Carbohydrates: .5g Proteins: 4g Fat: 20g Fiber: 0g

Homemade MCT Ice Cream (Ice Cream Maker)

Serves: 8, Preparation: 5 hours and 10 minutes

Ingredients

- 1/2 cup of MCT oil (Medium-chain triglyceride)
- 1 cup unsweetened almond milk
- 6 whole eggs
- 6 egg yolks
- 1 vanilla pod, seeds
- 1 tsp of Stevia glycerite (alcohol-free and a zero-calorie)
- 1 tsp salt
- 5 Tbsp of unsweetened cocoa powder

Instructions

1. Place all ingredients in a mixing bowl, and beat with a hand mixer.
2. Pour the ice cream mixture in a freezer-safe bowl, and freeze for one hour.
3. Then, pour the mass into the ice cream maker and work according to the manufacturer's instructions.
4. Keep in freezer for 4 - 5 hours.
5. Serve in chilled glasses or bowl.
6. Enjoy!

Nutrition information:

Calories: 223 Carbohydrates: 2.5g Proteins: 8g Fat: 22g Fiber: 1g

Iced Blueberry Granita

Serves: 8, Preparation: 10 minutes, Cooking: 15 minutes

Ingredients

- 1 1/4 cup of water
- Juice of 1/2 lemon
- 1 lb of blueberries (frozen)
- 1 cup of natural granulated sweetener such Stevia
- 1 tsp vanilla extract

Instructions

1. Make syrup: in a saucepan, combine water, stevia sweetener and lemon juice over medium-low heat.
2. Stir until becomes a thick syrup.
3. Remove from heat and let it cool on room temperature.
4. Place blueberries in a large bowl, and sprinkle with stevia.
5. Pour the syrup and stir.
6. Stir vanilla extract and pour the mixture in a freezer-safe container; freeze for 4 hours.
7. Serve in chilled bowls or glasses.

Nutrition information:

Calories: 45 Carbohydrates: 7g Proteins: 1g Fat: 1g Fiber: 2g

Lady Raspberry Ice Cream

Serves: 10, Preparation: 15 minutes, Cooking: 15 minutes

Ingredients

- 4 cups fresh raspberries
- 1 1/2 cups of natural sweetener (Stevia, Truvia, Erythritol...etc.)
- 2 Tbsp water
- 2 cups thick coconut cream

Instructions

1. In a saucepan, stir raspberries, sweetener and water over medium heat.
2. Reduce heat and cook, stirring, for 10 - 12 minutes or until raspberries melt.
3. Remove from heat and set aside to cool down.
4. Beat the coconut cream in a bowl with a mixer (on high).
5. Pour the syrup in a mixing bowl, and continue to beat for 45 - 60 seconds.
6. Place mixture in a freezer-safe bowl, and place in a freezer for 4 hours.
7. Every 30 - 45 minutes remove the ice cream in a mixing bowl and beat with a mixer.
8. This process will prevent ice crystallization.
9. Serve and enjoy!

Nutrition information:

Calories: 160 Carbohydrates: 7g Proteins: 2g Fat: 17g Fiber: 4g

Lemonita Granita
Serves: 10, Preparation: 10 minutes

Ingredients
- 4 fresh lemons, juice about 3/4 cup
- 1 ½ cups of natural sweetener (Stevia, Erythritol...etc.)
- 3 cups water
- 2 lemon peeled, pulp

Instructions
1. In a saucepan, heat all ingredients over medium heat.
2. Remove from heat, and let cool on room temperature.
3. Pour the mixture in a baking dish, wrap with plastic membrane and freeze for 6 - 8 hours.
4. Remove granita from the freezer, scratch with big fork and stir.
5. Serve in chilled glasses and enjoy!
6. Keep in freezer.

Nutrition information:
Calories: 13 Carbohydrates: 3g Proteins: 1g Fat: 1g Fiber: 0.2g

Low Carb Blackberry Ice Cream
Serves: 8, Preparation: 10 minutes

Ingredients
- 3/4 lb of frozen blackberries, unsweetened
- 1 1/4 cup of caned coconut milk
- 1/4 cup of granulated erythritol sweetener or to taste
- 2 Tbsp of almond flour
- 1 pinch of ground vanilla
- 1 Tbsp of MCT oil

Instructions
1. Put all the ingredients in a blender. Make sure blackberries are still frozen.
2. Blend until a creamy, homogeneous mass is formed.
3. Pour the blackberry mixture in a container and freeze overnight.
4. Serve in chilled glasses or bowls.

Nutrition information:
Calories: 83 Carbohydrates: 5g Proteins: 1g Fat: 8g Fiber: 2.5g

Murky Coconut Ice Cream
Serves: 8, Preparation: 15 minutes

Ingredients
- 2 can (11 oz) of frozen coconut milk
- 2 scoop powdered chocolate protein
- 4 Tbsp of stevia sweetener
- 2 Tbsp of cocoa powder

Instructions
1. In a high-speed blender, stir the iced coconut milk.
2. Blend for 30 - 45 seconds and then add the remaining ingredients.
3. Blend again until get a thick cream.
4. Pour the mixture in a container and store in freezer for 4 hours.
5. To prevent forming ice crystals, beat the mixture every 30 minutes.
6. Ready! Serve in chilled glasses.

Nutrition information:
Calories: 135 Carbohydrates: 3g Proteins: 4g Fat: 15g Fiber: 1g

Peppermint Chocolate Popsicles
Serves: 8, Preparation: 20 minutes

Ingredients
- 3 cups coconut milk (canned), divided
- 2 gelatin sheets
- 3 cup packed peppermint leaves
- 1 cup stevia granulate sweetener
- 1/4 tsp pure peppermint extract

- 3/4 cup of dark chocolate (60- 69% of cacao solid) melted

Instructions

1. Soak gelatin in a little coconut milk for 10 minutes.
2. In a saucepan, heat the coconut milk and peppermint leaves; cook for 3 minutes stirring constantly.
3. Add soaked gelatin and stir until completely dissolved.
4. Remove the saucepan from heat, cover and set aside for 20 - 25 minutes.
5. Strain the mint mixture through a colander into the bowl, and add the stevia sweetener: stir well. Pour the peppermint extract and stir.
6. Place bowl in the freezer for about one hour.
7. Remove from freezer and stir melted dark chocolate.
8. Pour into Popsicle molds, insert sticks in each mold, and freeze overnight.
9. Remove popsicles from the mold and serve.

Nutrition information:

Calories: 231 Carbohydrates: 8g Proteins: 3g Fat: 22g Fiber: 1g

Perfect Strawberry Ice Cream

Serves: 12, Preparation: 20 minutes

Ingredients

- 2 lbs of strawberries
- 2 1/4 cups of water
- 2 Tbsp of coconut butter, softened
- 1 1/2 cups of natural granulated sweetener (Stevia, Truvia, Erythritol...etc.)
- 2 egg whites
- 1 lemon squeezed

Instructions

1. Heat strawberries, water, coconut butter and stevia sweetener in a saucepan over medium-low heat.
2. When strawberries softened, remove the saucepan from heat, and allow it to cool on room temperature.
3. Whisk the egg whites until stiff; add the lemon juice and stir.
4. Add the egg whites mixture to strawberry mixture and gently stir with wooden spatula.
5. Refrigerate the ice cream mixture for 2 hours.
6. Pour cold ice cream mixture into ice cream maker, turn on the machine, and do according to manufacturer's directions.
7. In the case that you do not have ice cream maker, pour the mixture in a container and freeze for 8 hours.

Nutrition information:

Calories: 50 Carbohydrates: 6g Proteins: 1g Fat: 5g Fiber: 2g

Raskolnikov Vanilla Ice Cream

Serves: 8, Preparation: 10 minutes, Cooking: 20 minutes

Ingredients

- 3 sheets of gelatin sugar-free
- 2 US pints of cream
- 1/2 vanilla stick
- 1/2 cup stevia granulated sweetener
- 4 egg yolks
- 3 Tbsp of vodka

Instructions

1. Soak gelatin in some water (about 1 cup per 1 sheet of gelatin)
2. Heat the cream in a saucepan along with vanilla seeds and stevia sweetener; stir.
3. Add the egg yolks, and continue to stir for further 2 - 3 minutes.
4. Remove from heat, add gelatin and stir well.
5. Pour vodka and stir again; allow the mixture to cool.
6. Pour the mixture in a container and refrigerate for at least 4 hours.
7. Remove the mixture in an ice cream maker; follow manufacturer's instructions.
8. Or, pour the mixture in a freeze-safe container and freeze overnight.
9. Beat every 45 minutes with the mixture to prevent ice crystallization.
10. Serve and enjoy!

Nutrition information:

Calories: 118 Carbohydrates: 4g Proteins: 3g Fat: 10g Fiber: 0g

Traditional Spanish Cold Cream with Walnuts

Serves: 6, Preparation: 5 minutes, Cooking: 3 hours

Ingredients

- 3 cups of almond milk
- 3 cups of liquid cream
- 1 cup of ground walnuts
- 3/4 cup of natural sweetener (Stevia, Erythritol...etc.) or to taste
- 1 cinnamon stick

Instructions

1. Add all ingredients from the list above in your Slow Cooker.
2. Cover and cook on HIGH for 3 hours.
3. During cooking, stir several times with wooden spoon.
4. If your cream is too dense, add more almond milk.
5. Store cream in glass container and refrigerate for 4 hours.
6. Remove cream from the refrigerator 15 minutes before serving.

Nutrition information:

Calories: 193 Carbohydrates: 5g Proteins: 8g Fat: 20g Fiber: 2g

Sinless Chocolate Ice Cream

Serves: 6, Preparation: 15 minutes

Ingredients

- 1 can (15 oz) coconut milk
- 1/2 cup cocoa powder
- 1/4 cup natural sweetener (Stevia, Truvia, Erythritol...etc.)
- 1 tsp vanilla extract
- Chopped nuts or shredded coconut for serving (optional)

Instructions

1. Combine all ingredients in a bowl.
2. Use an electric mixer and beat the mixture until all ingredients combine well.
3. Transfer the mixture in a freezer-safe bowl and freeze for 4 hours.
4. To prevent ice crystallization, beat the ice cream with the mixer every hour.
5. Serve garnished with sliced nuts or shredded coconuts.

Nutrition information:

Calories: 204 Carbohydrates: 7g Proteins: 4g Fat: 21g Fiber: 4.5g

True Cinnamon Ice Cream

Serves: 8, Preparation: 10 minutes, Cooking:15 minutes

Ingredients

- 1 1/2 cup almond milk (or coconut milk)
- 1 cinnamon stick
- 1 1/2 cup natural granulated sweetener (Stevia, Truvia, Erythritol...etc.)
- 1 1/2 Tbsp lemon peel
- 8 egg yolks from free-range chicken
- 1 pinch of salt
- 1 1/2 Tbsp ground cinnamon
- 1 cup cream

Instructions

1. In a saucepan, heat almond milk, cinnamon stick, stevia sweetener and lemon peel.
2. Bring to boil, reduce the heat and stir over low heat for 10 minutes,
3. In a bowl, beat the egg yolks with the pinch of salt until frothy. Place the egg mixture in a glass bowl over the bain marie, and stir until thicken.
4. Remove the cinnamon stick and lemon peel, pour the almond milk in egg yolk mixture; continue to until the mixture becomes thick.
5. Remove the mixture from heat, add ground cinnamon, stir; set aside and allow it to cool on room temperature.
6. In a bowl, beat the cream until double in volume.
7. Combine the cream with egg mixture and gently stir with wooden spatula.
8. Place the ice cream in the freezer until frozen or for at least 6-8 hours.
9. Serve and enjoy!

Nutrition information:

Calories: 181 Carbohydrates: 6g Proteins: 4g Fat: 17g Fiber: 2g

Vanilla Coconut Ice Cream

Serves: 8, Preparation: 10 minutes

Ingredients

- 15 oz of coconut cream
- 2 Tbsp of coconut butter, softened
- 1/2 cup of stevia sweetener or to taste
- 1 pinch of salt
- 2 tsp vanilla extract
- 1 tsp vanilla powder

Instructions

1. Place all ingredients to the mixing bowl and beat for 3 - 4 minutes.
2. Pour the mixture in a container, cover with membrane and freeze for 4 - 5 hours.
3. After one hour, remove the mixture, place in a mixing bowl and beat it again for 3 - 4 minutes.
4. Repeat this process every half an hour in order to get smooth ice cream without the ice crystals.
5. When done, serve the ice cream in chilled bowls or glasses and serve.

Nutrition information:

Calories: 210 Carbohydrates: 3g Proteins: 3g Fat: 7g Fiber: 2g

Whole Coconut Ice Cream

Serves: 10, Preparation: 10 minutes

Ingredients

- 4 cups of coconut cream or full-fat coconut milk
- 2 Tbsp of coconut aminos
- 2 Tbsp of coconut extract
- 1/2 cup of natural sweetener stevia or to taste
- 1/2 cup of coconut flakes for serving (optional)

Instructions

1. In a large bowl, stir all ingredients.
2. Pour the ice cream mixture in container and freeze for 8 hours.
3. Stir every hour to avoid ice cream crystallization.
4. When done, remove the ice cream from freezer.
5. Serve in chilled glasses and sprinkle with coconut flakes.

Nutrition information:

Calories: 361 Carbohydrates: 6g Proteins: 4g Fat: 37g Fiber: 3g

"Stroganoff" Queso Fresco Cheese

Serves: 4, Preparation: 5 minutes, Cooking: 12 minutes

Ingredients

- 2 Tbsp of olive oil
- 1 of chopped green onion
- 1 cup of fresh button mushrooms
- 1 grated tomato
- 1 lb of Queso fresco- cheese cut into cubes
- 1 cup of fresh cream
- Salt to taste
- Worcestershire sauce to taste
- Mustard (Dijon, English, ground stone) to taste
- Ketchup to taste

Instructions

1. Heat the oil in a large skillet and sauté the onion until soft.
2. Add mushrooms and gently stir for 2 - 3 minutes.
3. Add grated tomato, and season with the salt, Worcestershire sauce, ketchup and mustard.
4. Bring to boil; add cheese cubes and stir well.
5. Cook just for one minute, to avoid the cheese melting.
6. Add the fresh cream and stir.
7. Remove from the heat, and allow it to cool for 5 minutes.
8. Serve.

Nutrition information:

Calories: 469 Carbohydrates: 5.7g Proteins: 19.5g Fat: 48g Fiber: 0.7g

Courgettes with Goat Cheese Cake

Serves: 4, Preparation: 15 minutes, Cooking: 2 hours

Ingredients

- Non-stick cooking spray for greasing
- 6 courgettes/zucchini grated
- 1 handful fresh mint roughly chopped
- 2 Eggs from free-range chickens
- 1 Tbsp of almond flour
- 1/2 tsp of baking soda
- 3/4 cup goat cheese, crumbled

Instructions

1. Grease the bottom and sides of your Crock Pot; set aside.
2. Grate the courgettes/zucchini and squeeze out all the excess water; place in a large bowl.
3. Add eggs, crumbled goat cheese, almond flour, baking soda and mint; stir through.
4. Pour batter in prepared Crock Pot.
5. Cover and cook on LOW for 2 – 3 hours.
6. Allow cake to cool, slice and serve.

Nutrition information:

Calories: 117 Carbohydrates: 2g Proteins: 8g Fat: 10g Fiber: 0.3g

Dark Nutty Chocolate Sauce

Serves: 8, Preparation: 5 minutes, Cooking: 4 hours

Ingredients

- 4 cups of almond milk
- 2 cups fresh cream
- 1 1/2 cups grated dark chocolate (70 - 80% cacao solid)
- 1 tsp of espresso coffee (two shoots)
- 2 Tbsp of ground almonds
- 1/2 tsp of ground cinnamon
- Pinch of ground red pepper (optional)
- Natural sweetener (Stevia, Truvia, Erythritol...etc.) to taste

Instructions

1. Place all ingredients in your Crock Pot.
2. Cover and cook on SLOW for 4 hours or HIGH for 2 hours.
3. Open lid and give a good stir.
4. Allow cream to cool before serving.
5. Keep refrigerated.

Nutrition information:

Calories: 263 Carbohydrates: 9g Proteins: 3.5g Fat: 22g Fiber: 2g

Irresistible Keto Lemon Cake

Serves: 10, Preparation: 15 minutes, Cooking: 3 hours and 15 minutes

Ingredients

- 1/3 cup almond butter, melted
- 2 cups almond flour
- 3/4 tsp baking soda
- 1 pinch of salt (optional)
- 1 cup of natural sweetener (Stevia, Truvia, Erythritol...etc.)
- 2 Eggs from free-range chickens
- 3 medium lemons
- 3 eggs from free-range chickens

Instructions

1. Line your Crock Pot with parchment paper.
2. In a bowl, combine the almond flour, sweetener, baking soda and a pinch of salt (optional).
3. In a separate bowl, whisk eggs; add lemon juice and the lemon zest.
4. Combine the flour mixture with egg mixture and stir until all ingredients combined well.
5. Pour the batter into Crock Pot.
6. Cover and cook on LOW setting for 3 - 3 1/2 hours.
7. Transfer cake to the plate, let it cool completely, cut in bars and serve.

Nutrition information:

Calories: 236 Carbohydrates: 6g Proteins: 835g Fat: 22g Fiber: 3g

Keto Blueberry Topping

Serves: 4, Preparation: 10 minutes, Cooking: 2 hours and 15 minutes

Ingredients

- 3/4 cup natural sweetener (Stevia, Truvia, Erythritol...etc.)
- 2 Tbsp of water
- 2 Tbsp of butter
- 1 cup fresh blueberries (or frozen blueberries)
- Juice from 1 lemon
- Zest from 1 lemon

Instructions

1. Heat the sweetener and water in a saucepan over low heat. Stir approximately 3 to 5 minutes until make nice, smooth syrup.
2. Add fresh butter, and stir to get smooth and shine surface.
3. Add blueberries in your Crock Pot and pour syrup evenly to cover blueberries.
4. Sprinkle the lemon zest, and drizzle with fresh lemon juice; gentle stir.
5. Cover and cook on LOW for 2 hours.
6. Open the lid and give a good stir.
7. Keep refrigerated.

Nutrition information:

Calories: 76 Carbohydrates: 6.5g Proteins: 0.5g Fat: 7g Fiber: 4g

Sinless Raspberries Cake

Serves: 6, Preparation: 15 minutes, Cooking: 2 hours

Ingredients

- 6 large eggs
- 1/4 cup natural sweetener (Stevia, Truvia, Erythritol...etc.)
- 1 tsp cinnamon
- 1/4 cup olive oil
- 2 cups fresh raspberries

Instructions

1. Line the bottom of your Crock Pot with parchment paper; set aside.
2. Beat eggs with a hand mixer in a bowl; add the sweetener oil and cinnamon.
3. Pour the egg mixture in prepared Crock Pot.
4. Sprinkle the raspberries over the egg mixture evenly.
5. Cover and cook on HIGH for 1 hour and 30 minutes, on LOW for 2 hours and 30 minutes.
6. Remove the cake from the Crock Pot, allow to cool, slice and serve.

Nutrition information:

Calories: 173 Carbohydrates: 5g Proteins: 15g Fat: 7g Fiber: 3g

Strawberry Ocean Sauce

Serves: 12, Preparation: 5 minutes, Cooking: 3 hours

Ingredients

- 2 lbs. of fresh strawberries
- 1 1/2 cups natural sweetener (Stevia, Truvia, Erythritol...etc.)
- 2 Tbsp of vanilla extract
- 1 1/4 cup water
- 1/2 lemon juice
- 2 cinnamon sticks

Instructions

1. Place all ingredients in your Slow Cooker and stir well,
2. Cover and cook on LOW for 3 hours.
3. Open lid and give and good stir.
4. Allow sauce to cool completely.
5. Remove cinnamon sticks and store into glass jar; keep refrigerated.

Nutrition information:

Calories: 35 Carbohydrates: 6g Proteins: 1g Fat: 11g Fiber: 1g

Chapter 15 Keto Grilling Recipes

Grilled Beef Fillet with Fresh Herbs
Serves: 4, Preparation: 15 minutes, Cooking: 10 minutes

Ingredients
- 2 lbs. beef eye fillet
- Salt and freshly ground black pepper to taste
- 1/4 cup oregano leaves, fresh and chopped
- 1/4 cup parsley, fresh and chopped
- 2 Tbsp rosemary leaves, fresh and chopped
- 2 Tbsp basil, fresh and chopped
- 1/4 cup olive oil

Instructions
1. Season beef fillets with the salt and pepper; place in a shallow container.
2. In a bowl, combine all remaining ingredients and rub the meat from all sides.
3. Cover and refrigerate overnight.
4. Remove meat from the fridge to room temperature 20 minutes before you put it on the grill.
5. Preheat your grill (pellet, gas, charcoal) to HIGH according to manufacturer instructions.
6. Place fillets on a grill and cook for about 8-10 minutes per side or to your preference for doneness.
7. When ready, let meat rest for 10 minutes and serve warm.

Nutrition information:
Calories: 591 Carbohydrates: 4g Proteins: 46g Fat: 54g Fiber: 3.5g

Grilled Chicken Breast with Stone-Ground Mustard
Serves: 4, Preparation: 15 minutes, Cooking: 25 minutes

Ingredients
- 4 chicken breasts, boneless and skinless
- 4 garlic cloves, minced
- 1/4 cup stone-ground mustard (gluten-free)
- 3 Tbsp olive oil
- 1 Tbsp fresh herb mix (basil, cumin, parsley, rosemary, thyme...etc.)
- Sea salt and ground black pepper to taste

Instructions
1. Place the chicken breasts in a shallow container.
2. In a bowl, combine all remaining ingredients and pour over the chicken.
3. Cover the container and refrigerate for 4 - 6 hours.
4. Preheat your grill (pellet, gas, charcoal) to HIGH according to manufacturer instructions.
5. Remove the chicken from the fridge.
6. Grill the chicken breasts for 10 - 12 minutes per side; flip them 3 - 4 times.
7. Serve hot.

Nutrition information:
Calories: 366 Carbohydrates: 1.5g Proteins: 50g Fat: 17g Fiber: 0.1g

Grilled Chicken in Sour Marinade

Serves: 8, Preparation: 15 minutes, Cooking: 10 minutes

Ingredients

- 4 lbs chicken breast boneless
- 6 lemons, in slices
- 2 Tbsp onion minced
- 1 Tbsp garlic minced
- 1/4 cup olive oil
- 1/2 tsp nutmeg grated
- 1/4 tsp of cinnamon
- Salt and freshly ground black pepper to taste

Instructions

1. In a large container, place chicken pieces and lemon slices.
2. In a small bowl, combine all remaining ingredients.
3. Pour the mixture evenly over the chicken. Refrigerate for 2 - 3 hours or overnight.
4. Preheat your grill (pellet, gas, charcoal) to HIGH according to manufacturer instructions.
5. Grill your chicken and lemon slices on direct heat for about 9 -10 minutes per side (internal temperature165° F).
6. Serve hot.

Nutrition information:
Calories: 338 Carbohydrates: 7g Proteins: 49.5g Fat: 14g Fiber: 1g

Grilled Chicken Legs in Bacon-Whisky Marinade

Serves: 4, Preparation: 25 minutes, Cooking: 20 minutes

Ingredients

For the sauce

- 4 slices of bacon cut into cubes
- 2 green onions finely chopped
- 1 Tbsp of chopped garlic
- 1/2 cup of mustard
- 3 Tbsp of coconut aminos
- 2 Tbsp of cinnamon
- 1/2 cup of whiskey
- 2 Tbsp of Worcester sauce
- 1 - 2 drops of Tabasco (optional)
- 4 chicken legs, skinless

Instructions

1. For the sauce: in a medium skillet fry bacon for about 5 - 6 minutes over medium heat.
2. Lower the heat: add the onion and garlic and sauté for 4 - 5 minutes.
3. Add the remaining ingredients, stir and cook for 5 minutes.
4. Remove the sauce from heat and let it cool down.
5. In a large plastic bag, add the chicken legs and drop the half of the sauce; shake to combine well.
6. Refrigerate the chicken to marinate overnight.
7. Remove the chicken from marinade.
8. Preheat your grill (pellet, gas, charcoal) to MEDIUM according to manufacturer instructions.
9. Grill the chicken breasts for about 20 minutes; flip every 5 - 6 minutes.
10. Brush the chicken with the rest of the sauce, and grill for further 15 minutes.
11. Let the chicken sit for 10 minutes before servings.

Nutrition information:
Calories: 573 Carbohydrates: 6.5g Proteins: 36g Fat: 7g Fiber: 3g

Grilled Chops in Dark Marinade

Serves: 6, Preparation: 15 minutes, Cooking: 8 minutes

Ingredients

- 3 Tbsp of sesame oil
- 3/4 cup coconut aminos (from coconut sap)
- 2 garlic clove, minced
- 1 Tbsp chili sauce
- 1 Tbsp stevia granulated sweetener
- 1/4 cup lemon juice fresh
- Salt and ground black pepper to taste
- 6 pork chops bone-in

Instructions

1. In a bowl, combine the sesame oil, coconut aminos, garlic, chili sauce, stevia, salt and pepper, and fresh lemon juice.
2. Place the marinade in a large resalable plastic bag along with pork; seal the bag and refrigerate overnight.
3. Remove the pork from the marinade, and par dry on kitchen paper.
4. Preheat your grill (pellet, gas, charcoal) to HIGH according to manufacturer instructions.
5. Place the pork chops on a grill and cook for 4 minutes per side.
6. Transfer the pork chops on a platter and let sit for 10 minutes. Serve warm.

Nutrition information:

Calories: 328 Carbohydrates: 4g Proteins: 29g Fat: 22g Fiber: 0.3g

Grilled Cuttlefish

Serves: 6, Preparation: 15 minutes, Cooking: 10 minutes

Ingredients

- 1/2 cup of olive oil
- 1 Tbsp of lemon juice
- 1 tsp of ground ginger
- 1 tsp oregano
- 2 pinch of salt
- 1 tsp five-spice powder
- 8 large cuttlefish cleaned
- 2 - 3 lemons for serving

Instructions

1. In a deep container add the cuttlefish.
2. In a bowl, combine all remaining ingredients and pour evenly over cuttlefish.
3. Cover and marinate for about 2 hours.
4. Remove the cuttlefish from marinade and pat dry them on kitchen paper.
5. Preheat your grill (pellet, gas, charcoal) to HIGH according to manufacturer instructions.
6. Place the cuttlefish on grill, and Grill the cuttlefish j 3-5 minutes on each side (depend of the size).
7. Serve hot with lemon wedges and lemon juice.

Nutrition information:

Calories: 301 Carbohydrates: 4g Proteins: 28g Fat: 19.5g Fiber: 2g

Grilled Lamb Chops with Flavored Marinade

Serves: 8, Preparation: 15 minutes, Cooking: 8 - 10 minutes

Ingredients

- 8 lamb chops
- For marinade / sauce
- 1 small white onion, cut into pieces
- 1 grated tomato
- 1 cup extra virgin olive oil
- 4 cloves of garlic
- 2 Tbsp of red wine vinegar
- 1 Tbsp of sweet paprika
- 1 Tbsp of dried thyme
- 1 Tbsp of coriander
- 2 tsp of cumin
- 2 tsp of salt
- 1 tsp of cayenne pepper
- 1 tsp of grated black pepper

Instructions

1. Combine the marinade ingredients and stir well.
2. Place the lamb chops in a shallow container next to each other, and cover with marinade.
3. Wrap the container with plastic membrane and refrigerate for 6 hours.
4. Remove the lamb chops 30 minutes before grilling; place them on a kitchen towel to pat dry
5. Preheat the grill for direct baking on high heat.
6. Place the lamb chops on grill, and cook, with lid closed, for about 4 minutes per side for medium-rare; turn them twice.
7. Remove from the grill, let rest for 5 minutes and serve hot.

Nutrition information:

Calories: 460 Carbohydrates: 4.5g Proteins: 28g Fat: 36g Fiber: 1.5g

Grilled Marinated Goat Skewers

Serves: 6, Preparation: 15 minutes, Cooking: 15 minutes

Ingredients

- 3 lbs. goat chops cut into large pieces
- 4 cloves garlic (minced)
- 2 tsp sweet paprika
- 1 tsp ground chilli
- 2 tsp ground cumin
- 2 tsp dried oregano
- 1/4 cup olive oil
- 1/4 cup white vine
- 1 tsp fresh basil finely chopped
- 1 tsp fresh mint finely chopped
- Kosher or sea salt to taste
- 1 lemon juice (freshly squeezed)

Instructions

1. Place the goat chops in a shallow container.
2. In a bowl, combine all remaining ingredients and pour evenly over chops.
3. Cover and refrigerate overnight.
4. Remove chops from fridge 30 minutes before grilling. Pat - dry the meet on a kitchen paper towel. Thread the meat cubes onto the skewers.
5. Preheat your grill (pellet, gas, charcoal) to HIGH according to manufacturer instructions.
6. Put skewers directly on grill grate and grill for 5 - 6 minutes from each side (Medium Rare - 145°F , Medium - 160°F
7. Well Done – 170°F), turning occasionally, until done.

Nutrition information:

Calories: 388 Carbohydrates: 4g Proteins: 45g Fat: 37g Fiber: 1g

Grilled Marinated Pancetta Strips

Serves: 8, Preparation: 15 minutes, Cooking: 8 - 10 minutes

Ingredients

- 5 - 6 lbs pancetta cut in strips
- 2 Tbsp of salt and black pepper or to taste
- 1 tsp smoked pepper
- 1 clove garlic minced
- 1/2 tsp of fresh oregano
- 1 Tbsp allspice (ground)
- 2 Tbsp of olive oil
- 1/2 cup of white wine
- 2 - 3 lemons for serving

Instructions

1. Place pancetta strips in a large container.
2. In a bowl, combine all remaining ingredients, and pour evenly over the pancetta strips.
3. Cover and shake the container; refrigerate it overnight.
4. Remove pancetta from fridge for at least half an hour before grilling.
5. Preheat your grill (pellet, gas, charcoal) to HIGH according to manufacturer instructions.
6. Place pancetta strips on a grill, and cook each side for 3 - 4 minutes or until done.
7. Remove grilled pork pancetta strips on a serving platter, and let sit for 10 minutes.
8. Serve with the lemon wedges.

Nutrition information:

Calories: 319 Carbohydrates: 4g Proteins: 0.5g Fat: 26g Fiber: 1.5g

Grilled Pork Chops with Ginger-Garlic

Serves: 4, Preparation: 15 minutes, Cooking: 14 - 16 minutes

Ingredients

- 4 pork chops
- 1/2 cup fresh cilantro, chopped
- 3 Tbsp fresh mint; more for garnish
- 2 Tbsp minced fresh ginger
- 2 Tbsp minced garlic
- 2 tsp grated lime zest
- 1/2 cup bone broth (or water)
- 1/4 cup coconut aminos (from coconut sap)
- 2 Tbsp Sesame oil
- Salt and freshly-ground black pepper to taste
- Lime wedges for serving

Instructions

1. Season pork chops with the salt and pepper, and place in a shallow container.
2. In a bowl, combine all remaining ingredients and pour evenly over chops; refrigerate overnight.
3. When you're ready to grill the chops, remove them from the marinade and discard the liquid.
4. Preheat your grill (pellet, gas, charcoal) to HIGH according to manufacturer instructions.
5. Set the chops directly over the heat. Cook them for about 2 minutes per side, and then remove the chops at a side. Cover the grill and cook the chops indirectly for further 4 to 6 minutes per side.
6. Transfer the chops to a clean platter and let them rest for 5 minutes before serving. Serve with the lime wedges.

Nutrition information:

Calories: 514 Carbohydrates: 4g Proteins: 52g Fat: 33g Fiber: 1g

Grilled Pork Ribs with Sweet Dark Sauce

Serves: 10, Preparation: 15 minutes, Cooking: 30 minutes

Ingredients

- 5 lbs pork ribs
- 1/4 cup coconut aminos
- 3 Tbsp sesame oil
- 2 Tbsp mustard (Dijon, English, ground stone)
- 2 Tbsp of stevia sweetener
- 1/2 cup water
- 2 garlic cloves, minced

Instructions

1. Cut the ribs into serving-size portions, and place them in a large container.
2. Combine all remaining ingredients and pour the sauce over the pork ribs.
3. Refrigerate for 6 hours or overnight.
4. Drain ribs and reserve marinade.
5. Preheat your grill (pellet, gas, charcoal) to HIGH according to manufacturer instructions.
6. Place the ribs on a grill (bone-side down), close the lid and cook for 30 - 35 minutes on 300 F.
7. Remove ribs to a plate, let sit for 5 minutes and serve hot.

Nutrition information:

Calories: 588 Carbohydrates: 4g Proteins: 36g
Fat: 57g Fiber: 0.3g

Grilled Sea bass with Hot Sauce

Serves: 4, Preparation: 10 minutes, Cooking: 12 - 15 minutes

Ingredients

- 1 lb Sea bass fillets
- 1 cup mayonnaise
- 1/2 cup of ground stone mustard
- 1/4 tsp of liquid smoking
- 1 lemon juice freshly squeezed
- 2 Tbsp hot sauce
- 2 cloves garlic minced

Instructions

1. Rinse and clean the fish; pat dry on kitchen paper.
2. In a bowl, combine all remaining ingredients and rub evenly the fish.
3. Preheat your grill (pellet, gas, charcoal) to MEDIUM-HIGH according to manufacturer instructions.
4. Place fish fillets on a grill and cook for about 5 - 6 minutes per side.
5. Serve hot.

Nutrition information:

Calories: 253 Carbohydrates: 8g Proteins: 24g
Fat: 14g Fiber: 0.5g

Grilled Spicy Shrimp with Coriander

Serves: 4, Preparation: 15 minutes, Cooking: 2 - 4 minutes

Ingredients

- 1 cup of olive oil
- 1 Tbsp of ground red hot peppers
- 1 Tbsp of coconut aminos
- 1 tsp of salt
- 2 lbs of large shrimp, cleaned
- 2 Tbsp of chopped fresh coriander leaves

Instructions

1. In a large bowl combine the olive oil, hot peppers with coconut aminos sauce and salt.
2. Add the shrimp and make sure to cover it evenly with the mixture.
3. Cover with membrane and marinate at room temperature for 30 minutes or in the refrigerator for 1 hour.
4. Prepare the grill for direct baking at HIGH temperature.
5. Remove the shrimp from the bowl and remove any marinade.
6. Thread shrimp onto skewers, three per skewer.
7. Grill shrimp, with lid closed, for 2 to 4 minutes, turning only once.
8. Remove shrimp from the grill and sprinkle with the chopped coriander.
9. Serve hot.

Nutrition information:

Calories: 334 Carbohydrates: 4g Proteins: 34g
Fat: 20g Fiber: 1g

Grilled Steak with Ginger and Sesame

Serves: 6, Preparation: 15 minutes, Cooking: 10 - 12 minutes

Ingredients

- 3 Tbsp of oil
- 2 Tbsp of grated fresh ginger
- 1 tsp of salt
- 1-1 / 2 tsp of ground black pepper
- 2 bone steaks (about 4lbs)

For the sauce

- 2 Tbsp sesame oil
- 4 Tbsp of sesame seeds
- 1 tsp of salt
- 1 tsp freshly ground black pepper
- 1 Tbsp
- of fresh lemon juice

Instructions

1. In a bowl, stir the oil, ginger, salt and pepper.
2. Rub the steaks with the ginger mixture and leave them at room temperature for about 15 to 30 minutes before baking.
3. Preheat your grill (pellet, gas, charcoal) to HIGH according to manufacturer instructions.
4. Heat non-stick saucepan over moderate heat and sauté sesame seeds, salt and black pepper for 4 - 5 minutes; stir with a wooden spoon. Place the sauce in a bowl and set aside.
5. Bake the steaks in direct heat with the lid closed 5 - 6 minutes per side for medium baking, turning 1 or 2 times.
6. Your stake is ready when a meat thermometer reads 140 degrees Fahrenheit
7. Serve hot with the sesame sauce.

Nutrition information:

Calories: 657 Carbohydrates: 2g Proteins: 54g
Fat: 52g Fiber: 1g

Grilled Swordfish Stuffed with Fresh Herbs

Serves: 4, Preparation: 15 minutes, Cooking: 16 minutes

Instructions

- 1 swordfish, whole fish or 2 smaller (well-cleaned)
- 2 lemon juice
- 2 Tbsp of freshly chopped herbs (thyme, oregano, onions, dill)
- 1 onion (small) finely chopped
- 1 small tomato chopped
- 1 clove of garlic
- 1 Tbsp of butter softened
- Salt and pepper to taste

Instructions

1. Preheat your grill (pellet, gas, charcoal) to HIGH according to manufacturer instructions.
2. Wash the fish and dry it.
3. Whisk the lemon juice, tomato, fresh herbs, garlic, butter and the salt and pepper to taste.
4. Fill the fish with the lemon-herbs mixture; rub the fish with a little salt, and brush the fish with the olive oil.
5. Place the fish on a grill, and lower the heat to MODERATE.
6. Grill for 8 minutes per side turning once. Serve hot.

Nutrition information:

Calories: 371 Carbohydrates: 4.5g Proteins: 45g Fat: 18g Fiber: 1g

Lemon Marinated Grilled Salmon

Serves: 4, Preparation: 15 minutes, Cooking: 10 -12 minutes

Ingredients

- 2 juice and zest of 2 lemons freshly squeezed
- 1/4 cup of olive oil
- 3 clove garlic, minced
- 1 tsp smoked paprika (mild)
- Salt and freshly ground black pepper
- 2 lbs salmon fillets with skin

Instructions

1. Combine the lemon juice and zest, olive oil, garlic, smoked paprika, and the salt and pepper.
2. Pour the mixture over the fish fillets.
3. Cover and refrigerate for 2 hours.
4. Preheat your grill (pellet, gas, charcoal) to HIGH according to manufacturer instructions.
5. Place the salmon fillets on grill (skin side down), and cover. Cook for 10 - 12 minutes or to preference.
6. Serve warm.

Nutrition information:

Calories: 459 Carbohydrates: 4g Proteins: 45g Fat: 28g Fiber: 1g

Oriental Chicken Skewers on Grill

Serves: 6, Preparation: 15 minutes, Cooking: 14 – 15 minutes

Ingredients

- 3 lbs of chicken fillet, cut in pieces
- 2 cloves of garlic, finely chopped
- 3 Tbsp of olive oil
- 1 lemon zest and juice
- 1/2 tsp of salt, pepper
- 1/4 tsp of coriander
- 1/4 tsp of cinnamon
- 1/4 tsp of turmeric
- 1/4 tsp of nutmeg
- Lemon wedges for serving

Instructions

1. Rinse the meat, pat dry on a kitchen paper, and cut in thin strips.
2. Peel and chop the garlic.
3. Place the chicken strips in a bowl.
4. Combine the olive oil, garlic, lemon, salt, pepper, coriander, cinnamon, turmeric and nutmeg, and pour over chicken.
5. With your hands mix the chicken with marinade, cover and refrigerate for 4 hours or overnight.
6. Drain the chicken and thread onto skewers.
7. Preheat your grill (pellet, gas, charcoal) to HIGH according to manufacturer instructions.
8. Place skewers on grill and cook for 5 - 7 minutes each side.
9. Serve hot with lemon wedges.

Nutrition information:

Calories: 332 Carbohydrates: 3g Proteins: 49g
Fat: 13g Fiber: 3g

Rib Eye with Chili Sauce and Garlic

Serves: 6, Preparation: 15 minutes, Cooking: 8 - 12 minutes

Ingredients

- 4 rib eyes (12 ounces each), cleaned
- For spread
- 2 Tbsp extra virgin olive oil
- 2 tsp of chili powder
- 2 tsp of coarse salt
- 1 Tbsp of ground red hot paprika
- 2 cloves of garlic grated
- 1 tsp of ground black pepper

For the sauce

- 1 medium chopped tomato
- 1 cup of spring onions finely chopped
- 1 chili pepper, sliced
- 1 cup fresh coriander leaves, chopped
- 2 Tbsp of fresh lime juice
- 3 tsp of coarse salt
- 1 tsp of grated black pepper
- 1 tsp of cumin
- 1 clove of garlic grated

Instructions

1. Stir all ingredients for the spread.
2. Rub the spread on both sides of the rib eye and allow to sit for 15 to 20 minutes before grilling.
3. In the meantime, combine all ingredients for the sauce; set aside.
4. Preheat your grill (pellet, gas, charcoal) to HIGH according to manufacturer instructions.
5. Bake Rib Eye on a high heat (direct baking with the lid closed) for about 4 - 6 minutes on each side for medium-rare.
6. Remove the steaks from the grill and let them rest for 10 minutes.
7. Serve warm with the sauce.

Nutrition information:

Calories: 611 Carbohydrates: 8g Proteins: 46g
Fat: 51g Fiber: 8g

Simple Grilled Marinated Chicken Fillets

Serves: 6, Preparation: 15 minutes, Cooking: 8 – 10 minutes

Ingredients
- 6 - 8 chicken fillets boneless

MARINADE
- 3/4 cup of olive oil
- 1/2 cup of fresh lemon juice
- 1 tsp of lemon zest
- 1 tsp of oregano, fresh or dry
- 2 Tbsp of bone broth
- Salt and ground black pepper

Instructions
1. Clean the fillets from their fiber, and then shred them.
2. Whisk with a fork all marinade ingredients to combine, and pour over the chicken fillets.
3. Cover with membrane and refrigerate for 6-8 hours or overnight.
4. Remove the chicken from the fridge 1 hour before grilling.
5. Preheat your grill (pellet, gas, charcoal) according to manufacturer's instructions.
6. Bake for 4 minutes from one side, turn them out, and grill for another 4 minutes.
7. Then turn them on and continue firing on the other side for 6-8 minutes.
8. The chicken is ready when internal temp reach 165F. Serve hot.

Nutrition information:
Calories: 446 Carbohydrates: 1.5g Proteins: 38g Fat: 32g Fiber: 0.2g

Stuffed Chicken Breasts with Olives and Feta

Serves: 6, Preparation: 20 minutes, Cooking: 15 - 20 minutes

Ingredients
- 4 chicken breasts
- 1 green onion finely chopped
- 2 cloves of garlic
- 2 tsp fresh thyme
- 1 sprig of rosemary
- 12 black olives, pitted
- 1/2 cup crumbled feta cheese
- 12 slices of bacon
- 3 Tbsp of olive oil
- Salt and ground pepper

Instructions
1. Clean and chop the onion and garlic.
2. Remove the leaves of thyme and rosemary from the stems and chop them very well.
3. Finally, clean olives and crumble feta cheese, and place into a bowl.
4. Place all remaining ingredients in a bowl, and combine well.
5. Open the chicken breasts and fill with the mixture.
6. Then, wrap the breasts in rolls and wrap them with bacon.
7. Preheat your grill (pellet, gas, charcoal) to HIGH according to manufacturer instructions.
8. Place wrapped chicken breasts on the grill and bake for about 15 - 20 minutes, turning them occasionally until the chicken reaches internal temperature of 150 ° F.
9. Serve hot.

Nutrition information:
Calories: 577 Carbohydrates: 4g Proteins: 5g Fat: 44g Fiber: 1g

Chapter 16 Keto-internation

Chinese

"Sweet" Pork and Mushrooms
Serves: 6, Preparation: 15 minutes, Cooking: 20 minutes

Ingredients
- 1/2 lb of pork loin, boneless
- 2 cups coconut aminos (from coconut sap)
- 1 cup of white wine
- 1 Tbsp of stevia
- 1 1/2 cups of avocado oil
- 1 large onion, finely chopped
- 1 lb of fresh mushrooms
- Salt and ground pepper to taste

Instructions
1. Rinse and cut mushrooms in thin strips.
2. Cut the onion in half and finely cut in cubes.
3. Cut the pork into thin strips.
4. Heat the oil in a large wok or frying skillet over high-moderate heat.
5. Sauté the onion with a pinch of salt for two minutes stirring continuously.
6. Add mushrooms and continue to sauté for further 3 minutes; stir.
7. Remove all ingredients in a bowl; set aside.
8. In a same wok or frying skillet heat the oil and fry the pork stirring continuously for 4 - 5 minutes or until meat is no longer pink.
9. Remove the mushrooms mixture to wok, pour the wine, stevia and continue to cook, stirring continuously, for further 3 - 4 minutes.
10. Taste and adjust salt and pepper; stir. Serve hot.

Nutrition information:
Calories: 380 Carbohydrates: 5g Proteins: 12g Fat: 32.5g Fiber:1g

Braised Qíncai with Coconut Aminos
Serves: 4, Preparation: 5 minutes, Cooking: 20 minutes

Ingredients
- 1 Tbsp of avocado oil
- 2 green onions, finely chopped
- 11 oz celery (stalks) sliced
- 1/2 cup water
- 11 oz white mushrooms, sliced
- 1/2 cup cauliflower rice
- 2 Tbsp Coconut Aminos
- Salt to taste

Instructions
1. Heat the avocado oil in a wok or in a frying skillet.
2. Add the chopped onions and sprinkle with a little salt; sauté for 3 - 4 minutes, stir.
3. Add sliced celery stalks and pour 1/2 cup water; simmer for 6 - 8 minutes.
4. Add white mushrooms and season with little salt; stir for 2 - 3 minutes.
5. Add cauliflower rice and Coconut Aminos and cook, stirring, for further 3 - 4 minutes. Serve hot.

Nutrition information:
Calories: 111 Carbohydrates: 1.5g Proteins: 4g Fat: 6g Fiber: 3.5g

Breaded Pork with Sour-Sweet Sauce
Serves: 4, Preparation: 15 minutes, Cooking: 15 minutes

Ingredients
- 1 lb pork without bone cut in strips

- 1/2 tsp salt or to taste
- 1/4 cup almond flour
- 2 egg yolks
- Olive oil for frying

Sauce
- 1 onion, cut into cubes
- 1 large tomato, finely chopped
- 1 tsp mustard
- 1 green pepper, finely chopped
- 2 Tbsp stevia sweetener
- 1/2 cup of fresh lemon juice

Instructions
1. Heat the oil in a wok over high heat.
2. Season pork strips with the salt evenly.
3. Roll the pork in almond flour, then in beaten egg yolks, and again in the almond flour.
4. Fry the pork strips in hot oil for 5 - 7 minutes.
5. Remove the pork on a plate covered with kitchen paper to drain.
6. In a meantime, in a same wok sauté the onion with a little salt.
7. Add the chopped tomato and stir for 2 - 3 minutes.
8. Add mustard, green pepper, stevia sweetener and some salt; stir for 2 - 3 minutes.
9. Remove the sauce from heat and pour the lemon juice; stir well.
10. Place the pork on a serving plate, pour the sauce over the meat and serve.

Nutrition information:
Calories: 469 Carbohydrates: 7g Proteins: 12g Fat: 47g Fiber: 2.5g

Chinese Chicken with Bamboo and Lemongrass
Serves: 6, Preparation: 5 minutes, Cooking: 25 minutes

Ingredients
- 2 tsp of sesame oil
- 2 Tbsp of coconut oil
- 1 lb chicken fillet cut into chunks
- 1 onion finely chopped
- 2 medium carrots, sliced
- 2 cloves of garlic minced
- 1 piece of fresh ginger cleaned and cut
- 1 Tbsp fresh lemongrass
- Bamboo slices (canned, unsalted)
- 2 fresh onions, sliced
- 1 chili pepper, finely chopped
- Fresh coriander finely chopped
- Salt and black pepper to taste

Instructions
1. Heat the coconut and sesame oil in a wok over moderate-strong fire.
2. Add the chicken with little salt and sauté for 3 - 4 minutes.
3. Put the onion in the wok and continue to sauté for further 2 - 3 minutes; stir.
4. Add the carrots and garlic and stir for 2 - 3 minutes.
5. Add ginger, lemongrass, chili and bamboo slices; continue to stir for further 3 minutes.
6. At the end, add fresh onion, coriander, and adjust salt and pepper to taste; cook for 3 - 4 minutes. Serve hot.

Nutrition information:
Calories: 108 Carbohydrates: 8g Proteins: 3g Fat: 7g Fiber: 2.5g

Five Spice Broccoli (Chinese)
Serves: 4, Preparation: 10 minutes, Cooking: 15 minutes

Ingredients
- 1 lb broccoli floweret
- 2 - 3 of avocado oil
- 2 1/2 cups of water
- Kosher salt to taste
- 1 Tbsp of Five Spice Powder

Instructions
1. Cut the broccoli into small pieces; rinse it and drain in a strainer.

2. Heat the avocado oil in a wok over high temperature.
3. Add the broccoli with a pinch of salt and sauté for 2 - 3 minutes.
4. Pour water and cook for 5 minutes; stir occasionally.
5. Remove broccoli to a serving plate, and sprinkle with Five Spice Powder

(blend of clover, peppercorns, fennel, cinnamon and star anise.
6. Serve immediately.

Nutrition information:
Calories: 55 Carbohydrates: 4g Proteins: 8g Fat: 3g Fiber: 1g

Fried Sour - Sweet Chicken Fillets
Serves: 4, Preparation: 10 minutes, Cooking: 6 - 8 minutes

Ingredients
- 1 1/2 lb chicken fillets cut in slices
- Salt to taste
- 1/2 cup fresh lemon juice
- 1/4 cup coconut flour
- 2 Tbsp stevia sweetener granulated
- 1/2 cup of olive oil for frying

Instructions
1. Place your chicken in a bowl, and season with salt to taste.
2. Pour the lemon juice over the chicken and stir well.
3. In a separate small bowl combine coconut flour and stevia sweetener.
4. Add coconut flour mixture to the bowl with the chicken; stir well.
5. Heat the oil in a wok and fry the chicken fillets for about 5 - 6 minutes.
6. Stir continuously to prevent sticking. Serve hot.

Nutrition information:
Calories: 381 Carbohydrates: 6g Proteins: 37g Fat: 21g Fiber: 0.5g

Instant Duck and Celeriac Soup

Serves: 6, Preparation: 5 minutes, Cooking: 35 minutes

Ingredients

- 1 - 2 Tbsp duck fat
- 2 big celery roots cut in cubes
- 4 - 5 cups water
- 1 lb duck meat, boneless, cut in small pieces
- 2 cups mushrooms (sliced)
- 2 green onions chopped (only green parts)
- Salt and pepper to taste

Instructions

1. Use a sharp knife to remove the tough skin of celeriac; cut in cubes.
2. Add the duck fat to your Instant Pot.
3. Add celeriac and all remaining ingredients and stir well.
4. Lock lid into place and set on the POULTRY setting for 30 - 35 minutes.
5. When ready, use Natural release about 15 - 20 minutes.
6. Taste and adjust salt and pepper to taste. Serve.

Nutrition information:

Calories: 155 Carbohydrates: 6g Proteins: 18g Fat: 6g Fiber: 2g

Marinated Pork Chops with Avocado Oil

Serves: 4, Preparation: 10 minutes, Cooking: 10 - 15 minutes

Ingredients

- 1/4 cup avocado oil
- 3 cloves garlic minced
- 1/2 cup lemon juice
- 1/2 cup coconut aminos
- 4 pork chops

Instructions

1. In a bowl, combine all ingredients except pork chops. Lay the pork in a baking pan and pour marinade over pork. Refrigerate for at least 4 hours or overnight.
2. Remove the pork chops from marinade and place on a kitchen paper to drain (reserve marinade).
3. Heat the marinade in wok over medium heat to simmer.
4. Cook the pork chops 10 minutes over medium heat.
5. Serve hot with marinade.

Nutrition information:

Calories: 361 Carbohydrates: 3g Proteins: 34g Fat: 15g Fiber: 0.3g

Spicy Marinated and Fried Chicken

Serves: 4, Preparation: 10 minutes, Cooking: 8 – 10 minutes

Ingredients

- 1 1/2 lbs of chicken fillet cut into strips
- Two pinch of salt (or to taste)
- 1 yogurt
- 1 Tbsp coriander (crushed seeds)
- 2 Tbsp coconut milk
- 1 Tbsp palm sugar or stevia sweetener
- 1 Tbsp curry powder
- 1 tsp ginger powder
- 1 tsp garlic powder
- 1 tsp hot mustard
- Olive oil for frying

Instructions

1. Season your chicken with a salt from all sides.
2. Place the chicken in a large resealable bag, and add all remaining ingredients.
3. Shake the bag to combine all ingredients evenly.
4. Refrigerate your marinated chicken for at least 3 hours.
5. Heat the oil in a wok or in a large frying skillet over moderate-high heat.
6. Remove the chicken from the bag, but do not clean the marinade.
7. Fry the chicken for 3 - 4 minutes per side or until done. Serve.

Nutrition information:

Calories: 211 Carbohydrates: 7g Proteins: 9g Fat: 18g Fiber: 1g

Stir Fry Vegetable Omelet with Mustard

Serves: 4, Preparation: 5 minutes, Cooking: 15 minutes

Ingredients

- 3 whole eggs from free-range chickens
- 3 egg whites
- 2 Tbsp coconut oil
- 2 cups mushrooms of your choice
- 2 small red chili peppers
- 1 grated carrot
- 2 cups of grated cabbage
- 1 courgette sliced
- 1/2 tsp cumin
- 1 tsp curry
- 1/3 tsp garlic powder
- 3 Tbsp of stone-ground mustard
- 1 Tbsp of sesame for garnish

Instructions

1. Beat the eggs and egg whites together in a bowl; set aside.
2. Heat the coconut oil in a wok over high heat.
3. Sauté the mushrooms and chili peppers with a pinch of salt.
4. Add carrot, cabbage, and zucchini and cook, stirring, for 4 - 5 minutes.
5. Then, add the egg mixture and stir well; cook for about 2 - 3 minutes; stir.
6. Season with cumin, curry, garlic powder, mustard and little salt; stir.
7. Remove from heat, serve and sprinkle with a sesame.

Nutrition information:

Calories: 194 Carbohydrates: 7g Proteins: 12g Fat: 13g Fiber: 4g

Mediterranean

Artichokes Stuffed with Gruyere and Capers
Serves: 4, Preparation: 20 minutes, Cooking: 1 hour

Ingredients
- 1/2 cup of olive oil
- 1 chopped onion
- 2 cloves garlic, chopped
- 2 tsp fresh thyme, chopped
- 1 tsp fresh fennel seeds
- 3/4 cup of finely ground almonds
- 1 cup of grated Gruyere cheese
- 2 Tbsp of capers
- 4 large artichokes, cleaned, without stalks
- 3 cup of white dry wine
- 3 cup water or bone broth
- Salt and ground pepper

Instructions
1. Preheat the oven to 400F/200 C.
2. Heat 3 tablespoon of oil in frying pan over medium heat.
3. Add the onion and sauté until soft for about 4 - 5 minutes.
4. Add the garlic, thyme, fennel and stir for 2 minutes.
5. Transfer to a bowl and allow to cool.
6. Add ground almonds, 1 cup of cheese, caper, and season with the salt the pepper; stir well.
7. With a spoon, take 2 tablespoons of the filling and place it in the center of each artichoke.
8. Put the artichokes in greased baking dish.
9. Sprinkle the artichokes with some oil and 1 cup of cheese.
10. Pour the wine and water or bone broth.
11. Cover with an aluminum foil and bake for about 1 hour.
12. Serve warm.

Nutrition information:
Calories: 459 Carbohydrates: 9g Proteins: 13g Fat: 38g Fiber: 7g

Baked Zucchini and Feta Omelet
Serves: 6, Preparation: 10 minutes, Cooking: 35 minutes

Ingredients
- 1/4 cup of olive oil
- 3 cloves garlic finely chopped
- 3 zucchini sliced
- 1 bunch of parsley
- 10 eggs from free-range chickens
- 1 cup Feta crumbled
- Sea salt and freshly ground pepper to taste

Instructions
1. Preheat the oven to 360 F/180C.
2. Grease a large baking dish and set aside.
3. Heat the olive oil in a frying skillet over medium heat. Sauté the garlic with the pinch of salt, stir gently, for 3 - 4 minutes.
4. Add zucchini and cook for further 3 - 4 minutes.
5. Transfer the zucchini mixture in a prepared baking dish.
6. Whisk the eggs with little salt and pepper, and stir crumbled feta. Pour the egg mixture evenly over zucchini.
7. Bake for about 25 - 30 minutes.
8. Allow to cool for 5 minutes, slice and serve.

Nutrition information:
Calories: 285 Carbohydrates: 5g Proteins: 16g Fat: 23g Fiber: 1g

Cretan Lamb Kiofta
Serves: 6, Preparation: 15 minutes, Cooking: 15 minutes

Ingredients
- 2 1/2 lbs of ground lamb meat

- 1 large onion, grated
- 4 cloves of garlic, grated
- 1 tsp of cumin
- 1 tsp of paprika
- 1 tsp of myrtle pepper (or allspice)
- 1 tsp of turmeric
- 3/4 cup chopped parsley
- 3/4 cup chopped mint leaves
- 1/2 cup of fresh rosemary leaves
- Salt and pepper to taste

Instructions
1. In a large bowl, combine all the ingredients.
2. Knead it with your hands until get a compact mixture.
3. Form the meat mixture into meatballs.
4. Line a platter with parchment paper, place meatballs, cover and refrigerate for 1 hour.
5. If you want you can grill your meatballs, or you can fry them in a frying skillet, 15 minutes in total. Serve hot.

Nutrition information:
Calories: 214 Carbohydrates: 1.5g Proteins: 27g Fat: 10g Fiber: 1,5g

Fried Mustard Mussels
Serves: 4, Preparation: 5 minutes, Cooking: 15 minutes

Ingredients
- 4 Tbsp olive oil
- 2 fresh spring onions, chopped
- 1/2 green pepper, chopped into small pieces
- 1 tsp oregano
- 1 1/2 lbs. mussels with shells, freshly cleaned
- 1 cup water
- 1/4 cup yellow mustard
- Freshly ground pepper to taste
- 2 lemons, juice, zest and slices

Instructions
1. Heat the oil in a large frying pan over medium-high heat.
2. Add chopped onion, pepper, and oregano; sauté for 2-3 minutes.
3. Add the mussels and water; toss the pan and cover.
4. Cook until all mussels opened.
5. Once opened, they are juicy and delicious.
6. Dissolve mustard with little water and pour over mussels. Cook for 1 minute and sprinkle with freshly ground pepper.
7. Serve with lemon juice and lemon zest.

Nutrition information:
Calories: 289 Carbohydrates: 8g Proteins: 22g Fat: 20g Fiber: 3,5g

Fried Sardines with Caper

Serves: 4, Preparation: 10 minutes, Cooking: 5 minutes

Ingredients

- 1 lb canned sardines
- 2 Tbsp wine vinegar
- 1 tsp fresh oregano
- 1/2 cup olive oil
- 1/2 cup caper
- 2 limes sliced

Instructions

1. Place sardines on the plate; sprinkle with the vinegar and oregano.
2. Place sardines in refrigerator for about 30 minutes.
3. Heat the oil in a large frying pan, and fry sardines for 2 minutes per side.
4. Serve sardines on the plate with lime and capers.

Nutrition information:

Calories: 453 Carbohydrates: 2g Proteins: 30g Fat: 42g Fiber: 1g

Grilled Sea Bream with Thyme

Serves: 4, Preparation: 15 minutes, Cooking: 20 minutes

Ingredients

- 2 Sea Bream fish
- 3 Tbsp olive oil
- Salt to taste
- 1 lemon
- 2 tsp of fresh chopped thyme

Instructions

1. Preheat your grill (charcoal, gas, and pellet).
2. Clean fish and rub with the oil, lemon, and the salt and fresh thyme mixture.
3. Grill the fish for 7 - 8 minutes per side.
4. Serve hot.

Nutrition information:

Calories: 315 Carbohydrates: 2.5g Proteins: 42g Fat: 15g Fiber: 1,5g

Grilled Seafood Basket

Serves: 5, Preparation: 10 minutes, Cooking: 1 hour and 10 minutes

Ingredients

- 2 lbs tentacles of octopus
- 1 lb squid
- 2 Tbsp garlic-infused olive oil
- 1 lemon juice fresh
- 1 lemon slices
- Sea salt and pepper
- Capers for serving

Instructions

1. Preheat the grill to 400F.
2. Season the octopus tentacles and squid with the salt.
3. Transfer the seafood on the grill.
4. Turn the octopus every 15 minutes and the squid / threshing once in 25 minutes.
5. Remove the squid after 40 minutes, and the octopus is ready after 1 hour and 10 minutes.
6. Sprinkle with olive oil and serve hot with lemon slices, fresh lemon juice and capers.

Nutrition information:

Calories: 258 Carbohydrates: 1.5g Proteins: 41g Fat: 10g Fiber: 0.2g

Haddock Napolitano (Italian)

Serves: 4, Preparation: 10 minutes, Cooking: 40 minutes

Ingredients

- 1/4 cup of Virgin olive oil
- 2-3 clove of garlic (whole but crushed)
- 1 red hot chili pepper
- 1 tomato, grated
- 1/2 cup of black olives, pitted
- 2 Tbsp of caper
- 2 Tbsp of almonds, chopped
- 1 1/2 lbs. of haddock
- 1 tsp of fresh oregano
- 1 Tbsp of fresh parsley finely chopped

Instructions

1. In a drying pan, heat the olive oil over medium-high heat.
2. Fry the haddock with skin side down for about 2 minutes per side.
3. Remove the fish from the pan, and place on a plate; set aside.
4. Heat the oil in a separate frying skillet, and sauté the garlic for 2 - 3 minutes.
5. Add the hot pepper, grated tomato and the capers; cook and stir for 3 - 4 minutes.
6. Add the almonds, black olives, and gently stir.
7. Cover and cook the sauce for 15 minutes over low heat.
8. Preheat the oven to 360F/180 C.
9. In a greased baking dish, put the pieces of haddock and pour them with the sauce (remove the garlic).
10. Bake for about 10 minutes.
11. Sprinkle fish with oregano, and bake for further 2 minutes.
12. Serve immediately with fresh parsley.

Nutrition information:

Calories: 201 Carbohydrates: 6,5g Proteins: 30g Fat: 6g Fiber: 3g

Mediterranean "Horta" Greens Patties

Serves: 4, Preparation: 15 minutes, Cooking: 5 minutes

Ingredients

- 1 1/2 cup Chervil (fine substitute would be fresh parsley or tarragon)
- 1/2 lb fresh spinach
- 1 fresh onion chopped
- 1 Tbsp mint leaves, freshly chopped
- 2 Tbsp anise
- 1/2 tsp baking powder
- Salt and ground black pepper
- 1 large egg from free-range chickens
- 1/2 cup almond flour
- Oil for frying

Instructions

1. Rinse and chop the chervil and spinach, and put them in a bowl with the remaining ingredients. Knead well the mixture and make small patties.
2. In a large frying skillet, heat the oil and fry patties for 2 minutes per each side.
3. Transfer the patties on a platter lined with kitchen paper. Serve hot.

Nutrition information:

Calories: 152 Carbohydrates: 6g Proteins: 6g Fat: 13g Fiber: 3g

Mediterranean Octopus "Meatballs"

Serves: 6, Preparation: 15 minutes, Cooking: 50 minutes

Ingredients

- 2 lbs octopus cleaned
- 1/4 cup of extra virgin olive oil
- 3 Tbsp chopped spring onion
- 2 Tbsp dill fresh dill finely chopped
- 3 Tbsp fresh parsley finely chopped
- 1/2 cup red wine
- 1 cup water
- 1 bay leaf
- 1 large egg from free-range chickens
- 1 cup almond flour
- Salt and freshly ground pepper to taste
- Olive oil for frying

Instructions

1. Rinse the octopus thoroughly.
2. Heat the olive oil in a pot over medium-high heat.
3. Cover the pot and sauté for 10 minutes, or until changes color (red).
4. Add the wine, water, bay leaf and cover the pot again; bring to boil, and cook for 35 minutes.
5. Allow the octopus to cool and cut into large pieces.
6. Place the octopus in a blender and mince.
7. Pour the octopus into a bowl and add all remaining ingredients.
8. From the mixture make balls.
9. Heat the oil in a frying skillet and fry the octopus balls for 3 - 4 minutes over medium heat.
10. Remove octopus balls into place lined with kitchen paper. Serve warm.

Nutrition information:

Calories: 377 Carbohydrates: 6g Proteins: 29g
Fat: 24g Fiber: 1.5g

Oven Baked Oysters and Mushrooms Frittata

Serves: 6, Preparation: 5 minutes, Cooking: 30 minutes

Ingredients

- 2 cups button mushroom, sliced
- 1/2 cup onion, chopped fine
- 1 Tbsp fresh butter
- 10 oysters, well drained
- 6 eggs from free-range chickens
- 1 cup almond milk
- 1/4 tsp paprika
- 1/4 tsp pepper
- 2 Tbsp cooked, crumbled bacon

Instructions

1. Preheat oven to 400F/200C.
2. Heat the butter in a skillet over medium heat.
3. Sauté mushrooms and onion for 2 - 3 minutes. Drain oysters and add to the mushroom mixture.
4. Cook for 1 - 2 minutes. Remove pan from heat and set aside.
5. In a bowl, beat eggs, almond milk, paprika and pepper.
6. Pour mixture over oyster mixture in skillet, and sprinkle with crumbled bacon.
7. Bake for 20 minutes or until set.
8. Cut into slices and serve.

Nutrition information:

Calories: 136 Carbohydrates: 3g Proteins: 11g
Fat: 10g Fiber: 0.5g

Roasted Asparagus with Garlic and Feta

Serves: 4, Preparation: 15 minutes, Cooking: 25 minutes

Ingredients

- 1 lb of fresh asparagus
- 1/2 cup of olive oil
- 3 cloves garlic
- 1 lemon zest + juice
- 1 Tbsp of dry oregano
- 1 tsp of hot pepper, ground
- 1 tsp salt and ground pepper
- 3/4 cup of feta cheese
- 3 Tbsp of fresh thyme leaves, finely chopped

Instructions

1. Preheat the oven to 400 F/ 200 C.
2. Clean the asparagus by cutting the hard place on its base (it is like wood), peel off from the waist and down.
3. Heat 2 tablespoon of oil in a frying pan over medium heat.
4. Add the garlic, lemon zest, oregano, and ground hot pepper; stir and sauté until the garlic is golden brown.
5. Remove from the heat.
6. In a large bowl put the asparagus with the remaining olive oil, salt, pepper and stir well.
7. Add the garlic mixture from the pan and stir well.
8. Add the asparagus in oiled baking dish, and sprinkle with feta cheese, and with the thyme.
9. Put in the oven, and bake for 10-15 minutes.
10. Remove from the oven, sprinkle with the lemon juice and serve.

Nutrition information:

Calories: 357 Carbohydrates: 8.5g Proteins: 11g Fat: 33.5g Fiber: 5g

Roasted Lamb Chops with Rosemary

Serves: 4, Preparation: 10 minutes, Cooking: 45 minutes

Ingredients

- 1/2 cup of almond flour
- 1 1/2 cup fresh rosemary
- 2 Tbsp of minced garlic
- 2 Tbsp of olive oil
- 1 tsp of yellow mustard
- Salt and ground pepper to taste
- 4 lamb chops

Instructions

1. Preheat the oven to 400 F/ 200.
2. In a deep bowl, combine almond flour, garlic, rosemary, and the salt and pepper.
3. Pour the olive oil and mustard and stir well.
4. Season the lamb chops with the garlic-rosemary mixture.
5. Place the lamb chops in oiled baking dish.
6. Bake for 20 minutes, and then turn chops over, reduce heat to 360F/180C, and bake for further 20 - 25 minutes.
7. Serve hot.

Nutrition information:

Calories: 391 Carbohydrates: 4g Proteins: 28g Fat: 39g Fiber: 02g

Spicy Seafood "Meatballs"

Serves: 6, Preparation: 15 minutes, Cooking: 10 minutes

Ingredients
- 1 lb octopus, ground
- 1 lb squid, ground
- 3 Tbsp ground almonds
- 1 bunch of parsley finely chopped
- 2 -3 drops of hot pepper sauce
- Salt and freshly ground pepper
- 1 cup olive oil for frying
- 2 Lemon slices and juice

Instructions
1. Cut octopus and squid into small pieces and blend in food processor or blender until minced well.
2. Transfer the minced seafood into bowl.
3. Add ground almonds, chopped parsley, red hot sauce, and little salt and pepper; knead the mixture until combine well.
4. Cover and refrigerate for 1 hour.
5. Remove the seafood mixture from the fridge and make balls.
6. Heat the oil in a frying skillet pan.
7. Fry your seafood "meatballs" until golden from one side.
8. Flip and fry from the other side for 1 minutes.
9. Drain on a kitchen pepper and serve immediately.

Nutrition information:
Calories: 489 Carbohydrates: 6g Proteins: 35g Fat: 40g Fiber: 0.5g

Zucchini with Scrambled Eggs

Serves: 4, Preparation: 10 minutes, Cooking: 10 minutes

Ingredients
- 6 medium-sized zucchini
- 2 green onions chopped
- 10 fresh eggs from free-range chickens
- Sea salt to taste
- 1/4 cup olive oil

Instructions
1. Rinse and peel zucchini; cut into thin slices and sprinkle with little salt.
2. Heat the oil in a skillet over medium heat.
3. Sauté onions with a pinch of salt; add zucchini slices and sauté for 2 - 3 minutes, gently stir.
4. In a bowl, whisk eggs and pour over garlic and zucchini.
5. Cook the omelet 2 minutes, and then use the spatula to turn omelet; cook for one minute and remove from the heat.
6. Serve hot.

Nutrition information:
Calories: 322 Carbohydrates: 6g Proteins: 16g Fat: 25g Fiber: 1g

Mexican

"Hot" Frutilla Ice Cream
Serves: 8, Preparation: 10 minutes, Cooking: 15 minutes

Instructions
- 1 lb strawberries, fresh or frozen
- 1 1/2 cups stevia powdered sweetener
- 2 Tbsp water
- 2 cups whipped cream
- 1/2 tsp cayenne pepper powder
- 1 Tbsp pure vanilla extract
- chopped almonds for decoration

Instructions
1. Combine the strawberries, stevia sweetener and 2 tablespoon of water in a saucepan.
2. Heat over medium heat and bring to a boil.
3. Reduce heat to low and stir for 3 - 4 minutes.
4. Remove from heat and add whipped cream; stir with spatula.
5. Add hot pepper powder and stir well.
6. Finally, pour the vanilla extract and give a good stir; set aside to cool.
7. Place the mixture in a freezer-safe bowl and freeze for 4 hours or overnight.
8. Let the ice cream at room temperature for 10 - 15 minutes before serving.
9. Serve decorated with chopped almonds.

Nutrition information:
Calories: 145 Carbohydrates: 5g Proteins: 10g Fat: 13g Fiber: 1,5g

Albóndigas (Keto Adaption)
Serves: 7, Preparation: 15 minutes, Cooking: 25 minutes

Ingredients
- 1 lb of ground beef
- 1/2 lb of minced pork
- 2 cloves garlic
- 3 eggs from free-range chickens
- 1 Tbsp of cumin, rosemary, thyme mixture
- 2 - 3 Tbsp of almond flour
- Salt and pepper to taste
- Olive oil for frying

SAUCE
- 2 - 3 Tbsp of olive oil
- 3 cloves of garlic sliced
- 2 ripe tomatoes, peeled
- Salt and black pepper to taste
- 1/2 cup of bone broth
- Fresh thyme finely chopped
- Salt and ground black pepper to taste

Instructions
1. In a bowl, add pork and beef meat, garlic, eggs, the salt and pepper and spices.
2. Knead with your hands to combine well.
3. Oil your hands, and make meatballs from dough.
4. Roll each meatball in almond flour and place on a plate.
5. Cover the plate with plastic membrane and refrigerate meatballs.
6. Make a sauce: Heat the oil in a deep pan, and sauté the garlic with a pinch of salt.
7. Add tomato pulp and season with the salt and pepper; stir with wooden spoon.
8. Add thyme and bone broth and stir.
9. Reduce heat and cook your sauce covered over low heat for 8 - 10 minutes.
10. In a meantime, fry your meatballs just 2 - 3 minutes to get a color.
11. Add meatballs in a sauce and cook for 10 minutes.
12. Serve hot.

Nutrition information:
Calories: 443 Carbohydrates: 5g Proteins: 22g Fat: 38g Fiber: 1,5g

Baked Mexican Meatballs with Anejo Cheese
Serves: 6, Preparation: 5 minutes, Cooking: 30 minutes

Ingredients
- 1 1/2 lb ground beef
- 1 onion, chopped fine
- 2 cloves garlic
- 1 cup shredded Anejo cheese (or Parmesan, Cotija)
- 1 Tbsp fresh butter
- 1 ¼ tsp chili powder
- 1 tsp ground coriander
- 1 ¼ tsp of ground cumin
- 2 eggs
- Sea salt and freshly ground pepper to taste

Instructions
1. Preheat oven to 350 degrees F/ 180 C.
2. Heat the butter in a frying pan and sauté onions and garlic for 3 minutes until translucent; season with the salt, stir and set aside.
3. In a bowl, whisk the eggs with a pinch of salt. Add the spices, salt, and pepper and stir.
4. Add onions and grated Parmesan, Cotija cheese; stir well.
5. Add beef and combine until all ingredients are well combined.
6. Make a meatballs and place on oiled baking pan.
7. Bake for 18 - 20 minutes. Serve hot.

Nutrition information:
Calories: 424 Carbohydrates: 3g Proteins: 27g Fat: 33g Fiber: 1g

Cold Mexican Coffee with Cinnamon
Serves: 4, Preparation: 10 minutes

Ingredients
- 4 cups espresso-style coffee
- 3/4 cup whipped cream
- 1 Tbsp liquid stevia (or to taste)
- 2 Tbsp of cocoa powder, unsweetened
- 1 tsp ground cinnamon
- 1/2 cup ice cubes crushed

Instructions
1. Combine all ingredients in your blender; blend for 30 - 45 seconds.
2. Pour coffee into cups, sprinkle with cinnamon and serve.

Nutrition information:
Calories: 117 Carbohydrates: 3g Proteins: 2g Fat: 12g Fiber: 1,5g

Enchiladas - Keto Version
Serves: 4, Preparation: 10 minutes, Cooking: 50 minutes

Ingredients
- 1/4 cup of olive oil
- 1 onion finely chopped
- 1 chili pepper finely chopped
- 2 cloves of garlic sliced
- 1 small tomato finely chopped
- 2 - 3 Tbsp of fresh water
- 1 chicken fillet boneless
- 1 green pepper finely chopped
- 2 Tbsp of grated Gouda cheese
- 2 Tbsp of grated mozzarella cheese
- Salt and ground black pepper to taste

Instructions
1. Heat the oil over medium heat, and sauté the onion, chili pepper, garlic and the tomato for 3 minutes.
2. Season with the salt and pepper and remove from heat.
3. Transfer the chili pepper mixture in a blender and pour little water; blend for 20 - 30 seconds.
4. Sprinkle generously the salt and pepper over chicken fillet,
5. Brush the chicken filet with chill mixture, wrap in plastic membrane and marinate for 3 hours in the refrigerator.
6. Preheat your oven to 360 F/180 C.
7. Place marinated chicken in oiled baking dish.
8. Sprinkle the green pepper over chicken, place in oven and bake for 25 minutes.
9. Remove chicken from the oven and sprinkle with grated mozzarella and Gouda cheese.
10. Bake for further 10 - 15 minutes or until cheese melt.
11. Serve hot.

Nutrition information:
Calories: 217 Carbohydrates: 6g Proteins: 7g Fat: 18g Fiber: 1.5g

Fajitas
Serves: 4, Preparation: 10 minutes, Cooking: 15 minutes

Ingredients
- 1 1/2 lbs. pork fillet cut into thin strips
- 1 tsp of garlic powder
- 1 tsp of red hot pepper
- 1 tsp of cumin
- 2 - 3 Tbsp of tequila
- 1/4 cup of olive oil
- 1 red pepper chopped
- 1 green pepper finely chopped
- 2 onions chopped
- 2 Tbsp of ketchup
- 2 Tbsp of mustard
- Salt and ground black pepper

Instructions
1. Combine pork with garlic powder, red hot pepper, cumin and tequila; refrigerate for one hour to marinate.
2. Heat the oil in a large frying skillet and sauté pork along with peppers and onion; season with the salt and pepper and cook for 3 - 4 minutes stirring from time to time.
3. Add the ketchup and mustard and stir well.
4. Cover and simmer on low heat for 5 - 7 minutes. Serve hot.

Nutrition information:
Calories: 587 Carbohydrates: 7g Proteins: 15g Fat: 54g Fiber: 2g

Keto Guacamole Dip

Serves: 4, Preparation: 15 minutes

Instructions

- 2 ripe avocados cut in small cubes
- 1 small onion, chopped
- 1 ½ Tbsp of lime, juice
- Zest from 1 lime
- 3 Tbsp of olive oil
- 4 - 5 sprigs of fresh cilantro leaves
- 2 red hot peppers, stems and seeds removed, sliced
- Coarse salt to taste
- 1/4 cup of fresh chopped coriander for serving (optional)

Instructions

1. Peel avocados and remove the pit; cut into small cubes.
2. Dump all ingredients in your food processor or into high-speed blender.
3. Blend until combined well or for about 30 - 45 seconds.
4. Taste and adjust salt and seasonings to taste.
5. Place in a glass bowl, sprinkle with coriander and refrigerate until serving.

Nutrition information:

Calories: 247 Carbohydrates: 8g Proteins: 10g Fat: 24g Fiber: 6g

Keto Serrano Avocado Dip

Serves: 8, Preparation: 15 minutes

Ingredients

- 4 ripe avocados
- Fresh juice of 2 limes
- 2 cloves of garlic finely chopped
- 1 small tomato cut into cubes
- 1 Serrano chili pepper sliced
- Salt and ground black pepper to taste
- 2 Tbsp of mustard
- 3 Tbsp of grated parmesan cheese

Instructions

1. Cut avocados in the middle, remove the stalk and, with a spoon, remove the flesh and place it in a bowl.
2. With a fork, melt the avocado, add the lime juice, garlic, salt, pepper, onion, tomato, and chili pepper; mix gently.
3. Refrigerate in a glass bowl for at least one hour. Serve.

Nutrition information:

Calories: 159 Carbohydrates: 7g Proteins: 6g Fat: 16g Fiber: 0.2g

Mexican Basil Avocado Pops

Serves: 6, Preparation: 15 minutes

Ingredients

- 2 avocados
- 1/4 can stevia natural sweetener or to taste
- 2 lemons, juice
- 3 cup of coconut milk
- 1 1/4 cup of water
- 20 fresh basil leaves finely chopped

Instructions

1. Place all ingredients in your fast-speed blender.
2. Blend until smooth or for about 30 - 45 seconds.
3. Pour the avocado mixture in Popsicle molds and insert wooden sticks in every mold.
4. Freeze until completely frozen. Serve and enjoy!

Nutrition information:

Calories: 162 Carbohydrates: 6.5g Proteins: 9g Fat: 17g Fiber: 4g

Spicy Coconut - Pork Tenderloin Stew

Serves: 4, Preparation: 10 minutes, Cooking: 25 minutes

Ingredients

- 1 1/2 lbs pork tenderloin
- Salt and ground pepper to taste
- 1 Tbsp chili powder or to taste
- 2 Tbsp olive oil
- 3 fresh onions finely chopped
- 1 onion finely chopped
- 1 cup of red wine
- 1/2 cup of coconut water (optional)

Instructions

1. Season the pork with the salt and a chili powder, and refrigerate for 3 - 4 hours.
2. When done, remove meat from the fridge.
3. Heat the oil in a frying pan and sauté the onion and fresh onion for 3 -4 minutes; stir.
4. Add marinated pork and sauté for 3 minutes; stir.
5. Pour the red wine and stir.
6. Cover and cook on low heat for about 15 minutes.
7. Pour the coconut water, stir and remove from heat.
8. Serve immediately.

Nutrition information:

Calories: 463 Carbohydrates: 8g Proteins: 52g Fat: 21g Fiber: 3g

Asian

Bacon Cooked in a Red Onion Peels (Siberia, Russia)
Serves: 6, Preparation: 5 minutes, Cooking: 25 minutes

Ingredients
- 2 cloves of garlic sliced
- Red onion peel (from 5 - 6 onions)
- About 1/2 cup of salt
- 4 bay leaves crumbled
- 4 whole cloves
- 6 grains of black pepper
- Water for cooking
- 2 lbs of bacon

Instructions
1. In a large pot full of salted water, boil the garlic, red onion peel, bay leaves, cloves, and black pepper for 10 minutes.
2. Add the bacon, cover and boil for 10 - 12 minutes.
3. Remove from the heat and let it rest 15 minutes (uncovered).
4. Remove the bacon and wrap in aluminum foil; refrigerate for 1 hour.
5. Remove from the fridge, slice and serve.

Nutrition information:
Calories: 584 Carbohydrates: 3g Proteins: 18g Fat: 22g Fiber: 2g

Baked Creamy Chicken with Vodka (Russia)
Serves: 7, Preparation: 15 minutes, Cooking: 40 minutes

Ingredients
- 4 chicken fillets, boneless
- 2 tsp of allspice
- 1/4 cup of olive oil, softened
- 1 clove of garlic, crushed
- 1 spring onion, chopped
- 2 Tbsp of vodka
- 1/2 cup of water
- 1 Tbsp fresh tomato, grated
- Salt and ground pepper to taste
- 1 cup cream
- 1/2 cup of goat cheese, softened
- 1 Tbsp of fresh parsley, chopped

Instructions
1. Season the chicken with allspice, and with the salt and pepper.
2. Heat the oil in a large frying skillet over high-moderate heat.
3. Sauté the chicken just until get nice golden color.
4. Remove the chicken from the skillet and place in a greased baking dish.
5. Preheat the oven to 360F/180C.
6. In a same frying skillet add little oil and sauté the onion and garlic with a pinch of salt for 3 - 4 minutes.
7. Add water, tomato pulp, cream goat cheese, and stir for 2 - 3 minutes over medium heat; stir frequently.
8. Remove the sauce from heat and pour vodka; stir well.
9. Pour the sauce over the chicken evenly.
10. Place in oven and bake for 30 minutes.
11. Serve hot with chopped parsley.

Nutrition information:
Calories: 470 Carbohydrates: 2.5g Proteins: 38g Fat: 33g Fiber: 0.3g

Frying Turmeric Salmon

Serves: 4, Preparation: 10 minutes, Cooking: 15 minutes

Ingredients

- 2 salmon fillets without skin
- 2 Tbsp olive oil
- 1 tsp of turmeric
- 1/2 tsp of smoked paprika
- 1/4 tsp Sea salt and black pepper, freshly ground
- 1 Tbsp coconut aminos (from coconut sap)
- 1 lemon, fresh juice

Instructions

1. Rinse and pat dry salmon on absorb paper.
2. Rub each fillet generously with salt, ground pepper, smoked paprika, turmeric
3. Heat a large frying pan over medium heat.
4. Fry the salmon fillets on both sides until golden brown, 4-5 minutes per side.
5. Remove salmon from the heat, and sprinkle with coconut aminos sauce, and drizzle with lemon juice. Serve.

Nutrition information:

Calories: 347 Carbohydrates: 1.5g Proteins: 40g Fat: 20g Fiber: 0.2g

Keto "Peking" Duck

Serves: 4, Preparation: 10 minutes, Cooking: 35 minutes

Ingredients

- 1/4 cup duck or chicken fat
- 3 scallions (only green parts) finely chopped
- 2 lb duck breasts, boneless
- 1 tsp ground paprika
- 1/2 cup water
- 1 tsp fresh ginger grated
- 1/2 tsp five spice powder
- 1/4 tsp ground nutmeg
- 2 whole Star Anise
- Salt and freshly ground pepper to taste

Instructions

1. Preheat the oven to 375 degrees F/190 C.
2. Rinse and pat dry the chicken breast; season with the salt and paprika.
3. Heat the duck or chicken fat in frying skillet, and sauté scallions with little salt for 5 - 6 minutes.
4. Add the duck breast, and sauté for 5 minutes; add water and spices and stir well.
5. Transfer the duck mixture to the oven and bake for 15 - 20 minutes.
6. Remove from the oven, cover and let sit for 15 minutes before serving.

Nutrition information:

Calories: 345 Carbohydrates: 2g Proteins: 45.5g Fat: 21g Fiber: 1g

Roasted Sour Duck with Horseradish & Ginger

Serves: 8, Preparation: 15 minutes, Cooking: 1 hour and 15 minutes

Ingredients

- 1 wild duck (about 4 - 5 lbs)
- Salt and ground pepper to taste
- 1 tsp of cumin
- 1 tsp of marjoram
- 1 tsp of horseradish
- 1 tsp of ground ginger
- 1 tsp of allspice
- 1 tsp of stevia granulated sweetener
- 1 Tbsp duck fat

Instructions

1. Combine cumin, marjoram, horse radish, ginger, allspice, stevia sweetener in a bowl.
2. Rinse and clean duck from fat inside, and season with the salt and pepper.
3. Rub the duck generously with the spice mixture inside and outside.
4. Wrap the duck in a foil.
5. On the stove place a large pot half-filled with water.
6. Take the colander in a pot and place the duck.
7. Bring to boil, and then cook the duck for 55 minutes.
8. Preheat the oven to 380F/190C.
9. Remove the duck from the foil, and cut in half.
10. Unwrap and place the duck in greased baking dish.
11. Bake for 15 -20 minutes.
12. Remove from oven and let it cool for 10 minutes. Serve.

Nutrition information:

Calories: 595 Carbohydrates: 0.5g Proteins: 54.5g Fat: 48g Fiber: 0.2g

Sautéed Duck Gizzards with Spices

Serves: 4, Preparation: 5 minutes, Cooking: 1 hour and 40 minutes

Ingredients

- 1 lb of duck gizzards
- 1/2 cup of duck fat (or lark)
- 4 leeks finely chopped
- 1 tsp fresh ginger grated
- 1/2 tsp cumin grated
- 1/2 tsp dry mustard
- 1/2 tsp chili powder
- 1/4 tsp turmeric ground
- Salt and ground pepper to taste
- Water

Instructions

1. Rinse the gizzards, pat dry and cut in pieces. In a frying pan add 1 of tablespoon coconut oil and add the gizzards.
2. Heat the fat in a wok or frying skillet over high heat; sauté gizzards with the salt and pepper.
3. Add chopped gizzards and sauté for 5 minutes.
4. Add all spices and pour water; stir well. Pour enough water to cover gizzards.
5. Cover and cook for 1 1/2 hours (or until done) over medium-low heat.
6. Serve hot.

Nutrition information:

Calories: 321 Carbohydrates: 7.5g Proteins: 21g Fat: 22g Fiber: 1.5g

Shashimi Coriander and Sesame Breaded Salmon

Serves: 4, Preparation: 15 minutes, Cooking: 10 minutes

Ingredients

- 1 bunch of fresh coriander, finely chopped
- 1 1/2 lb of fresh salmon (filleted, boneless)
- 1/4 cup white sesame
- 1/4 cup black sesame
- 2 Tbsp of coconut aminos
- 2 Tbsp of olive oil
- Lime juice

Instructions

1. Finely chop fresh coriander and place in a bowl.
2. Cut the salmon into 4 - 5 pieces and roll in coriander covering all sides.
3. Roll the salmon in a sesame seeds mixture.
4. Heat the oil in a frying skillet and fry the salmon for 7 - 10 minutes or until golden brown.
5. Remove salmon on a plate with absorbent paper.
6. Place on a serving plate, pour coconut aminos, sprinkle with lime juice and serve.

Nutrition information:

Calories: 409 Carbohydrates: 3g Proteins: 39g Fat: 26.5g Fiber: 1.2g

Snails in Parsley Sauce

Serves: 4, Preparation: 15 minutes, Cooking: 20 minutes

Ingredients

- 2 Tbsp of olive oil
- 2 spring onions (finely chopped)
- 1 green pepper, chopped into small pieces
- 3 clove garlic
- 1 grated tomato
- 1 lb snails (canned)
- 1/2 cup red wine
- 1/2 cup water
- 1 bunch of parsley finely chopped
- 1/2 cup lemon juice (freshly squeezed)
- Coarse salt and freshly ground black pepper

Instructions

1. Heat the oil in a frying pan, sauté spring onions, garlic and green pepper. Add grated tomato and pour the wine and water; stir.
2. Add snails and chopped parsley; stir.
3. Season salt and pepper, and pour the wine; stir.
4. Cover and cook for about 15-20 minutes over the low heat.
5. Serve with lemon juice.

Nutrition information:

Calories: 141 Carbohydrates: 5g Proteins: 21g Fat: 21g Fiber: 1.5g

Spicy Beef with Nuts

Serves: 6, Preparation: 10 minutes, Cooking: 30 minutes

Ingredients

- 2 lbs of beef fillets cut into stips
- 2 scallions finely chopped
- 2 cloves of garlic minced
- 2 green peppers cut into thin strips
- 3 Tbsp almonds chopped
- 1/2 cup of coconut aminos
- 1 cup of beef broth
- 3 Tbsp of sesame oil
- 1 tsp cumin
- 1 tsp cinnamon
- 1 tsp coriander
- 1 tsp allspice
- 1/2 cup of hot water
- Salt and ground black pepper

Instructions

1. Cut the beef into thin strips.
2. In a large skillet or wok, heat sesame oil.
3. Add beef strips and cook, stirring, just for 2 - 3 minutes.
4. Transfer beef on a plate and set aside.
5. In a same skillet or wok heat the oil and sauté scallions, garlic, pepper and ground almonds; season with the salt and pepper and stir for 3 - 4 minutes.
6. Add beef, bone broth, coconut aminos, spices, water, the salt and pepper, and bring to boil.
7. Reduce heat to moderate-low, cover and cook for 20 - 25 minutes; stir occasionally.
8. Serve hot.

Nutrition information:

Calories: 437 Carbohydrates: 4g Proteins: 37g Fat: 32g Fiber: 2g

Spicy Chicken in Pakistani Way

Serves: 4, Preparation: 10 minutes, Cooking: 25 minutes

Ingredients

- 3 Tbsp of olive oil
- 1 onion finely chopped
- 1 clove of garlic
- 1 tsp of freshly ground ginger
- 2 - 3 Tbsp of yogurt
- 1 tsp of ground coriander
- 1 -1 tsp chili powder
- 1 tsp of turmeric
- 3 Tbsp of ground mustard
- Salt to taste
- 1/2 cup water
- 1 lb chicken boneless cut in slices
- 1 tsp garam masala
- 10 grains of black pepper
- 4 - 6 whole cloves
- Fresh chopped parsley to taste

Instructions

1. Heat the oil in a wok or in a frying skillet and sauté the onion and garlic with a pinch of salt.
2. Add the ginger, yogurt, coriander, chili, curcuma and ground mustard, salt and water; stir to combine well, and cook for 2 - 3 minutes.
3. Add sliced chicken and stir for 2 minutes.
4. Add the remaining ingredients, lower heat to moderate-low, and cook for 15 - 17 minutes. Serve hot with chopped parsley.

Nutrition information:

Calories: 134 Carbohydrates: 4g Proteins: 6g Fat: 13g Fiber: 1.5g

Middle Eastern

Anchovies with Fig Leaves
Serves: 6, Preparation: 15 minutes, Cooking: 6 minutes

Ingredients
- 1 Tbsp of red ground paprika
- Salt and ground pepper to taste
- Juice of 1 lemon
- 1/2 cup olive oil for marinade
- 2 lbs of anchovies
- 1 1/4 cups of almond flour
- 5 - 6 large fig leaves
- 1 cup olive oil for frying

Instructions
1. Combine the paprika, salt, pepper, lemon juice and olive oil; stir well.
2. Place anchovies in a large container and pour marinade over the fish evenly.
3. Cover the container and place in fridge for 1 hour.
4. Rinse and pat dry the fig leaves.
5. Remove anchovies from marinade, and roll each fish in almond flour.
6. Heat the oil in a frying skillet and place the anchovies.
7. Cover fish with fig leaves.
8. Cook anchovies for 2 - 3 minutes per side.
9. Flip fish once, one by one, and cove again with fig leaves.
10. Remove fig leaves and serve immediately.

Nutrition information:
Calories: 443 Carbohydrates: 1.5g Proteins: 1g Fat: 54g Fiber: 0.5g

Arab Fattoush Salad
Serves: 8, Preparation: 15 minutes

Ingredients
- 1 grated tomato (medium)
- 1/4 cup almonds chopped
- 1 medium hot pepper
- 1 cucumber (medium)
- 1/2 lettuce head (medium)
- 1 cup fresh onions slices
- 2 Tbsp fresh parsley
- 1 tsp fresh mint

Dressing
- 1 Tbsp lemon juice fresh
- 4 Tbsp olive oil
- Salt and black pepper to taste
- 1 tsp of cumin

Instructions
1. Rinse the tomato and cut into cubes.
2. Rinse, peel and cut the cucumber in cubes.
3. Clean the pepper from the seeds and cut into cubes.
4. Finely chop the onions, parsley and mint.
5. Finally, clean the leaves of lettuce from any dirt and chop.
6. Add all ingredients in a large salad bowl and stir.
7. Beat the olive oil with the lemon juice, cumin, and salt and pepper to taste.
8. Pour the salad with the sauce, toss to combine well, cover and refrigerate one hour before serving.

Nutrition information:
Calories: 122 Carbohydrates: 7g Proteins: 3g Fat: 10g Fiber: 2.5g

Arabian Baba Ghanoush Eggplant Salad

Serves: 6, Preparation: 15 minutes, Cooking: 45 minutes

Ingredients

- 1 large eggplant
- 4 cloves of garlic unpeeled
- 2 Tbsp of lemon juice
- 3 Tbsp of tahini or ground sesame seeds
- 1/2 tsp of ground cumin
- 1/4 tsp of salt or to taste
- Olive oil for serving
- Fresh parsley or coriander for serving
- Ground red paprika for serving

Instructions

1. Preheat oven to 400 F/200 C.
2. Pick the eggplant with a fork; place it on a baking sheet along with the garlic.
3. Bake the eggplant for 45 minutes, but remove after 30 minutes, peal them and continue to bake.
4. When the eggplant is ready, remove it from the oven and leave it for 10 minutes to cool.
5. Add the eggplant, garlic and tahini in a food processor and beat very well.
6. Transfer the eggplant mixture to a bow, and season with the salt the pepper, cumin, and fresh lemon juice; stir well.
7. Serve with olive oil and ground red paprika.

Nutrition information:

Calories: 106 Carbohydrates: 3g Proteins: 3g Fat: 10g Fiber: 3.5g

Baked Mustard-Almond Breaded Fillet

Serves: 4, Preparation: 5 minutes, Cooking: 55 - 65 minutes

Ingredients

- 2 lbs of beef fillet cleaned
- Salt and black ground pepper
- 2 - 3 Tbsp of ground mustard seeds
- 1 Tbsp of yellow mustard
- 1 tsp turmeric powder
- 4 Tbsp of almond flour
- 1/2 cup of olive oil

Instructions

1. Season your fillet with the salt and pepper, mustard powder, yellow mustard, oil and sprinkle with turmeric.
2. Roll each fillet in almond flour, place on a plate and refrigerate for one hour.
3. Preheat the oven to 400 F/200 C.
4. Place the fillet in oiled baking pan and bake for about 55 - 65 minutes.
5. Remove from the oven, and let sit for 10 minutes. Serve hot.

Nutrition information:

Calories: 612 Carbohydrates: 1.5g Proteins: 41g Fat: 59g Fiber: 0.6g

Cyprian Lamb Riffi

Serves: 6, Preparation: 10 minutes, Cooking: 50 - 60 minutes

Ingredients

- 1/2 cup of olive oil
- 3 lbs of lamb chops
- 1 Tbsp salt or to taste
- 1 cup of water
- 4 bay leaves
- 2 cloves of crushed garlic
- 1 lemon (the juice)

Instructions

1. Heat the oil in the saucepan over medium-high heat.
2. Season the lamb chops with the salt and brown evenly on all side.
3. Pour the water and place the bay leaves and garlic between the lamb chops.
4. Reduce heat to low, and cook covered for 40 - 45 minutes.
5. Check if your lamb is well cocked, and if not, pour some boiling water and cook for further 10 - 15 minutes.
6. Remove the lamb chops on a serving platter. Serve hot with fresh lemon juice.

Nutrition information:

Calories: 588 Carbohydrates: 1.5g Proteins: 42g Fat: 49g Fiber: 0.1g

Egyptian Spinach with Coriander Sauce

Serves: 4, Preparation: 10 minutes, Cooking: 20 minutes

Ingredients

- 3/4 lb fresh spinach
- 2 Tbsp of olive oil
- 1 onion finely chopped
- 1 leek finely chopped
- 3 cloves garlic
- 3 cup of water
- 4 Tbsp of grated tomato
- 1 cup fresh coriander finely chopped
- 1 Tbsp of fresh butter
- Salt and ground pepper to taste

Instructions

1. Put the spinach in boiled salted water and cook for 3 to 5 minutes.
2. Remove from heat and place in colander.
3. In a frying skillet heat the oil, add the onion garlic and leek; sauté for 2-3 minutes.
4. Pour water and grated tomato, coriander, the salt and pepper to taste; stir.
5. Transfer spinach, stir, cover and cook for 6 - 8 minutes over low heat.
6. Transfer the spinach mixture to your high-fast blender, add butter and blend for 30 seconds.
7. Taste and adjust salt and pepper. Serve.

Nutrition information:

Calories: 145 Carbohydrates: 5.5g Proteins: 5g Fat: 11g Fiber: 4g

Grilled Spicy Kebabs

Serves: 4, Preparation: 10 minutes, Cooking: 10 minutes

Ingredients

- 1 lb of minced beef and lamb (or only beef)
- 1 small onion finely chopped
- 2 cloves of garlic minced
- 2 Tbsp of fresh parsley
- 2 Tbsp of fresh mint
- 1 tsp of cumin
- 1 tsp of ground sweet paprika
- 1 tsp of vinegar
- 1 Tbsp of cold water
- 1 Tbsp of sesame oil
- 1 pinch of nutmeg
- 1 pinch of cayenne pepper
- Salt and freshly ground pepper
- Fresh chopped parsley for garnish

Instructions

1. In a bowl, add all ingredients from the list above and knead vigorously for 5-7 minutes.
2. Cover the bowl with a plastic membrane and refrigerate for 2 hours.
3. Take a small amount of minced meat to our palm and stab it on a skewer.
4. Place on a grill and cook for 3-4 minutes on each side.
5. Garnish with chopped parsley. Serve with yogurt or tzatziki.

Nutrition information:

Calories: 348 Carbohydrates: 4g Proteins: 21g Fat: 27g Fiber: 0.6g

Halloumi with Basil Sauce

Serves: 4, Preparation: 10 minutes, Cooking: 5 minutes

Ingredients

- 1 lb Halloumi cheese cut into sticks
- Basil sauce
- 1 1/2 or fresh basil leaves
- 1 cup of olive oil
- 1 tsp of ground almonds
- 2 cloves of garlic
- 1/4 cup grated parmesan

Instructions

1. Fry the halloumi sticks in a skillet for 1 to 2 minutes. Remove from heat and set aside.

Basil sauce

1. Place all the ingredients in the blender and blend unttil the mixture is completely smooth.
2. Serve halloumi stick with basil sauce and enjoy!

Nutrition information:

Calories: 668 Carbohydrates: 3g Proteins: 27g Fat: 64g Fiber: 0.4g

Keto Lahmajoun Dish

Serves: 4, Preparation: 10 minutes, Cooking: 20 minutes

Ingredients

- 3/4 lb ground beef
- 2 Tbsp of olive oil
- 1 tomato peeled and grated
- 3 Tbsp of tomato juice, unsweetened
- 1 spring onion finely chopped
- 2 cloves of garlic chopped
- Pinch of red hot pepper
- 1 Tbsp of cumin
- 1 tsp of ground sweet paprika
- 1/2 bunch of parsley finely chopped
- 2 Tbsp of fresh mint finely chopped
- Salt and ground pepper to taste
- Yogurt for serving

Instructions

1. In a large frying skillet heat the olive oil.
2. Sauté the ground beef with a pinch of salt until it changes a color.
3. Add the onion, garlic and season with cumin, paprika and chili.
4. Continue the sauté for one minute and add the tomato and tomato juice.
5. Season the salt the pepper, stir, and cover; let simmer for about 15 minutes.
6. Finally, add fresh parsley and mint and stir.
7. Serve hot with Greek yogurt.

Nutrition information:

Calories: 302 Carbohydrates: 3g Proteins: 25g Fat: 16g Fiber: 1g

Mousahan Chicken

Serves: 6, Preparation: 10 minutes, Cooking: 45 minutes

Ingredients

- 3 lbs of chicken
- 2 small onions finely chopped
- 1/2 cup of olive oil
- 1/2 cup of dry sumac spice (or lemon zest)
- 1/2 Tbsp of spices mix (cloves, basil, thyme)
- 10 cardamom seeds
- 3 bay leaves
- 1 cinnamon stick
- Salt and ground black pepper to taste

Instructions

1. Cut the chicken into 4 pieces, and season generously with the salt.
2. Place the chicken in a pot, and add water until totally covered.
3. Add all remaining ingredient and simmer for about 25 minutes over low heat.
4. Preheat the oven to 360F/180 C.
5. Remove the chicken from the saucepan and lay in an oiled baking dish.
6. Sprinkle with the salt and pepper, and add little sumac; bake for about 20 minutes. Serve hot.

Nutrition information:

Calories: 217 Carbohydrates: 6g Proteins: 8g Fat: 20g Fiber: 2.5g

Sardines Saganaki

Serves: 4, Preparation: 10 minutes, Cooking: 10 - 12 minutes

Ingredients

- 2 lbs fresh sardines cleaned
- 2 Tbsp of mustard
- Juice of 3 large lemons
- 1/4 cup of olive oil
- 2 - 3 Tbsp of water
- 4 cloves garlic
- 1 hot pepper finely chopped
- Salt to taste
- 1 Tbsp fresh chopped parsley

Instructions

1. Season sardines with the salt; set aside.
2. In a bowl, beat the mustard with the lemon juice; set aside.
3. Cut the garlic and the hot pepper into small pieces.
4. Heat the oil in a frying skillet and sauté garlic and hot pepper with a pinch of salt.
5. Add sardines and water; toss the skillet to combine well.
6. Cover and cook (without stirring) for 10 minutes over medium-low heat.
7. Add the mustard-lemon juice mixture, shaking the pan gently.
8. Put the sardines on a platter, sprinkle with chopped parsley and serve.

Nutrition information:
Calories: 140 Carbohydrates: 1.5g Proteins: 4g Fat: 15g Fiber: 0.5g

Sephardic Eggs Haminados

Serves: 10, Preparation: 10 minutes, Cooking: 15 minutes

Ingredients

- 20 eggs from free-range chickens
- Onion peels
- 1 cup of vegetable oil
- Salt and ground pepper to taste
- 4 cups of water

Instructions

1. In a saucepan pour water, salt and pepper, oil and add onion peels.
2. Add eggs in saucepan and cover with onion peels.
3. Cook on medium heat for 15 minutes.
4. Remove from heat, cover and let sit for 2 hours.
5. Rinse eggs, peel and place on a platter. Serve.

Nutrition information:
Calories: 239 Carbohydrates: 0.8g Proteins: 13g Fat: 21g Fiber: 0.05g

Shakshuka - Baked Eggs in Sauce (Keto version)
Serves: 6, Preparation: 5 minutes, Cooking: 25 minutes

Ingredients

- 1/4 cup of olive oil
- 2 green onions, thinly sliced
- 1 bell pepper, seeded and thinly sliced
- 2 - 3 clove garlic, thinly sliced
- Pinch of cayenne, or to taste
- 1 tsp ground cumin
- 2 tomatoes, peeled and coarsely chopped
- Salt and ground pepper to taste
- 6 large eggs from free-range chickens
- 1 1/2 cup of feta cheese, crumbled
- Fresh cilantro and basil leaves finely chopped, for serving

Instructions

1. Preheat oven to 400 F/200 C.
2. Heat the oil in a large heat-proof skillet over medium heat.
3. Sauté the onion and pepper with the pinch of salt for 3 -4 minutes; stir occasionally.
4. Add the garlic, cayenne and cumin and stir for further 2 minutes.
5. Add the tomato and stir for 6 - 8 minutes until mixture has thickened.
6. Finally, add crumbled feta cheese and stir.
7. Crack the eggs into skillet, one by one, and sprinkle with pinch of salt and pepper.
8. Place skillet to oven and bake for 8 minutes or until eggs are set.
9. Remove skillet from oven, sprinkle with fresh cilantro and basil and serve.

Nutrition information:
Calories: 402 Carbohydrates: 6.5g Proteins: 19g Fat: 33g Fiber: 2g

Shish Taouk - Lebanese Marinated Chicken
Serves: 4, Preparation: 10 minutes, Cooking: 40 minutes

Ingredients

- 2 lbs chicken breast cut in cubes

For the marinade:

- 1/2 cup fresh tomato juice
- 2 Tbsp mayonnaise
- 1 Tbsp of olive oil
- 1 - 2 fresh lemon juice
- 1 tsp garlic powder
- 1 tsp fresh thyme
- Salt and black pepper to taste
- 1/2 tsp hot ground paprika
- 1/2 tsp fresh ginger
- 1/2 tsp fresh coriander
- 1/2 tsp white pepper
- 1/2 tsp cinnamon

Instructions

1. Stir all marinade ingredients until combined well.
2. Put the chicken into large bowl, cover evenly with marinade and refrigerate overnight.
3. Preheat oven to 350 F/170 C.
4. Remove chicken from the fridge and place in a oiled baking dish.
5. Bake for about 30 - 35 minutes.
6. Serve hot.

Nutrition information:
Calories: 331 Carbohydrates: 5g Proteins: 49g Fat: 12g Fiber: 1g

Turkish Tas Kebap

Serves: 6, Preparation: 5 minutes, Cooking: 1 hour and 40 minutes

Ingredients

- 2 lbs beef shoulder boneless, cut into small pieces
- 2 large onions, finely chopped
- 2 cloves of garlic, melted
- 1/3 cup of olive oil
- 2 Tbsp fresh parsley, finely chopped
- 2 small ripe tomatoes, peeled and mashed
- 1 cup of white dry wine
- 1 tsp of cinnamon
- 1 tsp of dried oregano
- 1 bay leaf
- 2 - 3 cloves (whole)
- Salt and black ground pepper to taste

Instructions

1. In a deep frying skillet, heat the olive oil to moderate heat and sauté the meat for 2 minutes per side.
2. Transfer meat to a plate, cover and set aside.
3. In the same frying skillet, sauté the onion and garlic with a pinch of salt for 5 - 7 minutes; stir.
4. Return the meat to the skillet.
5. Add all remaining ingredients from the list and stir well: cover and cook for 1 1/2 hours over low heat.
6. Remove the cloves and bay leaves from the pot. Serve hot.

Nutrition information:

Calories: 419 Carbohydrates: 6g Proteins: 41g Fat: 24g Fiber: 2g

Scandinavian

Baked Tuna "Meatballs"
Serves: 4, Preparation: 10 minutes, Cooking: 20 minutes

Ingredients
- 1 can (11 oz) tuna (canned and drained)
- 1 green onion finely chopped
- 2 cloves garlic (finely chopped)
- 1 Tbsp grated ginger (about a 1 1/2" piece)
- A handful if fresh cilantro, chopped
- 2 green chilies finely sliced
- 2 cardamom seeds
- 1/4 tsp cinnamon
- 2 cloves
- 1 tsp coriander (crushed seeds)
- 3 Tbsp ground almonds
- 1 large egg
- Grated hard cheese (optional)
- 1 pinch of sea salt
- Oil - 2 to 3 tbsp

Instructions
1. Drain and add tuna in a bowl.
2. Combine tuna fish with all remaining ingredients.
3. Knead the mixture until combine well.
4. Cover the bowl with foil and refrigerate for 1 hour.
5. Preheat the oven to 365 degrees F or 180 degrees C
6. Remove tuna mixture from the fridge, and make balls (10 - 12).
7. Place tuna balls in oiled baking dish.
8. Bake for 15 - 18 minutes. Serve hot.

Nutrition information:
Calories: 245 Carbohydrates: 7g Proteins: 15g
Fat: 19g Fiber: 1.5g

Chilled Salmon Soup
Serves: 6, Preparation: 10 minutes, Cooking: 35 minutes

Ingredients
- 1 salmon fillet
- 5 cups of water
- 1/2 cup of white wine
- 1 small onion cut in cubes
- 1 leek, only white part
- 2 Tbsp of fresh butter
- 2 cups of cauliflower
- 3 Tbsp of fresh celery finely chopped
- 1 1/4 cup of cream
- 2 pinch of sea salt

Instructions
1. Cut the fish in pieces.
2. Add fish in a pot with boiling salted water and vine.
3. Reduce the heat and cook fish for about 10 minutes.
4. Remove fish on a plate, cover and set aside; reserve broth.
5. Heat the butter over medium heat, and sauté the leek and onion with a pinch of salt for 4 to 5 minutes; stir.
6. Add cauliflower and celery, and stir for further 5 - 6 minutes.
7. Add the fish and reserved broth in a pot, and cook for 10 minutes on low heat.
8. Remove the pot from the heat and stir the cream.
9. Place the fish mixture in a large container, cover and refrigerate for 2 to 3 hours. Serve.

Nutrition information:
Calories: 276 Carbohydrates: 5g Proteins: 10g
Fat: 24g Fiber: 1.5g

Creamy Cucumber and Egg Salad

Serves: 6, Preparation: 10 minutes, Cooking: 25 minutes

Ingredients

- 2 large eggs hard boiled
- 3 cucumbers sliced
- 2 Tbsp of olive oil
- 1 cup of whipped cream
- 2 Tbsp mayonnaise
- 3 stalks of fresh fennel
- Salt and ground pepper to taste

Instructions

1. Boil the eggs, clean and set aside.
2. Rinse and slice the cucumber into slices.
3. Boil the cucumber slices for 5 minutes, and removed to drain.
4. Heat the oil in a pan, and combine cream, mayonnaise, fennel, and a pinch of salt and pepper.
5. Add the cucumber slices and gently stir.
6. Add sliced eggs and stir.
7. Cook all ingredients for 5 minutes over moderate-low heat or until thick.
8. From the yolk, salt and black pepper, make sauce by crushing it in a water bath to thicken.
9. Add the cream a little, then add mayonnaise and sprinkle with sliced dill.
10. Taste and adjust salt and pepper to taste.
11. Serve immediately.

Nutrition information:
Calories: 143 Carbohydrates: 6g Proteins: 5g Fat: 14g Fiber: 2.5g

Grilled Tuna Fish with White Wine

Serves: 4, Preparation: 10 minutes, Cooking: 5 minutes

Ingredients

- 1 lemon juice, freshly squeezed
- 1 Tbsp dried parsley
- 1 tsp minced garlic
- 1 cup dry white wine
- Salt and pepper to taste
- 2 lbs tuna fish
- Olive oil for frying

Instructions

1. Pour lemon juice, parsley, garlic, wine, and salt and pepper in a large plastic bag.
2. Place tuna and close the bag; shake.
3. Marinate tuna for 4 hours.
4. Heat the oil in a large frying skillet over medium-strong heat.
5. Remove tuna from marinade and dry on kitchen paper.
6. Fry tuna for 1/2 to 2 minutes per side. Serve hot.

Nutrition information:
Calories: 343 Carbohydrates: 2.5g Proteins: 54g Fat: 10g Fiber: 0.1g

Marinated Salmon with Alfalfa Sprouts

Serves: 4, Preparation: 15 minutes

Ingredients

- 1 lb salmon, cleaned
- 1/2 Tbsp of fresh dill, chopped
- 2 pinches sea salt
- 1 tsp of granulated stevia
- 2 lemons
- 2 limes
- 2 to 3 Tbsp of olive oil
- Ground black pepper to taste
- 1/4 cup of Alfalfa spouts
- 2 Tbsp fresh celery, chopped

Instructions

1. Cut the salmon in thin slices and season with the salt, sweetener and dill.
2. Wrap the fish slices in foil and refrigerate for about 6 hours or overnight.
3. Remove salmon from the fridge and rinse with cold water.
4. Place the salmon on a kitchen paper to drain, and then, transfer the fish in a bowl.
5. Pour lemon and lime juice, olive oil, black pepper and Alfalfa sprouts over the salmon; gently stir.
6. Sprinkle with chopped celery and serve.

Nutrition information:

Calories: 261 Carbohydrates: 7g Proteins: 26g
Fat: 15g Fiber: 4g

Smoked Salmon Omelet with Fresh Chives

Serves: 4, Preparation: 5 minutes, Cooking: 10 minutes

Ingredients

- 8 large eggs from the free range chickens
- Salt and pepper to taste
- 1/4 cup of olive oil
- 1 large onion, finely chopped
- 8 oz of smoked salmon, chopped
- 3 Tbsp of cream
- Finely chopped chives for serving

Instructions

1. Beat the eggs with a pinch of the salt and pepper.
2. Heat the oil in a skillet over medium-high heat and sauté onion for 3 - 4 minutes.
3. Add salmon and gently stir.
4. Pour the egg mixture and cook for 2 to 3 minutes.
5. Flip the omelet and cook for 1 minutes.
6. Transfer the omelet to the plate, generously sprinkle with chopped chives and serve.

Nutrition information:

Calories: 343 Carbohydrates: 3.5g Proteins: 22g
Fat: 26g Fiber: 0.5g

Smoked Salmon Spread

Serves: 4, Preparation: 10 minutes

Ingredients

- 1 spring onion, finely chopped
- 1 cup of cream cheese
- 2 Tbsp of sour cream
- 12 oz smoked salmon
- 1 tsp of Worcester sauce
- 2 drops of Tabasco (optional)
- 1 tsp of fresh dill

Instructions

1. Combine all ingredients in a deep bowl.
2. Stir gently with wooden spoon until the mixture combine evenly.
3. Cover with foil and keep refrigerated.

Nutrition information:

Calories: 312 Carbohydrates: 3g Proteins: 20g Fat: 24g Fiber: 0.2g

Stewed Mackerel Fillets with Celery

Serves: 4, Preparation: 5 minutes, Cooking: 15 minutes

Ingredients

- 2 mackerel filets, cut in small pieces
- 1 Tbsp of wine vinegar
- 1 carrot, sliced
- 1 cup of fresh celery chopped
- 1/2 cup of vegetable oil
- 6 - 7 stalks fresh parsley finely chopped
- 1/4 tsp of sea salt
- 1/2 cup water
- 2 lemons for serving

Instructions

1. Pour oil in a large pot and add mackerel fish; sprinkle with a pinch of salt and pour vinegar.
2. Sauté for 2 minutes, and combine all remaining ingredients from the list above and pour water.
3. Cook for 10 -12 minutes over the medium heat; stir 2 - 3 times.
4. Serve hot with lemon slices.

Nutrition information:

Calories: 378 Carbohydrates: 6.5g Proteins: 14g Fat: 35g Fiber: 1.5g

Stuffed Cucumbers with Tuna

Serves: 8, Preparation: 15 minutes

Ingredients

- 3 large cucumbers
- 3/4 cup of olive oil
- 1 can (11 oz) tuna in oil, drained
- 1/2 cup mayonnaise
- 2 Tbsp of mustard
- 1 fresh lemon juice
- 2 tsp of fresh chopped dill
- Salt to taste
- Lemon slices for serving

Instructions

1. Rinse cucumbers and cut into thick slices.
2. With a teaspoon hollow out the inner part of cucumbers, and add in a bowl.
3. Add all remaining ingredients in a bowl, and combine well.
4. Place the cucumber slices on a large platter.
5. Fill cucumber with a little spread.
6. Decorate with lemon slices and refrigerate for 30 minutes. Serve.

Nutrition information:

Calories: 310 Carbohydrates: 7.5g Proteins: 11g
Fat: 27g Fiber: 1.5g

Swedish Baked Creamy Meatballs

Serves: 4, Preparation: 25 minutes, Cooking: 3 minutes

Ingredients

- 3/4 lb of ground beef
- 1/4 lb of minced pork
- 1 onion red, finely chopped
- 1 tsp of natural sweetener like stevia
- Salt and pepper to taste
- 1/2 tsp of nutmeg
- 1 large egg
- 2 Tbsp of fresh butter
- 3/4 cup of cooking cream
- 1/4 cup of bone broth

Instructions

1. Preheat the oven to 350 F/175 C.
2. In a pan, melt the teaspoon of butter and
3. In bowl, combine ground beef, pork, onion, stevia, nutmeg, egg, and the salt and pepper.
4. Knead with your hands until get compact mixture.
5. From the mixture make meatballs; place them in oiled baking dish.
6. Heat the butter in a pan over medium heat; add the cooking cream and bone broth.
7. Cook the mixture only for 2 - 3 minutes.
8. Pour the butter mixture over meatballs and place in oven.
9. Cover with foil and bake for 20 minutes.
10. Serve hot.

Nutrition information:

Calories: 496 Carbohydrates: 3.5g Proteins: 25g
Fat: 42g Fiber: 0.5g

Japanese

Baked Pork Loin with "Tonkatsu" Sauce

Serves: 4, Preparation: 15 minutes, Cooking: 20 minutes

Ingredients

- 1/2 cup almond flour
- 1 Tbsp extra virgin olive oil
- 4 pork loin chops, boneless
- 1 tsp salt and freshly ground black pepper
- 1 large egg from free-range chickens
- 3 Tbsp of Worcester sauce
- 1 Tbsp of roasted sesame seeds

Instructions

1. Preheat the oven to 400 F/200 C.
2. Preheat the olive oil in a skillet over medium-low heat and stir the almond flour for 2 minutes.
3. Remove the almond flour on a plate and let it cool.
4. Remove any fat from the pork chops, and season with the salt and pepper.
5. Beat the egg in a bowl.
6. Dip each pork chop in egg, and then roll into almond flour.
7. Bake the pork in a baking sheet lined with parchment paper for about 15 - 20 minutes.
8. Remove the pork chops on a plate, and cut in small pieces; place the meat on a platter.
9. In a bowl, combine the Worcester sauce with the roasted sesame, and with the pinch of ground pepper.
10. Serve the pork chops with the sauce.

Nutrition information:

Calories: 471 Carbohydrates: 6g Proteins: 57g Fat: 24g Fiber: 2.2g

Baked Turmeric Salmon Patties

Serves: 6, Preparation: 15 minutes, Cooking: 10 minutes

Ingredients

- 2 can (11 oz) salmon drained, skin and bones removed
- 1 tsp turmeric ground
- 1 cup sesame seeds toasted
- 2 organic eggs
- 1 Tbsp of olive oil for batter
- 1 cup scallions, chopped
- 1 Tbsp fresh lemon juice

Instructions

1. 1. Preheat your oven to 380F/ 190 C.
2. 2. In a deep bowl, combine all ingredients from the list above. Stir the mixture until a combine well.
3. 3. Form mixture into 6 equal patties.
4. 4. Place patties in one oiled baking sheet, and bake for 10 minutes, turning once.
5. 5. Transfer patties to a serving plate lined with absorbent paper and serve hot.

Nutrition information:

Calories: 281 Carbohydrates: 3g Proteins: 31g Fat: 17g Fiber: 1.5g

Delicious Keto Oyakodon

Serves: 4, Preparation: 15 minutes, Cooking: 15 minutes

Ingredients

- 6 chicken thighs, boneless and cut into strips
- Pinch of salt and ground black pepper
- 1 green onion finely sliced
- 4 large eggs, beaten
- 2/3 cup bone broth
- 1/4 cup of coconut aminos
- 1 Tbsp of stevia granulated sweetener

Instructions

1. Season the chicken strips with the salt and ground pepper.
2. In a bowl, combine bone broth, coconut aminos and stevia; stir until sweetener dissolves well.
3. Heat a wok and stir finely sliced green onion with a pinch of salt.
4. Add the chicken strips and sauté for 4 - 5 minutes.
5. Pour the bone broth mixture, stir, cover and cook for 5 minutes over low heat.
6. In a bowl, whisk the eggs and pour in wok; stir with the wooden spoon.
7. Cook for 4 - 5 further minutes or until eggs are set. Serve hot.

Nutrition information:

Calories: 352 Carbohydrates: 7g Proteins: 28g Fat: 23g Fiber: 1g

Eggs Stuffed with Creamy Salmon

Serves: 4, Preparation: 15 minutes, Cooking: 15 minutes

Ingredients

- 8 eggs, hard boiled
- 1 cup salmon, finely chopped
- 1 scallion, finely chopped (only green parts)
- 1 Tbsp mustard (Dijon, English, or whole grain)
- 2 Tbsp mayonnaise (without honey)
- 1 tsp of fresh lemon juice
- Salt and ground pepper to taste
- Fresh dill for garnish

Instructions

1. Pour water in a saucepan, turn the heat on to high, and bring the water to a boil.
2. Boil the eggs for 12-15 minutes; clean and cut the eggs in the middle. Remove the yolks.
3. Combine together the eggs, salmon, chopped scallions (only green parts), mayonnaise, lemon and mustard.
4. Stir well with the fork to achieve a puree mixture.
5. Season the salt and pepper to taste.
6. Fill the eggs with the salmon/mayo mixture and sprinkle with dill.
7. Refrigerate eggs until serving.

Nutrition information:

Calories: 232 Carbohydrates: 3g Proteins: 21.5g Fat: 14g Fiber: 0.2g

Grilled Gouda Topped and Marinated Pork Roast

Serves: 4, Preparation: 15 minutes, Cooking: 8 -10 minutes

Ingredients
- 1 1/2 lb of pork roast, sliced in pieces 0.4 inch
- 1/4 cup of coconut aminos
- 2 oz Gouda cheese cut in cubes

Instructions
1. Cut the pork meat in pieces and spread with coconut aminos.
2. Wrap in plastic membrane and refrigerate overnight.
3. Remove the pork from the fridge and place on kitchen paper.
4. Preheat your grill (any) on HIGH temperature.
5. Place the pork on a grill and cook for about 4 minutes.
6. Flip the pork oven, and cover with the Gouda cheese.
7. Grill until cheese melt or about 3 - 4 minutes.
8. Serve immediately.

Nutrition information:
Calories: 434 Carbohydrates: 0.3g Proteins: 46g Fat: 27g Fiber: 0g

Grilled Salmon with Lemon Marinade

Serves: 3, Preparation: 10 minutes, Cooking: 15 minutes

Ingredients
- 1 lb salmon fillets with skin
- 3 juice and zest of 2 lemons
- 2 Tbsp extra-virgin olive oil
- 3 cloves garlic, minced
- Salt and freshly ground black pepper, to taste

Instructions
1. In a bowl combine lemon juice, olive oil and minced garlic.
2. Place the salmon in a container, pour with lemon juice mixture, cover and refrigerate for 4 hours.
3. Preheat your grill (any) to HIGH.
4. Take the fish out of the fridge, and pour marinade in a saucepan.
5. Grill the fish for 5-7 minutes per side.
6. In a meantime, boil the marinade mixture and simmer over low heat.
7. Serve grilled fish warm with the marinade sauce.

Nutrition information:
Calories: 341 Carbohydrates: 7.5g Proteins: 34g Fat: 20g Fiber: 2g

Hoikoro - Japanese Pork and Cabbage
Serves: 4, Preparation: 5 minutes, Cooking: 20 minutes

Ingredients
- 1 Tbsp of olive oil
- 1 clove garlic, minced
- 1 1/2 lb of pork belly cut into long strips
- 2 cups shredded cabbage
- 1 green bell pepper, sliced
- 1/2 cup water
- 2 Tbsp of coconut aminos
- 1/2 tsp chili pepper (optional)

Instructions
1. Heat the olive oil in a frying pan over medium heat.
2. Add minced garlic and sauté for about 2 minutes.
3. Add the pork strips, water and coconut aminos.
4. Stir and fry for about 4-5 minutes.
5. Add shredded cabbage and chopped green pepper.
6. Stir and cook for 8 -10 minutes.
7. Add the chili pepper (optional) and stir well. Serve immediately.

Nutrition information:
Calories: 599 Carbohydrates: 0.3g Proteins: 12g Fat: 63g Fiber: 2g

Keto Beef Gyudon
Serves: 4, Preparation: 10 minutes, Cooking: 15 minutes

Ingredients
- 1 Tbsp of sesame oil
- 1 small red onion finely chopped
- 2 green onions, finely chopped
- 1 1/2 lb beef, thinly sliced in strips
- 2 tsp stevia granulated sweetener
- 2 Tbsp of red wine
- 1 Tbsp of coconut aminos
- 3 large eggs from free-range chickens
- Salt and ground black pepper

Instructions
1. Heat the oil in a large skillet over medium heat.
2. Sauté the red onion and green onions with the pinch of salt.
3. Add the beef slices and sweetener and stir for 2 minutes.
4. Pour the red wine and coconut aminos; stir well.
5. Cook over low heat for 3 - 4 minutes.
6. Whisk the eggs in a bowl with the pinch of salt and pepper, and pour over meat and onions.
7. Cover and cook for 5 minutes or until the eggs are done. Serve immediately.

Nutrition information:
Calories: 591 Carbohydrates: 6.5g Proteins: 36g Fat: 27g Fiber: 0.5g

Rib eye Steak with Keto Adapted Teriyaki Sauce

Serves: 4, Preparation: 10 minutes, Cooking: 15 minutes

Ingredients

- 2 beef rib eye steaks
- 1 tsp almond flour
- 1 tsp water
- 1 Tbsp roasted sesame seeds
- 1 green onion/scallion
- Teriyaki Adapted Sauce
- 1/4 cup of Coconut aminos
- 1/2 cup of red wine
- 1 Tbsp ginger juice
- 2 tsp granulated stevia sweetener

Instructions

1. In a bowl, whisk together the coconut aminos, red wine, ginger juice and sweetener.
2. Place the steaks in a plastic bag, and add 4 tablespoon of coconut aminos sauce.
3. Refrigerate and marinate steaks for 1 hour.
4. Remove the meat from the fridge and let sit for 10 minutes on room temperature.
5. Pour adapted Teriyaki sauce in saucepan, add sliced onions and roasted sesame.
6. In a small bowl, whisk the almond flour and water, and pour in a saucepan; stir for 10 minutes.
7. In a wok heat the oil and cook steaks for 2 minutes per side.
8. Serve steaks with the hot sauce.

Nutrition information:

Calories: 528 Carbohydrates: 2.3g Proteins: 50g Fat: 35g Fiber: 0.6g

Shogayaki - Ginger Pork Loin

Serves: 4, Preparation: 5 minutes, Cooking: 20 minutes

Ingredients

- 2 lb thinly sliced pork loin
- 1/2 of onion, chopped
- 1 clove garlic, grated
- 1 inch ginger (about 1 tsp.)
- Kosher salt and freshly ground black pepper
- 1 Tbsp of olive
- 1 spring onion, finely chopped
- 2 Tbsp of bone broth
- 2 Tbsp of coconut aminos
- Shredded cabbage for serving

Instructions

1. Season the pork meat with the salt and pepper.
2. In a bowl, combine the onion, garlic and ginger; set aside.
3. Heat the oil in a skillet and cook the pork for about 4 - 5 minutes (do not overcook).
4. Add the onion mixture and gently stir for 2 - 3 minutes,
5. Sprinkle spring onion and cook for further 2 - 3 minutes over medium-low heat.
6. Pour the bone broth and coconut aminos; stir and cook for 2 minutes.
7. Serve immediately with freshly shredded cabbage.

Nutrition information:

Calories: 364 Carbohydrates: 3.4g Proteins: 52g Fat: 15g Fiber: 1g

Fareast

Arugula and Beef Salad with Sesame Dressing

Serves: 4, Preparation: 10 minutes

Ingredients

- 4 Tbsp of sesame oil
- 2 Tbsp of wine vinegar
- 2 tsp of granulated stevia (optional)
- 6 oz fresh arugula finely chopped
- 1 roasted beef fillet (cut into small strips)
- 2 green onions sliced
- Salt and ground black pepper to taste
- 1 Tbsp of sesame seeds

Instructions

1. In a small bowl, whisk the sesame oil, vinegar, the salt and pepper, and stevia if used.
2. In a separate large bowl combine arugula, green onions and the beef fillet; sprinkle little salt and pepper.
3. Pour the sesame oil dressing and toss to combine evenly.
4. Sprinkle with sesame seeds and serve immediately.

Nutrition information:

Calories: 414 Carbohydrates: 5g Proteins: 29g Fat: 31g Fiber: 4g

Bulgogi Beef (South Korea)

Serves: 4, Preparation: 10 minutes, Cooking: 12 minutes

Ingredients

- 1 1/2 lbs of beef steak cut into small pieces
- 1/4 cup of coconut aminos
- 2 Tbsp of granulated stevia
- 1 medium onion finely chopped
- 2 garlic cloves minced
- 2 Tbsp of sesame seeds
- 4 Tbsp of sesame oil

Instructions

1. Place the beef in a deep container.
2. In a bowl, stir coconut aminos, sweetener, onion, garlic, sesame seeds, and sesame oil.
3. Pour the sweet sauce over the beef, and toss to combine evenly.
4. Refrigerate the beef for 3 - 4 hours to marinate.
5. Remove the meat from the fridge and grill or bake it for 10 – 12 minutes in the oven on 350F.
6. Serve hot.

Nutrition information:

Calories: 476 Carbohydrates: 4.5g Proteins: 41g Fat: 34g Fiber: 1.1g

Cantonese Lobster

Serves: 6, Preparation: 5 minutes, Cooking: 20 minutes

Ingredients

- 4 oz butter
- 1 large onion chopped
- 2 cup chopped celery
- 2 1/2 lb lobster meat
- 8 oz coconut water
- 1 inch ginger sliced thinly
- 1/4 cup almond flour
- 1 quart water
- Salt

Instructions

1. Heat butter in a wok or frying skillet over medium heat.
2. Sauté the onion and celery with a pinch of salt for about 3 - 4 minutes.
3. Add lobster meat and coconut water, and cook for 2 - 3 minutes; toss the wok.
4. Add sliced ginger and gently stir.
5. Add slowly the almond flour and gently stir.
6. Pour water and toss the wok; cover and cook for about 5 - 6 minutes.
7. Taste and adjust seasonings. Serve.

Nutrition information:

Calories: 338 Carbohydrates: 5g Proteins: 34g Fat: 20g Fiber: 2g

Cantonese Roasted Char Siu

Serves: 6, Preparation: 10 minutes, Cooking: 2 hours

Ingredients

- 3 pork baby back ribs
- A pinch of salt and pepper
- 2 tsp of liquid stevia sweetener
- 3 Tbsp coconut aminos
- 2 Tbsp sesame oil
- 1 tsp fresh ginger (minced)
- 2 clove garlic finely sliced
- 1 tsp hot chili pepper sauce

Instructions

1. Preheat your oven to 350F.
2. Line a baking dish with aluminum foil.
3. Season your ribs with the pinch of salt and pepper.
4. Place the ribs in a prepared baking dish, cover with foil and bake for 1 ½ - 2 hours.
5. Make a sauce; In a bowl, whisk all remaining ingredients.
6. Baste your ribs every 30 minutes with the sauce.
7. Remove from oven, and let ribs rest for 10 minutes. Serve.

Nutrition information:

Calories: 605 Carbohydrates: 0.7g Proteins: 51g Fat: 48g Fiber: 0g

Chilo Raita Sauce (India)

Serves: 4, Preparation: 5 minutes

Ingredients

- 2 cup full-fat yogurt
- 2 Tbsp onion, finely chopped
- 1/4 cup cucumber, grated
- 2 tsp lemon juice
- 1/2 tsp ginger powder
- 2 tsp fresh mint, finely chopped
- 1 1/2 tsp chili pepper powder
- Salt to taste

Instructions

1. Place all ingredients in your blender.
2. Blend for 30 - 45 seconds or until smooth.
3. Taste and adjust seasonings.
4. Place in a glass bowl and refrigerate until serving.

Nutrition information:

Calories: 15 Carbohydrates: 1g Proteins: 1g Fat: 1g Fiber: 0.5g

Chinese Oriental Shrimp with Sauce (Hong Kong)

Serves: 4, Preparation: 5 minutes, Cooking: 15 minutes

Ingredients

- 1/2 cup of olive oil
- 4 plum tomatoes cut into quarters
- 3 tsp minced garlic
- 1/2 onion chopped
- 2 green onions chopped
- 1/4 cup red wine
- 1/2 cup of grated tomato
- Salt and ground pepper to taste
- 1 tsp garlic powder
- 1/4 cup stevia sweetener
- 24 oz of peeled and devein white prawns

Instructions

1. Heat the oil in a frying skillet and cook tomato, garlic, onion and green onion; sprinkle with the pinch of salt and pepper, and sauté for 5 minutes stirring.
2. Pour the wine, grated tomato, garlic powder, stevia, and the salt and pepper; stir.
3. Add shrimps and cook for 4 - 5 minutes over medium heat.
4. Transfer shrimp to serving plate, pour with sauce and serve.

Nutrition information:

Calories: 305 Carbohydrates: 4g Proteins: 7g Fat: 27g Fiber: 1g

Egg Salad with Curry Dressing (Japan)

Serves: 6, Preparation: 20 minutes

Ingredients

- 3/4 cup of mayonnaise
- 1 Tbsp of curry
- 1/2 tsp of turmeric powder
- Salt and ground black pepper to taste
- 1/2 cup of extra-virgin olive oil
- a few leaves of green salad
- 1 cup of red cabbage, shredded
- 8 eggs, hard boiled, cut in half or quarter
- 1 lb of asparagus

Instructions

1. In the bowl, stir the mayonnaise, curry, turmeric powder, salt and pepper, and olive oil; set aside.
2. Cover the serving plate with green salad leaves, and shredded red cabbage.
3. Add boiled eggs and asparagus over salad.
4. Sprinkle eggs with little salt, and drizzle with olive oil.
5. Pour the curry-mayo sauce and toss to combine well.
6. Refrigerate for 20 minutes and serve.

Nutrition information:

Calories: 228 Carbohydrates: 7g Proteins: 10g Fat: 17g Fiber: 2g

Fried Mongolian Chicken

Serves: 6, Preparation: 15 minutes, Cooking: 10 minutes

Ingredients

- 3 chicken fillets, boneless
- 1/2 cup of almond flour
- 1 cup of olive oil
- 2 cloves garlic minced
- 1 onion finely chopped
- 2 spring onions sliced
- Salt and ground black pepper to taste

Marinade

- 1/2 cup of water
- 1 Tbsp of ground almonds
- 3 Tbsp of coconut aminos
- 1 Tbsp of oyster sauce
- 2 tsp of stevia sweetener
- 2 tsp of ground red peppers
- 2 tsp of apple cider vinegar

Instructions

1. In a bowl, whisk all ingredients for the marinade.
2. Cut the chicken fillets into strips and generously season with the salt and ground pepper.
3. Roll the chicken in almond flour, and then add into sauce; cover the chicken evenly, cover and refrigerate for 2 hours to marinate.
4. Heat the oil in a wok and sauté the garlic and onion with the pinch of salt.
5. Add spring onions and cook for 3 - 4 minutes; stir.
6. Add marinated chicken and cook for 3 - 5 minutes or until done.
7. Serve hot.

Nutrition information:

Calories: 534 Carbohydrates: 3.5g Proteins: 26g Fat: 47g Fiber: 1g

Mongolian Sour-Sweet Ukhriin makh (beef)

Serves: 2, Preparation: 15 minutes, Cooking: 10 minutes

Ingredients

- 1 cup of vegetable oil
- 1 tsp of fresh grated ginger
- 1 Tbsp of finely chopped garlic
- 1/4 cup coconut aminos
- 1/2 cup of water
- 2/3 cup of stevia granulated sweetener
- 1 lb of beef steak finely sliced
- 1 cup almond meal
- 3 fresh onions (only the green part), finely sliced

Instructions

1. Heat the vegetable oil in a skillet over moderate-low heat.
2. Add grated ginger and garlic and sauté about 2 minutes.
3. Pour the coconut aminos sauce, water and sweetener, and stir for 3 -4 minutes.
4. Remove the sauce from heat and set aside.
5. Combine the beef slices with almond flour; let sit for 10 minutes.
6. Heat the oil in a wok or frying skillet over high heat.
7. Fry the beef slices for about 3 minutes until golden yellow but not overcooked.
8. Transfer beef on a parchment paper to drain.
9. Place the meat on a serving plate, pour with the ginger sauce and sprinkle with sliced green parts of fresh onions.
10. Serve immediately.

Nutrition information:

Calories: 418 Carbohydrates: 3g Proteins: 19g Fat: 38g Fiber: 0.3g

Pak Choi and Chicken Stir-fry

Serves: 4, Preparation: 5 minutes, Cooking: 25 minutes

Ingredients

- 1/4 cup olive oil
- 2 green onions finely chopped
- 2 chicken breasts cut into cubes
- 1 lb Pak Choi, finely chopped
- 2 tsp fresh dill chopped
- 2 tsp fresh parsley (chopped)
- 1 Tbsp ginger powder
- 1/2 tsp chili powder
- 2 Tbsp apple cider vinegar or fresh lemon juice
- Salt and pepper to taste

Instructions

1. Heat the oil in the wok or in a frying skillet, and sauté the onions with a pinch of salt.
2. Add the chicken pieces and cook for 3-4 minutes, stirring occasionally.
3. Add Pak Choi along with all remaining ingredients; gently stir, cover and cook for 10 minutes.
4. Remove from the heat and let rest for 10 minutes.
5. Taste and adjust seasonings. Serve.

Nutrition information:

Calories: 280 Carbohydrates: 4g Proteins: 28g Fat: 17g Fiber: 2g

Pancit Canton with Lap Ceung

Serves: 2, Preparation: 5 minutes, Cooking: 50 minutes

Ingredients

- 4 cups of water
- 1 chicken breast boneless cut in strips
- 1/2 lb pork, cubed
- 2 Tbsp sesame oil
- 2 Tbsp of minced garlic
- 1/2 cup chopped onion
- Salt and ground pepper to taste
- 1/2 lb shrimp, deveined, and cut lengthwise
- 1/2 cup lap ceung - Chinese sausage, sliced
- 2 cup cauliflower (divided into flowerets)
- 2 cups of shredded cabbage
- 1 carrot diced
- 1 cup celery finely chopped
- 1/4 cup fresh onions sliced
- 2 Tbsp of coconut aminos

Instructions

1. In large pot, boil chicken and the pork until tender, about 15 - 20 minutes over medium-low heat.
2. Remove meat from the pot and place on a plate; reserve 3 cups of broth.
3. Heat the oil in wok or frying skillet and sauté the garlic and onion until translucent: season with the pinch of salt.
4. Add pork, chicken and shrimp, and cook for 15 minutes over low heat.
5. Pour reserved broth and add all remaining ingredients; gently stir.
6. Cover and cook for further 10 - 12 minutes over low-medium heat.
7. Serve in bowls, and sprinkle with fresh onion slices.

Nutrition information:

Calories: 296 Carbohydrates: 5g Proteins: 17g Fat: 23g Fiber: 2g

Seolleongtang (Korea)

Serves: 8, Preparation: 15 minutes, Cooking: 6 hours

Ingredients

- 3 lbs beef leg (marrow and knuckle) bones, cut up
- 2 lbs beef shank
- Salt and pepper to taste
- Water
- 4 chopped scallions for serving

Instructions

1. Soak the bones in cold water for about 2 - 3 hours.
2. In a separate bowl soak the beef meat for several hours; keep refrigerated.
3. Remove bones from the bowl and put in large and deep pot; cover with water completely.
4. Cook on a high heat; bring to boil, and then reduce the heat to medium-low, and cook for 10 minutes.
5. Drain and rinse the bones.
6. Rinse and clean the pot and return the bones.
7. Pour the water enough to cover the bones, and cook on medium heat for 4 - 6 hours.
8. Add the soaked meat, and cook until meat is tender, for 2 hours about.
9. Remove the bones and the meat; pour the broth trough the colander and place in another pot.
10. Slice the meat and add to the soup; season with the salt and pepper to taste.
11. Serve with chopped scallions.

Nutrition information:

Calories: 459 Carbohydrates: 0.3g Proteins: 27g Fat: 38g Fiber: 0.2g

Shurinpu Stew (Japan)
Serves: 6, Preparation: 5 minutes, Cooking: 15 minutes

Ingredients
- 1/4 cup sesame oil
- 2 fresh onions finely chopped
- 2 cups fresh celery, sliced
- 1 green peppers, sliced
- 1 1/2 lb frozen shrimp, peeled and deveined
- 3/4 lb fresh mushrooms sliced
- 1/2 cup coconut aminos (from coconut sap)
- 2 Tbsp natural sweetener (Stevia, Erythritol...etc.)
- 1/2 cup water

Instructions

1. Heat the oil in a frying skillet over medium-high heat.
2. Sauté onions, celery, green pepper with a pinch of salt until softened.
3. Add shrimp and mushrooms and sauté for 1 - 2 minutes.
4. Pour coconut aminos sauce, stevia sweetener and water; stir.
5. Reduce heat and simmer for about 10 - 12 minutes or until shrimp turn pink.
6. Serve.

Nutrition information:
Calories: 191 Carbohydrates: 4g Proteins: 22g Fat: 11g Fiber: 2g

Spicy Mongolian Lamb
Serves: 6, Preparation: 15 minutes, Cooking: 25 minutes

Ingredients
- 2 lbs of frozen lamb, boneless
- Chinese cabbage leaves
- 1 lbsp of fresh spinach leaves
- Olive oil for baking

Sauces ingredients
- 4 green onions finely chopped
- 2 Tbsp of fresh ginger
- 1/2 cup of sesame paste
- 3 Tbsp of sesame oil
- 3 Tbsp of coconut aminos
- 2 Tbsp of chili sauce
- 1/4 cup of fresh chopped coriander

Instructions
1. Let the lamb to thaw; cut into very thin slices, and season with the salt and pepper.
2. Preheat oven to 400°F.
3. Grease the baking dish with the olive oil and place the lamb slices.
4. Bake for 25 minutes or until done.
5. Remove the lamb from the oven and let sit for 5 - 10 minutes.
6. Cover the large plate with the cabbage and spinach leaves.
7. Place the lamb slices over the salad.
8. Combine the green onions and ginger in one small bowl.
9. In a separate bowl, whisk the sesame paste and sesame oil.
10. In a third small bowl, combine the coconut aminons with colander; stir well.
11. Serve the lamb with sauces and enjoy!

Nutrition information:
Calories: 501 Carbohydrates: 6g Proteins: 32g Fat: 28.5g Fiber: 2.5g

Yangnyeom-tongdak Chicken (Korea)

Serves: 8, Preparation: 5 minutes, Cooking: 15 minutes

Ingredients

- 24 chicken wings
- Salt and ground black pepper to taste
- 1/4 cup of almond flour
- 1 egg
- 1/2 tsp baking soda
- 3/4 cup of olive oil
- 2 - 3 cloves garlic minced
- 2 Tbsp of hot pepper paste
- 4 Tbsp cider vinegar; more to taste

Instructions

1. In a deep container, combine the salt and pepper, almond flour, baking soda and one egg.
2. With your hand cover the chicken wings with this mixture.
3. Heat the oil in a large frying skillet over high heat until bubbles.
4. Fry the chicken wings for 15 minutes or until golden brown.
5. In the case that your skillet is not large enough, divide the chicken into batches.
6. Remove the chicken wings on a platter lined with parchment paper to drain.
7. In a meantime prepare the sauce: in a bowl, stir the oil, garlic, hot pepper sauce and vinegar.
8. Transfer the chicken wings on a serving plate and cover with the sauce evenly.
9. Serve.

Nutrition information:

Calories: 354 Carbohydrates: 0.3g Proteins: 14.5g
Fat: 33g Fiber: 0.1g

Printed in Great Britain
by Amazon